An Introduction to Ethics

This book examines the central questions of ethics through a study of theories of right and wrong that are found in the great ethical works of Western philosophy. It focuses on theories that continue to have a significant presence in the field. The core chapters cover egoism, the eudaimonism of Plato and Aristotle, act and rule utilitarianism, modern natural law theory, Kant's moral theory, and existentialist ethics. Readers will be introduced not only to the main ideas of each theory but also to contemporary developments and defenses of those ideas. A final chapter takes up topics in meta-ethics and moral psychology. The discussions throughout draw the reader into philosophical inquiry through argument and criticism that illuminate the profundity of the questions under examination. Students will find this book to be a very helpful guide to how philosophical inquiry is undertaken as well as to what the major theories in ethics hold.

JOHN DEIGH is Professor of Philosophy and Law at the University of Texas at Austin. He is the author of *The Sources of Moral Agency* (Cambridge, 1996) and of *Emotions, Values, and the Law* (2008).

An Introduction to Ethics

JOHN DEIGH

University of Texas at Austin

CAMBRIDGE
UNIVERSITY PRESS

CAMBRIDGE UNIVERSITY PRESS
Cambridge, New York, Melbourne, Madrid, Cape Town, Singapore,
São Paulo, Delhi, Dubai, Tokyo

Cambridge University Press
The Edinburgh Building, Cambridge CB2 8RU, UK

Published in the United States of America by Cambridge University Press, New York

www.cambridge.org
Information on this title: www.cambridge.org/9780521775977

First published 2010

Printed in the United Kingdom at the University Press, Cambridge

A catalog record for this publication is available from the British Library

Library of Congress Cataloging in Publication data
Deigh, John.
An introduction to ethics / John Deigh.
   p.   cm. – (Cambridge introductions to philosophy)
ISBN 978-0-521-77246-4 (hardback) – ISBN 978-0-521-77597-7 (pbk.)
1. Ethics. I. Title. II. Series.
BJ1012.D43   2010
170–dc22

                                                                 2009050368

ISBN 978-0-521-77246-4 Hardback
ISBN 978-0-521-77597-7 Paperback

To the memory of my father and mother

Maurice Deigh (1913–2004)

Dorace B. Deigh (1915–2006)

Contents

Preface

Ethics is one of the main branches of philosophy. Its range, extending from fundamental questions about the nature of our humanity and freedom to very practical questions about the morality of physician-assisted suicide and experiments on animals, is vast. An introduction must, therefore, be selective in its coverage. I have chosen, as a way of covering the central questions of ethics, to concentrate on different theories of right and wrong that we find in the great works of Western philosophy and that continue to have a large presence in the field. Sustained study of these theories illuminates systematic connections among the field's central questions and the ideas the philosophers who produced the theories invented to answer them.

A good introduction to a branch of philosophy not only surveys its major ideas and theories but also exemplifies philosophical inquiry into them. I have tried to do both. In doing so, I hope to draw the reader into inquiry of the kind that philosophers undertake when they examine a philosophical question as well as to inform him or her about the major ideas and theories in which philosophers who study ethics traffic. Philosophical inquiry requires argument and criticism, and the reader needs to be aware that some of the arguments and criticism I make in the course of examining these different ethical theories represent my own reflections on them rather than settled opinion among the experts. Some of what I say, then, is bound to be controversial. And if it provokes objection or skepticism, I will then have succeeded in the second of my two aims.

I have benefited from the advice of several friends who read some of the chapters in draft. I am indebted to Reid Blackman, Daniel Brudney, George Graham, Hugh LaFollette, and Martha Nussbaum, all of whom gave me valuable comments and suggestions. Brad Cokelet read the entire manuscript and offered many perceptive pointers and observations that helped me prepare the final draft. I am very grateful to him for his efforts and wisdom. I also wish to thank my editor, Hilary Gaskin, not only for the advice she gave me throughout the project on how to improve my exposition, but also for her patience and kindness. The book has had a lengthy gestation. My greatest debt is to the teachers of ethics with whom I studied as an undergraduate and who introduced me to the subject. Thomas E. Hill, Jr., in particular, taught me not only to appreciate the intricacies and subtleties in the works of Hume, Kant, Mill, and others, but how to read these works at once critically and sympathetically. It gives me pleasure to think that with this book I have in part discharged my debt to him.

John Deigh
Austin, Texas

1   What is ethics?

1. The problems of ethics: an example

Ethics, like other branches of philosophy, springs from seemingly simple questions. What makes honest actions right and dishonest ones wrong? Why is death a bad thing for the person who dies? Is there anything more to happiness than pleasure and freedom from pain? These are questions that naturally occur in the course of our lives, just as they naturally occurred in the lives of people who lived before us and in societies with different cultures and technologies from ours. They seem simple, yet they are ultimately perplexing. Every sensible answer one tries proves unsatisfactory upon reflection. This reflection is the beginning of philosophy. It turns seemingly simple questions into philosophical problems. And with further reflection we plumb the depths of these problems.

Of course, not every question that naturally occurs in human life and proves hard to answer is a source of philosophical perplexity. Some questions prove hard to answer just because it is hard to get all the facts. Whether there is life on Mars, for instance, and whether the planet has ever supported life are questions people have asked for centuries and will continue to ask until we have enough facts about the Martian environment to reach definite answers. These are questions for the natural sciences, whose business it is to gather such facts and whose problems typically arise from difficulties in finding them and sometimes even in knowing which ones to look for. The questions with which ethics and other branches of philosophy begin are different. They resist easy answers, not because of difficulties in getting the relevant facts, but because of difficulties in making sense of them and how they bear on these questions. We reflect on the matters in question and discover that our ordinary ideas contain confusions and obscurities and have surprising implications. We discover, as a result,

1

that our ordinary beliefs about these matters are shaky and have complicating consequences we did not realize and are reluctant to endorse. Philosophical study, which begins with seemingly simple questions, uncovers these difficulties and then, through close, critical examination of our ideas and beliefs, seeks to overcome them.

Here is an example. You are strolling through a neighborhood park on a free afternoon when something in the bushes nearby catches your eye. It's a woman's purse, presumably lost. Or perhaps it was stolen and then discarded. You look inside and find a driver's license. You also see a huge wad of cash. The purse wasn't stolen. What should you do? Being an honest person, you look on the license for an address or look to see whether there is an identification card with a phone number you could call. In other words, you begin taking the steps necessary to returning the purse, with all of its contents, to its owner. A dishonest person would take the cash and toss the purse back into the bushes. "Finders keepers, losers weepers," he might think as he stuffed the cash into his pockets. And even an honest person, especially one who was down on his luck or struggling to make ends meet, might think about taking the cash. "Why should I be honest and return the money?" he might wonder. "After all, there is no chance of my being caught if I keep it and am careful about how I spend it, and the satisfaction of doing the honest thing hardly compares to the relief from my troubles that this money will bring. It is true that honesty requires returning the purse and its contents to the owner, but it is also true that honesty, in these circumstances, does not appear to be nearly as profitable as dishonesty." Still, any honest person suppresses such thoughts, as he looks for a way to return the purse with its contents intact. The thoughts, however, are troubling. Is there nothing to be said for doing the honest thing, nothing, that is, that would show it to be, in these circumstances, the better course of action?

In asking this question we are asking whether you have a stronger reason to return the cash to the purse's owner than you have to keep it. After all, a huge wad of cash – let's say four thousand dollars – is more than just handy pocket money. Just think of the many useful and valuable things you could buy with it. Or if you've already bought too many things on credit, think of how much of your debt it could help pay off. Plainly, then, you have a strong reason to keep the money. At the same time, keeping the money is dishonest, and this fact may give you a strong and even overriding reason to return it. But we cannot simply assume that it does. For the question we are asking is whether honesty is the better course of action in these circumstances, and since asking it entails asking whether an action's being the honest thing to do gives you a strong or indeed any good reason to do it, to assume that it does would just be to beg the question. That is, you would be taking as a given something for which a sound argument is needed before you can assume its truth. So our question in the end is really a question about what you have good reason to do in circumstances where dishonest action is safe from detection and apparently more profitable than honest action. Could it be that doing the honest thing in such circumstances is to act without good reason? Could it be that only ignorant and weak-minded people act honestly in them? It may seem strange to suggest that it could. But unless one can show that you have good reason to be honest even in circumstances in which you could keep your dishonesty secret and profit from it, this strange suggestion is the unavoidable conclusion of these reflections.

The question about what you should do in such circumstances thus leads us first to wonder whether you have stronger reason to do the honest thing than to do what is dishonest and then to wonder whether you even have a good reason to do the honest thing. Both questions are troubling, but the second is especially so. This is because we commonly think an excellent character is something worth having and preserving even at significant costs to one's comfort or wealth, and we take honesty to be one of its essentials. Consequently, while the first question might lead us to reconsider the wisdom of placing such high value on possessing an excellent character, the second forces us to question whether honesty is one of the essentials of an excellent character. And to think one could have an excellent character even though one was not honest is a very unsettling result. It not only threatens to undermine the confidence we have in the moral rule that calls for doing the honest thing even when dishonesty could not be detected, but it also puts into doubt basic feelings and attitudes we have toward others and ourselves that help to create the fabric of our relations with friends, neighbors, colleagues, and many others with whom we interact in our society. In particular, it puts into doubt the admiration and esteem we feel for those of unquestionable honesty and the pride we take in our own honesty and trustworthiness.

After all, when people prove to be honest in their dealings with us, we praise and think well of them for not having taken advantage of us when they could. And similarly when our own honesty is tested and we meet the test, we feel proud of ourselves for not having yielded to the temptations to cheat or to lie that we faced. In short, we take honesty to be an admirable trait in others and a source of pride. But now the trouble our question causes becomes evident, for how could doing something that you had no good reason to do be a sign of an admirable trait or a trait in which you could justifiably take pride? To the contrary, it would seem, such action is a sign of ignorance or a mind too weak to choose by its own lights, and there is nothing admirable about ignorance or a slavish conformity to other people's opinions; nothing that would justify pride. Hence, the basic feelings and attitudes towards others and ourselves that honesty normally inspires must be misguided or bogus if we can find no good reason to act honestly except in those circumstances where dishonesty is liable to be found out and punished. Yet how odd it would be if the high regard we had for friends and colleagues in view of their honesty and the self-regard that our own honesty boosted were entirely unwarranted, if they were found to be based on the mistaken belief that honesty was essential to having an excellent character. Could it be that the people who warrant our admiration are not those of impeccable honesty but rather those who do the honest thing only when it is advantageous or necessary to avoiding the unpleasant consequences of being caught acting dishonestly?

2. Socrates and Thrasymachus

We have come, by reflecting on a common test of a person's honesty, to one of the seminal problems in moral philosophy. It is the problem at the heart of Plato's *Republic*. Plato (427–347 BC) sets his study of the problem in motion with an account of an exchange between Socrates (469–399 BC) and the sophist Thrasymachus.[1] Initially, the exchange concerns the nature of justice and centers on Thrasymachus' cynical thesis that *justice* is the name of actions that the powerful require the rest of us to perform for their benefit. Under the pressure of Socrates' cross-examination, however, Thrasymachus falls into contradiction and then, rather than revise his ideas, shifts the conversation from the question of what justice is to the question of whether the best life, assuming success in that life, is one of justice and honesty or the opposite. Thrasymachus boldly declares for the latter. People who

---

[1] Plato, *Republic*, bk. I, 336b–354b.

act with complete injustice, he argues, provided they can make themselves invulnerable to punishment, live decidedly better lives than people who are completely just and honest. The reason, he says, is that just and honest people always come out on the short end in their relations with unjust people. Just people, for instance, take only their fair share while unjust people take as much as they can get away with. Likewise, just people fulfill their responsibilities even when doing so requires them to sacrifice money or time, whereas unjust people find ways to evade their responsibilities whenever evading them is to their advantage. In general, then, Thrasymachus maintains, to act justly is to act for another's good and not one's own, and the unjust person is not so foolish as to ignore his own good for the sake of another's. The unjust person therefore gains riches and seizes opportunities that the just person forgoes, and the life of greater riches and more opportunities is surely the better life.

Thrasymachus' ideal is the tyrant whose power over others is supreme and who, by confiscating his subjects' property and extorting their labor, uses that power to make himself inordinately prosperous at their expense. Kings and emperors who set themselves up as deities and compel their subjects to enrich and glorify them are a common example. Another, more familiar in the modern world, is the military dictator who rules by terror and fraud, who loots his country's wealth, and who lives opulently while stashing additional spoils in foreign bank accounts and other offshore havens. This type of individual, the one who practices injustice on a very large scale and succeeds, is for Thrasymachus the most happy of men. Moreover, unlike small-time criminals, who are scorned as thugs, crooks, and cheats, the tyrant who overreaches on a grand scale is hailed as masterful and lordly and treated with much deference and respect. Here, Thrasymachus thinks, is proof positive of the tyrant's great happiness. These are signs, he concludes, that the completely unjust man who succeeds at dominating and deceiving others is admirably strong, wise, and free. The completely just individual, by contrast, is at best a good-hearted simpleton.

Thrasymachus, unfortunately, proves to be as bad at defending these views as he was at defending his initial thesis about the nature of justice. Plato, it seems, who depicts Thrasymachus throughout the exchange as arrogant and belligerent, did not want him to be mistaken for a skillful thinker too. Skillful thinking is what Socrates teaches, and his lessons would be lost if so rude an intellectual adversary were allowed to display it as well. Consequently, when Socrates renews his cross-examination and presses Thrasymachus on the merits of his claims about the advantages of living an unjust life, Thrasymachus crumbles and withdraws. Yet his defeat does not end the discussion. It leads, instead, to a restatement of his claims by participants in the conversation much friendlier to Socrates and less sure of themselves. Glaucon and Adeimantus take up Thrasymachus' challenge to the value of justice and put it in a way that moves the discussion forward. Whatever Plato's purpose in having such an ill-tempered participant introduce this challenge, it was not in order quickly to dismiss it. In the *Republic* the curtain falls on Thrasymachus at the end of book I, but the discussion of his claims continues for another nine books.

Glaucon and Adeimantus, to sharpen Thrasymachus' claims, subtly change their focus. Where Thrasymachus emphasized the benefits of practicing injustice and acclaimed the excellence of the man who successfully lives a completely unjust life, Glaucon and Adeimantus emphasize the seeming absence of benefits intrinsic to practicing justice and make the case for thinking that whatever good one can gain from living a just life one can also gain by fooling people into believing that one is just when one isn't. Rather than promote the ideal of being a tyrant with supreme power over others, Glaucon points to the advantages of being a sneak with a magical ring that gives whoever wears it the power to become invisible at will.[2] Such a sneak could enrich himself by theft and advance his ambitions by murder while remaining above suspicion, and consequently he could enjoy both the advantages of being esteemed by others as just and honest and the fruits of real crime. Like Thrasymachus' tyrant, he too can practice injustice with impunity, and for this reason he seems to live a better life than the truly just individual. But in addition, he seems also, by virtue of being able to appear to others as just, to reap the very benefits of being so. Hence, even more than Thrasymachus' tyrant, this sneak puts the value of justice into doubt. If he can truly gain all its benefits by virtue of appearing to be just when he isn't, then he shows that justice has no intrinsic merit and is therefore not worth practicing for its own sake. By introducing the fable of Gyges' ring, Plato thus turns Thrasymachus' challenge into one of the main problems of ethics: on what basis, if any, can we understand justice as

---

[2] Ibid., bk. II, 359b–360d.

admirable in itself, as something one has good reason to practice even in circumstances in which one would profit from injustice without the least fear of being found out.

3. The subject of ethics

The main problems of ethics arise, as our example of your finding a lost purse containing a huge wad of cash illustrates, from reflection on situations in life that involve matters of morality. Ethics is the philosophical study of morality. It is a study of what are good and bad ends to pursue in life and what it is right and wrong to do in the conduct of life. It is therefore, above all, a practical discipline. Its primary aim is to determine how one ought to live and what actions one ought to do in the conduct of one's life. It thus differs from studies in anthropology, sociology, and empirical psychology that also examine human pursuits and social norms. These studies belong to positive science. Their primary aim is not to prescribe action but rather to describe, analyze, and explain certain phenomena of human life, including the goal-directed activities of individuals and groups and the regulation of social life by norms that constitute the conventional morality of a community. They do not, in other words, seek to establish conclusions about what a person ought to do but are only concerned with establishing what people in fact do and the common causes and conditions of their actions. Nor is this difference between ethics and certain social sciences peculiar to these disciplines. It can be seen as well in the contrast between medicine and physiology, or between agriculture and botany. The former in each pair is a practical discipline. Both are studies of how best to achieve or produce a certain good, health in the one case, crops in the other, and each then yields prescriptions of what one ought to do to achieve or produce that good. By contrast, the latter in each pair is a positive science whose studies yield descriptions and explanations of the processes of animal and plant life but do not yield prescriptions for mending or improving those processes.

The definition of ethics as 'the philosophical study of morality' gives the chief meaning of the word. It has other meanings, to be sure, some of which are perhaps more usual in general conversation. In particular, the word is commonly used as a synonym for morality, and sometimes it is used more narrowly to mean the moral code or system of a particular tradition, group, or individual. Christian ethics, professional ethics, and Schweitzer's ethics are examples. In philosophy, too, it is used in this narrower way to mean a particular system or theory that is the product of the philosophical study. Thus philosophers regularly refer to the major theories of the discipline as Hume's ethics, Kant's ethics, utilitarian ethics, and so forth. In this book, unless the word is so modified, it will be used solely with its chief meaning.

To grasp this meaning, however, we must be certain of what is meant by *morality*. This word, too, is used to mean different things, and consequently, to avoid confusion and misunderstanding, we need to pin down what it means when ethics is defined as the philosophical study of morality. We could of course fix the right meaning by defining morality as the subject of ethics, but obviously, since our interest in fixing the right meaning is to determine what the subject of ethics is, this definition would get us nowhere. At the same time, it does suggest where to look for clues. It suggests that we look to the contrast we just drew between ethics and certain studies in anthropology and sociology. For that contrast, besides serving to distinguish ethics as a practical discipline, also makes salient two distinct notions of morality. One is that of morality as an existing institution of a particular society, what is commonly called the society's conventional morality. The other is that of morality as a universal ideal grounded in reason. The first covers phenomena studied in anthropology and sociology. The second defines the subject of ethics.

Admittedly, that there are two notions of morality is not immediately evident. It should become so, however, from seeing that no conventional morality could be the subject of ethics. A conventional morality is a set of norms of a particular society that are generally accepted and followed by the society's members. These norms reflect the members' shared beliefs about right and wrong, good and evil, and they define corresponding customs and practices that prevail in the society. As is all too common, sometimes these beliefs rest on superstitions and prejudices, and sometimes the corresponding customs and practices promote cruelty and inflict indignity. It can happen then that a person comes to recognize such facts about some of the norms belonging to his society's conventional morality and, though observance of these norms has become second nature in him, to conclude nonetheless that he ought to reject them. Implicit in this conclusion is a realization that one has to look beyond the conventional morality of one's society to determine what ends to pursue in life and what it is right to do in the conduct of life. And it therefore follows that a conventional morality cannot be the subject of a study whose principal aims are to determine what are good and bad ends to pursue in life and what it is right and wrong to do in the conduct of life. It cannot be the subject of ethics.

A concrete example may help to flesh out this implication. Not that long ago the conventional morality in many if not most sections of the United States condemned interracial romance and marriage, and even today in small pockets of this country norms forbidding romance and marriage between people of different racial backgrounds are still fully accepted and vigorously enforced. Imagine then someone raised in a community whose conventional morality included such norms coming to question their authority as it became increasingly clear to him that they were based on ignorance and prejudice and that the customs they defined involved gratuitous injuries. His newfound clarity about the irrational and cruel character of these norms might be the result of a friendship he formed with someone of another race, much as Huckleberry Finn's epiphany about the untrustworthiness of his conscience resulted from the friendship he formed with the runaway slave Jim. Huck, you may remember, suffered a bad conscience about helping Jim escape from bondage but then quit paying it any heed when he discovered that he could not bring himself to turn Jim in and would feel just as low if he did.[3] That we think Huck's decision to disregard the reproaches of his conscience – the echoes, as it were, of the conventional morality of the slaveholding society in which he was raised – perfectly sound, that we think equally sound a decision to go against norms in one's society that prohibit interracial romance and marriage, shows that we recognize the difference between what a particular society generally sanctions as right action and generally condemns as wrong and what one ought to do and ought not to do. Ethics, being concerned with the latter, does not therefore take the former as its subject.

The possibility of a sound decision to go against the norms of the conventional morality of one's society implies standards of right or wise action that are distinct from those norms. The reason why is plain. A sound decision requires a basis, and the basis, in this case, cannot consist of such norms. It cannot, in other words, consist of norms whose authority in one's thinking derives from their being generally accepted and enforced in one's society. A decision to go against such norms, a decision like Huck Finn's, represents a

---

[3] Mark Twain, *The Adventures of Huckleberry Finn*, ch. 16.

conclusion that a norm's being generally accepted and enforced in one's society is not a sufficient reason to follow it, and consequently it could be sound only if its basis did not consist of standards whose authority was that of custom. Its basis must consist instead of standards that derive their authority from a source that is independent of custom. These standards may of course coincide to some extent with the norms of a conventional morality. That is, they may require or endorse many of the same acts as those norms do. But coincidence is not identity. However coincident they may be with the norms of a conventional morality, they nonetheless derive their authority in practical thought from a different source and therefore constitute a distinct set of moral standards.

What could this different source be? Since the standards in question can form the basis of a sound decision to go against the norms of the conventional morality of one's society, they must be standards that rational and reflective thinking about one's circumstances support. Accordingly, the source of their authority can fairly be said to be rational thought or reason. Here then is the second notion of morality. It is the notion of morality as comprising standards of right and wise conduct whose authority in practical thought is determined by reason rather than custom. Unlike the first notion, that of morality as an existing institution of a particular society, it represents a universal ideal. The standards it comprises are found, not by observing and analyzing the complex social life of a particular society, but rather by reasoning and argument from elementary facts about human existence taken abstractly. Morality, conceived in this way, is the subject of ethics. Its philosophical study consists in finding the standards it comprises, expounding them systematically, and establishing the rational grounds of their authority in practical thinking. And unless otherwise indicated, subsequent references to morality in this book should be taken, not as references to some conventional morality, but rather as references to the set of standards that this ideal comprises.

Having arrived at this understanding of ethics, we can now see immediately why the problem at the heart of Plato's *Republic* is central to the study. For it would be disconcerting, to say the least, if it turned out that the authority that basic standards of justice and honesty had in our practical thinking derived from custom only and was not backed by reason. It would be disconcerting, that is, if no ethical theory could show that these standards were integral to morality. Yet this possibility is clearly implied by our reflections on the example of your finding a lost purse containing a huge wad of cash as well as by Glaucon's restatement of Thrasymachus' position. Both represent arguments for the proposition that basic standards of justice and honesty are standards of conventional morality only. The challenge, then, that they create for ethical theory is to find rational grounds for the authority that basic standards of justice and honesty carry in practical thought. It is to justify on rational grounds taking these standards as ultimate guides to what one ought to do in the conduct of one's life. Such a justification would show that one had good reason to do the honest thing for its own sake. It would thus answer the doubts that the example of your finding a lost purse containing a huge wad of cash and Glaucon's restatement of Thrasymachus' position raise about the reasonableness of doing the honest thing in circumstances in which one could profit materially from dishonesty without the least fear of being found out.

4. An alternative conception of morality

Nothing is ever quite this pat in philosophy. Many people, for instance, think of morality as a list of universal "Do"s and "Don't"s corresponding to which are universal truths about what it is right and wrong to do. The basic standards of justice and honesty appear on this list in the form of injunctions like "Tell the truth!" "Keep your promises!" "Don't cheat!" "Don't steal!" and so forth, and the truths that those who think of morality in this way see as corresponding to these injunctions are propositions in which truth-telling and promise-keeping are said to be right actions, cheating and stealing wrong actions. Indeed, on this conception of morality, the very way in which our ideas of right and wrong are connected to matters of justice and honesty guarantees the truth of these propositions. Thus, because justice and honesty are a matter of what we owe others and what we are obligated to do for them, there can be no question about whether it is right to do what justice and honesty require. If you borrow a thousand dollars from me, for example, then you owe me a thousand dollars and are obligated to repay the loan. To renege would be dishonest. It would be a violation of the duty you have assumed by accepting the loan, and to violate a duty is to do something wrong, unless of course it is necessary in order to avoid violating a more important or stringent duty. By the same token, because reneging would be a violation of the duty you have assumed by accepting the loan, you ought not to renege, unless of course you have to in order to avoid violating a more important or stringent duty. Clearly, then, if this conception of morality defined the subject of ethics, the problem at the heart of Plato's *Republic* would have to be re-evaluated.

The call for such re-evaluation is, in fact, an important theme among philosophers for whom this conception defines the subject of ethics. To these philosophers, the problem is based on a mistake.[4] The mistake, they maintain, consists in confusing the question of whether the basic standards of justice and honesty are authoritative with the question of whether they are ultimate guides to achieving one's ends or satisfying one's interests. A standard of conduct, they point out, can have authority in one's practical thinking even though it does not guide one toward achieving one's ends or satisfying one's interests. It is enough that the standard defines a duty. Thus, when you recognize that, having borrowed a thousand dollars from me, you have a duty to repay the loan, you see that you are obligated to repay it, that the duty binds you to repay me whether or not you want to and whether or not you would benefit from doing so. And to understand that the duty so binds you is to recognize the authority of the standard that defines it. Confusion sets in, however, when one thinks of circumstances in which you might be tempted to renege and so might ask yourself "Should I repay this loan?" for it is easy to misconstrue this question as a challenge to the authority of the standard that requires repayment. But the question can only represent such a challenge if it expresses uncertainty about whether you have a duty to repay the loan, and you cannot be uncertain about this. It cannot, in other words, represent such a challenge if it is merely a question you put to yourself on realizing that you might be better off defaulting. Even if you would be better off defaulting, even if you decided that defaulting was more in your interest than repaying, you would still have the duty to repay. The standard would still be an authoritative rule by which the rightness and wrongness of your conduct was measured.

Philosophers who make this criticism of the *Republic*'s core problem take morality to be a system of standards whose authority in practical thought is independent of the desires and interests of those whose conduct the system regulates. The key element in this conception of morality is the idea that the standards define duties, for to have a duty to do something is to be bound to

---

[4] H. A. Prichard, "Does Moral Philosophy Rest on a Mistake?" *Mind* 21 (1912): 21–37.

do it regardless of one's attitudes about doing it or the effect on one's interests of doing it. The familiar predicament of being bound by a duty to do something that is both unpleasant and disadvantageous – a duty, say, to keep a promise to visit your cantankerous Uncle Bob when you really can't spare the time – makes this point clear. Recognizing your duty to visit Uncle Bob, you think that it would be wrong to cancel the visit, that you ought to keep your promise, even though you have no desire to see him and know that you would find the visit a nuisance as well as a loss of valuable time. The thought here that you ought to keep the promise expresses the sense of being bound by it. That your desires would be better satisfied, your interests better served, by canceling the visit therefore gives you no reason to abandon the thought as false or mistaken. If you nevertheless wonder whether you ought to keep the promise, you must, it seems, have a different sense of 'ought' in mind in asking this question. Else the question would be idle. Accordingly, philosophers who favor this conception of morality draw a sharp distinction between two uses of 'ought', one that captures the sense of being duty-bound to do something and one that captures the sense of being well-advised to do it in view of what would best serve your ends and interests. The distinction both reflects and reinforces the conception's central theme: that morality's authority in practical thought is not answerable to the desires and interests of those whose conduct it regulates.

The distinction, then, solidifies the criticism of the *Republic*'s core problem that the conception supports. The gist of the criticism is that the problem rests on a mistake about the import of asking whether one ought to be just, as Glaucon did when he restated Thrasymachus' position, or whether one ought to do the honest thing, as we imagined you might do upon finding a lost purse containing a huge wad of cash. One can easily construe such questions as challenging the authority of basic standards of justice and honesty, but only, so the criticism goes, because of confusion over the sense in which 'ought' is used in asking them. Thus, for them to challenge that authority, 'ought' must be used in the sense in which to say that one ought to do x is to say that one is duty-bound to do x. But this is not the sense in which you or Glaucon would use 'ought' to ask them. The sense in which you or he would use 'ought' to ask them is the sense in which to say that one ought to do x is to say that one would be well-advised in view of one's ends and interests to do x. This is the sense 'ought' has when such questions are asked as a result of reflection on the advantages of acting unjustly or dishonestly. But when 'ought' is used in this sense to ask such questions, they fail to challenge the authority of basic standards of justice and honesty. However advantageous acting unjustly or dishonestly might be in some circumstances, one may still be duty-bound to act justly and honestly in them. In short, the criticism comes down to the charge of misdirection. Plato put ethics on the wrong track, according to this criticism, when he sought to justify the authority basic standards of justice and honesty have in a person's practical thinking on the basis of what best serves his ends and interests.

5. Two types of ethical theory

The opposition between Plato and the philosophers who make this criticism – let us call them Plato's critics – corresponds to a major division among ethical theories. This division, like the opposition between Plato and his critics, reflects a disagreement over the proper conception of morality. Accordingly, theories that side with Plato support the conception that his critics regard as the source of his error. On this conception, morality comprises standards of right and wrong conduct that have authority in practical thought in virtue of the ends or interests served by the conduct that these standards guide. These theories are teleological. The opposing theories, then, support the conception on which Plato's critics base their criticism. On this conception, morality comprises standards of right and wrong that have authority in practical thought independently of the ends or interests of those whose conduct they guide. These theories are deontological. *Teleology* and *deontology* are technical terms in ethics, and as is typical of such terms, their etymology explains their meaning. 'Telos' is Greek for end or purpose. 'Deon' is Greek for duty. Thus, on a teleological conception of ethics, the study of what it is right to do and wrong to do follows and depends on the study of what are good and bad ends to pursue or what one's real interests are. By contrast, on a deontological conception, the former study is partly if not wholly independent of the latter. That is, on this conception of ethics, determining what it is right to do and wrong to do does not always require knowing what are good and bad ends to pursue or what one's real interests are.

To see more clearly this difference between teleology and deontology, consider how each conceives of ethics as a practical discipline. A practical discipline, recall, is one whose primary aim is to prescribe action relevant to its area of study. Its chief conclusions, therefore, are prescriptions of what one ought to do in various circumstances within that area. In some practical disciplines, the chief conclusions are prescriptions in which 'ought' has the second of the two senses we distinguished above. That is, 'ought' is used in them in the sense in which to say that one ought to do *x* is to say that one would be well-advised to do *x* in view of certain ends or interests. These disciplines are teleological. Medicine is a prime example. Its chief conclusions are prescriptions about what actions one ought to take to prevent illness and improve health. In other words, they specify actions one would be well-advised to do to protect and promote one's own health or the health of those in one's care. Health, then, is the ultimate end within medicine, and accordingly its study is the study of right and wrong ways to pursue this end. Alternatively, one could characterize health as a good and medicine as the study of how to achieve this good. By analogy, on a teleological conception of ethics, a certain end is taken to be ultimate – pleasure, perhaps, or happiness, or the welfare of humankind. It is the highest good for human beings, what philosophers call the *summum bonum*. The object of ethical study, then, is to determine how to achieve it, and the study of what it is right and wrong to do in the conduct of life thus follows and depends on the study of what this good consists in or, put differently, what are good and bad ends to pursue in life.

On a deontological conception of ethics, its chief conclusions are prescriptions in which 'ought' has the first of the two senses we distinguished above. That is, 'ought' is used in these prescriptions in the sense in which to say that one ought to do *x* is to say that one is duty-bound to do *x*. This alters significantly the way in which ethics is conceived as a practical discipline. Medicine, in particular, is no longer an apt model. One must look to a different discipline. Historically, following the tradition of Christian ethics, this has been jurisprudence. Accordingly, one understands moral standards, the standards of right and wrong, as analogous to the laws of a community that regulate its members' conduct. Thus, just as a jurisprudential study of the laws of a community yields conclusions about what actions its members are legally obligated to perform, so on a deontological conception of ethics, the study of what it is right and wrong to do in the conduct of life yields conclusions about what actions a person is duty-bound to perform. And just as the determination of what actions a community's laws obligate its members to do does not depend entirely on determining what public or even private good is realized by the observance of those laws, so too the determination of what actions moral standards bind a person to do does not depend entirely on determining what good would be realized by their observance. These standards have authority in practical thought in virtue of the authority of their source, just as a community's laws have authority in virtue of the authority of the legislator or legislative body that enacted them. And in either case they have such authority independently of the ends and interests of those whose conduct they regulate.

Plato's critics believe the *Republic*'s core problem is inherent in a teleological conception of ethics. A deontological conception, they think, avoids the problem. The reason they think so is plain. If the chief conclusions of ethics are prescriptions about what one ought to do in the sense of being duty-bound rather than being well-advised in view of certain ends and interests, then no fact about the advantages or benefits one would gain from violating a duty of justice or honesty in a given situation challenges the truth of the prescription that one ought to do the just or honest thing in that situation. Its truth is unchallenged by such facts since none of them is relevant to whether one is duty-bound to do the just or honest thing. All such facts, that is, are consistent with one's being duty-bound to do it. Plato's critics, then, treat the *Republic*'s core problem as resting on a mistake because they believe the teleological conception of ethics it presupposes is false. The problem, however, is deeper than they recognize. A deontological conception of ethics does not avoid it.

6. The problem of deontology

Consider again the problem as it arises from our example of your finding a lost purse containing a huge wad of cash. When, having found this purse, you wonder what you ought to do, your question, according to Plato's critics, can either be about what duty requires you to do or about what you would be well-advised to do in view of your ends and interests. Ethics, they would say, concerns the former and not the latter, and therefore, since it is the latter and not the former that bids you to forsake basic standards of honesty as guides to conduct, the problem is due to a simple confusion over the meaning of the question you are asking. Yet this diagnosis is too quick. The problem, remember, arises when the question leads you to search for a good reason to be honest, and if a deontological conception of ethics avoids this problem, as Plato's critics believe, then either you must have such a reason just by virtue of your having a duty not to take what doesn't belong to you or your search for such a reason is itself a mistake. Either, that is, your having a duty to do the honest thing is itself a good reason to do it, or you don't need to search for such a reason to recognize the authority that basic standards of honesty have in practical thought. Neither of these alternatives, however, is free of difficulties. Quite the contrary, both are open to serious objection. Neither, then, allows a deontological conception of ethics to escape from the *Republic*'s core problem.

Thus suppose Plato's critics took the first alternative. Suppose, that is, they maintained that you have a good reason not to take the cash from the purse just in virtue of your having a duty not to take it. Your having a duty to do something, they might say, is itself a good reason to do it. But on what grounds could they defend this view? "Well," they might argue, "as we have pointed out, if you have a duty to do something, if you are duty-bound to do it, then you ought to do it, and plainly it makes no sense to say that someone ought to do something unless he has a good reason to do it." But this response would be a nonstarter. It would amount to begging the question. No doubt, before Plato's critics drew their distinction between a use of 'ought' that signifies being duty-bound to do some action and a use that signifies being well-advised to do an action in view of one's interests and ends, we might have accepted, as a general thesis about the use of 'ought' to prescribe action, that to say that someone ought to do *x* is to imply that the person has a good reason to do *x*. But once they draw their distinction, acceptance of this general thesis requires separate consideration of the two cases. Hence, they cannot use the thesis to defend their view without first showing that it holds for each of the specific uses of 'ought' they have identified, particularly, the use that signifies being duty-bound to do some action. In other words, before they can use the thesis they must first show that if one is duty-bound to do some action, one has a good reason to do it. And this just puts them back to square one.

In response to this criticism, Plato's critics might try a new tack. "Admittedly," they might say, "we could not use the general thesis to defend our view if the reasons people had to do things were all of one kind. For in that case it would be wrong for us to assume that saying that someone ought to do *x* implies that he has a reason to do *x* regardless of which sense of 'ought' one uses to say this. But the reasons people have for doing things are not all of one kind. Specifically, corresponding to the distinction we draw between the two uses of 'ought,' there is a distinction between moral reasons and personal reasons. The point is that just as ethics, on our conception of it, is concerned with what people ought to do in the sense of what they are duty-bound to do rather than what they would be well-advised to do in view of their ends and interests, so too it is concerned with what people have moral reasons to do rather than what they have personal reasons to do. Accordingly, saying that someone ought to do something, if one is using 'ought' in the sense of being duty-bound to do it, is to imply that the person has a moral reason to do it. Or in other words, your having a duty to do something gives you a moral reason to do it."

With this response Plato's critics would clear themselves of the charge of begging the question. But in doing so, they would be shifting the grounds on which they hold that a deontological conception of ethics avoids the *Republic*'s core problem. They would be giving up the first of the two alternatives we identified and taking the second. This should be plain, for they would be arguing, in effect, that to search for good reasons to do the honest thing, in circumstances such as yours, is to search for good personal reasons, and such a search, whatever the outcome, has no bearing on the authority that basic standards of honesty have in practical thought. To think that it does would be to make the same mistake as the original one of thinking that asking whether you ought to do the honest thing in these circumstances challenges the authority of the standards. That is, just as this question could not challenge the standards' authority if what you were asking was whether you would be well-advised to do the honest thing in view of your ends and interests, so too your search for good reasons to do the honest thing could not challenge that authority since what you would be after would be good personal reasons to do the honest thing. To challenge the authority of these standards the question you were asking would have to be whether you were duty-bound to do the honest thing and the reasons you were after would have to be moral reasons. But to ask whether you were duty-bound to do the honest thing is to ask an idle question, and similarly there is no point in searching for moral reasons to be honest. You have such reasons because the standards have authority in practical thought, because they define duties that bind you to do certain actions, and not the other way round. Or so Plato's critics, in shifting to the second alternative, would argue.

On this view, one recognizes the moral reasons one has to do certain actions by recognizing the authority that moral standards have in practical thought, and not vice versa. How such authority is to be understood, however, is not immediately clear. An explanation, though, comes directly from the way Plato's critics conceive of ethics as a practical discipline. For their conception of ethics as a practical discipline is modeled on jurisprudence. Accordingly, they see the standards of morality as analogous to the laws of a community. Such laws have authority over every member of the community and, in virtue of that authority, give each member legal reasons to do what they require him or her to do. By analogy, then, moral standards have authority over those whose conduct they regulate and, in virtue of that authority, give them moral reasons to act as the standards direct. In this way, Plato's critics can explain moral reasons as following from and dependent on the authority of moral standards and not vice versa. Thus, on this explanation, the basic standards of honesty, in virtue of the authority they have in practical thought, would give you a moral reason to do the honest thing in the circumstances you faced independently of your having any good personal reasons to do it. Yet to advance this explanation, Plato's critics would have to assume that you belonged to a community in which the standards of morality, rather than some code of positive law, say, were the authoritative standards of conduct and in which each member was subject to the authority of those standards in virtue of his or her membership in the community. And herein lies the difficulty with their view. After all, it would not be mere querulousness on your part to ask, "What community is this? And how did I become a member?"

7. The idea of a moral community

The impulse to think of all human beings as joined together in a moral community almost certainly lies behind the belief that morality has authority in our lives regardless of our having personal reasons to be moral. It is one source of the powerful attraction that a deontological conception of ethics has. There is a global community of all human beings, it is frequently said, a global village, as it were, and a person qualifies as a member of this village just in virtue of being human. The community's laws are the universal standards of morality, and the members have duties and rights according to these laws. This thought or something like it, let us then suppose, is what lies behind the way Plato's critics explain how the authority of moral standards precedes and certifies moral reasons. Accordingly, the thought would supply them with answers to your questions, for it specifies the community to which they would think you belonged and sets out the conditions of your membership. But the thought itself would have to be justified before Plato's critics could claim to have shown by this explanation that a deontological conception of ethics avoids the *Republic*'s core problem. Communities of different human beings exist all over the globe, and evidence of their existence consists in their written laws, published rules, territorial markers, governing institutions, financial arrangements, communal celebrations, ensigns and other symbols of communal unity, and written and oral histories. Yet there seems to be no such evidence of a global community to which all human beings belong. How then could Plato's critics justify the thought that there was such a community? How could they show that the thought did not merely reflect their aspiration to a universal morality?

Lacking empirical evidence of such a community, they must turn to what they affirm as the universal truths about right and wrong that correspond to the basic standards of morality. On their conception of morality, these truths are propositions about what fulfills and what violates one's duties, since on this conception matters of right and wrong are matters of what one ought and ought not to do in the sense of what one is duty-bound to do. These truths, moreover, are universal inasmuch as the human practices that create duty would be found in any society. These include such practices as lending and borrowing, promising and consenting, buying and selling, making friends, entering into marriage, establishing a family, offering and accepting aid, and so forth. Since a society that lacked such practices is scarcely conceivable, one might then infer from this observation that, even though no moral community of all human beings had ever been realized, the basic standards of morality nonetheless constituted a framework for such a community. One might infer, that is, that because they corresponded to universal truths about right and wrong that any reflective person would affirm, they represented valid principles governing all human social relations both within and across real communities. Such an inference appears to be the best, if not the only way Plato's critics could justify the thought on which their understanding of the authority of moral standards depends.

Still, it falls short of justifying that thought. Although it may appear that the universal truths about right and wrong that Plato's critics affirm correspond to standards of conduct that constitute a framework for a moral community of all human beings, the appearance is misleading. These truths may correspond to such standards, but then again they may not. For what makes them true (if they are true) is the existence in every human society of practices that create duties, and consequently we would need some further reason to think they corresponded to standards of morality that constituted a framework for a moral community of all human beings. Without such a reason we cannot assume such correspondence and therefore cannot assume that they correspond to standards whose authority goes beyond that of custom. The standards they correspond to may just be the social norms of a conventional morality. These, too, define duties.

Consider marriage, for example. Marriage may be a practice in every human society, and if it is, then it is a universal truth that being faithless to your spouse is wrong inasmuch as the duties that marriage creates include duties of fidelity to one's spouse. Yet this truth may correspond only to the social norms that define such duties, norms that differ among themselves according as the society to whose conventional morality they belong practices monogamy or polygamy, enforces patriarchal or egalitarian relations among the sexes, permits or prohibits widows to remarry, and so forth. Consequently, what Plato's critics represent as the standard of morality to which this truth corresponds may come to nothing more than a generalization of these different norms, in which case no standard corresponding to it would have authority in practical thought that went beyond the authority of custom. The same points, then, apply to the other universal truths about right and wrong that Plato's critics affirm. Hence, these truths do not provide sufficient grounds for justifying the thought on which the critics' understanding of the authority of moral standards depends.

The problem at the core of Plato's *Republic* has traditionally been a problem about justice. The philosophical study of morality is a study of standards of right and wise conduct whose authority in practical thought is determined by reason rather than custom, and the problem is how to understand the basic standards of justice as having such authority. How are these standards to be explained as part of morality? Critics of Plato have insisted that this problem rests on a mistake. In their view, no conception of morality that left open the question of whether morality included these standards could ever be right. Thus, on the correct conception, as they see it, the basic standards of justice are paradigm moral standards. This idea is the essence of deontology. But in putting it forth deontologists invite the charge of infecting morality generally with the problem of finding rational grounds for the authority of standards of justice. That they invite this charge is obscured by their various efforts to insulate morality, as they conceive of it, from embarrassing questions: their distinction between two senses of 'ought', the corresponding distinction between moral and personal reasons, their supposition of a moral community of all human beings, their appeal to universal truths about matters of right and wrong. But, as we've now seen, these efforts serve only to postpone the time at which deontologists must answer the charge. Full insulation of morality from these embarrassing questions is not possible. To answer the charge, then, they must show that the authority moral standards have in practical thought, on their conception of morality, is determined by reason and not custom. Otherwise their conception comes down to nothing more than a piece of abstract anthropology. Hence, far from avoiding the *Republic*'s core problem, it faces that problem writ large.

8. Ethical theories and moral ideals

To answer the *Republic*'s core problem requires explaining how justice and honesty qualify as excellences of character. This requires in turn explaining how acts of justice and honesty are in themselves reasonable, that is, how an act's being the just or honest thing to do gives one, by that fact alone, a good reason for doing it. Developing these explanations is a task of ethical theory, and one can find among the many theories that philosophers, since Plato, have put forward a broad range of different explanations. The explanations that teleological theories offer connect acting justly with the achievement of the good that is taken to be the ultimate end of right and wise action, the *summum bonum*. What this end is varies from one teleological theory to another, but on any of them, the explanation must be that acting justly and honestly are necessary means, or perhaps the best means to achieving it. Deontological theories, by contrast, must offer explanations of a different kind. Since on these theories the rightness of acting justly and honestly is not a matter of whether such actions contribute to the achievement of some end but rather a matter of their conforming to standards that have authority in practical thought independently of a person's ends, the explanations they offer must bring to light some point to acting justly and honestly. They must, in other words, so enlarge our understanding of those standards and their place in human life that we see a point to our conforming to them. If, instead, a deontological theory offered no such explanation, it would leave us in the dark about why we conform to them. It would ask us to take their authority on faith and to obey it blindly. It would therefore fail to show that they had authority in practical thought that was backed by reason rather than custom and would thus fall short of a central aim of ethical theory.

Implicit in every theory's answer to the *Republic*'s core problem is an ideal of human life. Indeed, no ethical theory could be complete if it did not imply such an ideal. A complete ethical theory not only formulates and system- atizes the standards of morality, but also justifies them by laying out the rational grounds of their authority in practical thought. Such justification, at a minimum, requires explaining conformity to these standards as mean- ingful conduct, for you would be at a loss to understand how the authority of these standards could have rational grounds if you could not find any meaning to your conforming to them. A complete ethical theory, then, as part of its justification of moral standards, explains how conformity to them is meaningful, and it does so by showing how such conduct contributes to your realizing an ideal of human life. Ideals, generally, serve to make actions meaningful in our lives. Many, like those of athletic prowess, artistic creativity, commercial prosperity, romantic love, family togetherness, tri- umph over the elements of nature, and so forth, give meaning to common activities of life by presenting models of success in those activities. Having a model or picture of what success in them consists in enables us to see their pursuit as something important, worthwhile, or fulfilling. To be sure, none of these ideals serves to make conformity to moral standards meaningful. While they present models of success in activities that moral standards regulate, conformity to moral standards is not what success in those activ- ities consists in, and therefore to explain such conformity as meaningful an ethical theory must incorporate an ideal that applies directly to it. Let us call such an ideal a moral ideal. It is moral ideals, then, that ethical theories imply in their answers to the *Republic*'s core problem.

Needless to say, many people in daily life are seldom if ever troubled about the meaningfulness of their conforming to moral standards. By and large, they recognize that general conformity to moral standards by the members of a community is necessary if people are to live together peacefully and that conforming to them also brings such personal advantages as an untarnished reputation and the goodwill of others. Asked, then, the point of following such standards, they would likely respond by citing one or another of these advantages and not some moral ideal. Still, there are times when one's circumstances invite acts of dishonesty or injustice that would neither disrupt social life, tarnish one's reputation, nor cause one to lose the goodwill of others. Our example of your finding a lost purse containing a huge wad of cash is a case in point. At these times, one realizes, if one is sufficiently reflective, that the point of one's conforming to moral standards cannot be the necessity of such conformity for social harmony or for maintaining a sterling reputation and the goodwill of others. At these times, to find meaning in one's conforming to them, one must seek a fuller understanding of their place in one's life, and the search, if successful, leads one to affirm some moral ideal.

By the same token, then, an ethical theory, if it succeeds in justifying moral standards, affirms a moral ideal. Its justification of them consists in laying out the rational grounds of their authority in practical thought, and it cannot do this without giving meaning to a person's following them in circumstances in which neither social peace nor personal advantage would be harmed by his ignoring them. It cannot, that is, lay out such grounds without implying a moral ideal. In this regard, an ethical theory articulates the thinking of a reflective person who finds himself in such circumstances and who, having been brought up to act justly and rightly, now wonders whether there is a point to doing so. His thinking might take any one of a number of different avenues. Each one would correspond to a different moral ideal guiding his thought. Accordingly, there are a number of different ethical theories that articulate these different avenues of thought and that affirm these different ideals.

It will be the project of the next several chapters to examine these different theories. The first ones we will examine are teleological. (See Appendix for a diagram of these.) Afterwards we will take up those that are deontological. Once our survey is complete, we will turn to an important twentieth-century skeptical attack on these theories and the alternative ethics it offers. Our examination of the latter will lead to general questions about practical reason and ethical knowledge, whether either is possible and if it is, how shall we understand it. The final chapter will deal with these issues.

2 Egoism

1. The wise pursuit of happiness

The question that leads us into the study of different ethical theories concerns the reasons we have to be honest and just in circumstances that invite dishonesty or injustice without risk of disrupting social peace, tarnishing one's reputation, or losing the goodwill of others. One thought a person who was faced with such circumstances might have is that his happiness is best served in the long run by adhering to the standards of honesty and justice. "The cash is very tempting," he might say to himself as he looked at the wad of bills in the purse he had just found, "but it would be stupid to take it. The costs and risks involved make it likely to be more trouble than it's worth." The ideal that a person who thought along these lines would affirm is that of wisdom in the pursuit of happiness. In ethics, the theory that affirms this ideal is *egoism*. The popularity of this theory among people unfamiliar with moral philosophy suggests that no other theory has more immediate intuitive appeal. The theory, in addition, has a secure and important place in the history of ethics. Arguably, it is the theory Plato worked out in the *Republic* to answer Thrasymachus' challenge to the value of justice. In any case, it certainly had other champions in the ancient world. The most noteworthy of these is the great Hellenistic philosopher Epicurus (341–271 BC). Its place in modern philosophy is no less prominent. In the early modern period its defenders included such major thinkers as Thomas Hobbes (1588–1679) and Benedict de Spinoza (1632–77), and it continued to receive strong and important support in the eighteenth and nineteenth centuries. Only in the twentieth century did its vitality begin to wane, although even today it still has active and influential defenders.

Egoism is a teleological theory. Its fundamental principle is that the highest good for each person is his or her own happiness. From this principle it follows that right action consists in looking out for and furthering one's happiness, wrong action consists in neglecting it. The theory, in other words, answers all questions about what a person ought to do by prescribing the action by which he can best promote his own happiness. Stated so baldly, the theory sounds like a recipe for selfishness. But it would be a mistake to interpret it in this way. Selfishness means that one pursues one's own interests without regard to the interests of others. A selfish person thinks only of himself; nobody else matters to him. Egoism, while its fundamental principle identifies a person's own happiness as the highest good for that person, does not prescribe the pursuit of that good without regard to the interests of others or concern for their well-being. Indeed, wherever one's own happiness depends on other people's goodwill or their doing well, it would be foolish not to promote their interests or be concerned about their well-being. And given how pervasive such dependence is in life, it would be especially foolish not to cultivate friendships, help one's neighbors, show kindness to strangers, contribute to the good of one's community, and so forth. Egoism, then, far from being a recipe for selfishness, encourages behavior and attitudes that are just the opposite. Its defenders advance it in the belief that basic standards of justice, honesty, kindness, charity, and the like can be seen to have authority in practical thought that is grounded in reason when one comes to see that a person's happiness depends on his following them. Thus the thought that inspires the theory is that applying intelligence and forethought to the aim of achieving happiness shows that the best way to realize this aim is to live one's life by such standards.

The thought reflects the ideal of wisdom in pursuit of happiness. This is the ideal that egoism affirms. A mature understanding of the conditions necessary for achieving happiness and of the practices, skills, and habits that make it possible over an entire life shows that one could not have any realistic hope of achieving it if one lived without regard to the interests of others or the rules they expect one to follow. Wisdom in the pursuit of happiness means taking account of one's long-term as well as one's short-term interests and one's limitations and vulnerabilities as well as one's powers and opportunities. Accordingly, a wise person does not squander his resources on immediate pleasures and transitory benefits but rather saves a good portion of them as protection against hardship that might arise in the future. Nor does he indulge his appetites and emotions to excess, risking injury to his health or damage to valuables whose loss he would later regret. Rather he resists their pressure and keeps a level head. Similarly, then, such a person does not ignore others or trample on their interests for the sake of paltry rewards and temporary advantages. Instead, he cultivates friends and tries not to make enemies, for he knows that, however prosperous and well-liked he is now, there may come a time when he needs the help of friends and to be free of threats from enemies. And he knows, too, that the comforts and joys of friendship are among the greatest of human pleasures. Such wisdom is nothing more than common sense, of course, but it is no strike against an ethical theory that it draws on common sense. Egoism is such a theory. Its program is to find in these and similar pieces of common sense a justification for adherence to basic standards of justice and honesty, kindness and charity, as well as those of thrift and frugality, self-control and level-headedness.

Clearly, then, egoism sharply opposes a view like Thrasymachus'. Both, to be sure, affirm the ideal of wisdom in the pursuit of happiness. They agree, that is, in their identification of happiness as the highest good. Where they disagree is on the question of what wisdom requires for successful pursuit of this good. Egoism, in answering the question, seeks to justify morality as a set of universal standards of right and wrong adherence to which is the best, if not the only means, to achieving happiness. Thrasymachus' view, by contrast, represents a kind of skepticism about morality. It denies that there is a set of universal standards of right and wrong whose authority in practical thought is backed by reason. At most, Thrasymachus would say, there is a loose set of maxims about always keeping your promises, telling the truth, helping those in need, and so forth that the weak would be wise to follow. But the strong, he would declare, would not, for they can ignore these maxims with impunity and, as a result, can gain riches they would otherwise have to forgo. On Thrasymachus' view, in other words, these maxims do not constitute a set of universal standards that could be the object of ethical theory, nor do any others. Hence, his view represents a challenge to the very project of ethical theory, and this challenge is particularly sharp in the case of egoism. Before taking it up, however, we need to develop further our exposition of egoism, to examine the chief arguments for its taking happiness to be the highest good, and to lay out and assess its program for grounding the basic standards of justice, honesty, kindness, charity, and the like in its fundamental principle.

2. The concept of happiness

One thing essential to understanding egoism is clarification of its central concept, that of happiness. The clarification is essential because the word 'happiness' is ambiguous. On the one hand, it is sometimes used to denote a mood, which can be short-lived and even momentary. Thus we talk of moments of happiness or describe events as bringing a little happiness into our lives. On the other hand, the word is sometimes used to denote a condition of a person's life as a whole or at least over a significant stretch of it. Thus, when we describe someone as finding happiness or achieving happiness, we have some such condition in mind. 'Happiness,' when used in the first sense, means something like elation or joy. Its opposite is sadness. 'Happiness,' when used in the second sense, means something like a permanent or long-lasting state of well-being and satisfaction with one's situation. Its opposite is misery. This second sense, and not the first, is the sense we intend when we speak of the pursuit of happiness. The pursuit of happiness is not the pursuit of elation or joy. It is the pursuit of a durable state of well-being and satisfaction with one's life. This pursuit is what egoism takes to be the context of right and wise action, and accordingly it is in this second sense of 'happiness' that the word is used to formulate the fundamental principle of egoism. This sense is the theory's central concept.

The concept combines the idea of living well with the idea of being satisfied with one's life. Its two elements, then, are well-being and self-satisfaction. Many philosophical discussions of happiness focus exclusively on the first element and ignore the second. Indeed, a common assumption of these discussions is that the concepts of happiness and well-being are identical. This assumption, however, is mistaken. Happiness is, in part, a concept of psychology; well-being is not. To say that someone is happy is to attribute to him a certain attitude toward himself or his life, whereas no such attitude is attributed to someone in saying that he is living well. Accordingly, a full account of the concept of happiness includes an element that captures this attitude. Contrary, then, to what is commonly assumed, the concept is not identical to that of well-being. Nonetheless, it does not follow that a philosophical discussion of happiness necessarily goes wrong if it focuses on well-being. What does follow is that in making well-being the focus of such a discussion one must keep in mind that one is focusing on only a part of happiness. The main question in such a discussion is what happiness consists in, and the point is that the answer one comes to may not be complete if one comes to it from consideration of what a person's well-being consists in. Be this as it may, consideration of what well-being consists in is the principal means to determining what happiness consists in.

What a person's well-being consists in is among the oldest questions in ethics. Traditionally, the main answers have been pleasure and excelling at things worth doing. *Hedonism* is the theory that supports the first answer. *Perfectionism* is the theory that supports the second. According to hedonism, human well-being consists in pleasure and the absence of pain. The more a person's life is filled with pleasure and is free of pain the better that life is. Perfectionism, by contrast, takes human well-being to consist in activity that is both worth doing and excellently done. The more a person's life is filled with such activity and is free of both trivial actions and failures the better that life is. In short, hedonism measures a person's well-being by the quality of his subjective states, whereas perfectionism measures it by the worth and character of the activities in which he engages. Hedonism takes well-being as consisting in pleasant and agreeable experiences unspoiled by painful and disagreeable ones. Perfectionism takes it as consisting in engaging in worthwhile activities and doing well in them.

These different accounts of well-being then apply directly to the question of what happiness consists in, though each factors in the second element of the concept of happiness differently. Thus, because satisfaction with one's life is itself a kind of pleasure, dissatisfaction with one's life a kind of pain, the hedonist's account can encompass the second element and therefore give a complete answer on its own. Hedonism, in other words, can hold that how satisfied one is with one's life contributes as much to one's well-being as it does to one's happiness, and therefore the two concepts fall together. By contrast, because one could be dissatisfied with one's life even though it consisted of activities that were worth doing and one was excelling at them, the perfectionist's account must be coupled with the second element to arrive at a complete answer. Perfectionism, in other words, holds that satisfaction with one's life is not a factor of one's well-being, and therefore the concepts of well-being and happiness need not extend to all the same people. The person who is never satisfied with his accomplishments no matter how extraordinary they are may be doing very well in life yet not have achieved happiness.

Egoism can draw on either hedonism or perfectionism for an account of happiness that guides its determination of right action. The theory's central concept, in other words, can be given either a hedonistic or a perfectionistic interpretation. Nonetheless, there is a theoretical advantage to giving it a hedonistic interpretation. As we just saw, the hedonist's account of happiness can unify the concept's two elements, whereas the perfectionist's account cannot, and it stands to reason that a theory will be more coherent if its central concept is unified. In this case, the disunity in the perfectionist's account means that one renders egoism an indeterminate theory when one takes this account as the one that guides its determination of right action. The theory is not, by contrast, similarly indeterminate when one takes the hedonist's account as the one that guides the theory's determination of right action. Hence, giving a hedonistic interpretation to the theory's central concept yields the more coherent and therefore the more powerful version of egoism.

Consider, for example, the situation of someone who has decided to seek happiness in music. She has a talent for the violin, let us suppose, and would regret not pursuing it. At the same time, she may be unsure of how high to aim in this pursuit. What degree of virtuosity should she strive to achieve? Of course, she can expect to achieve a greater degree the more talent she has, but even knowing how talented she is, she may still be uncertain. In principle, she can resolve her uncertainty if she takes the hedonist's account of happiness as her guide. Thus she knows that she would get a great deal of pleasure from playing the violin well, and the better she played the more pleasure she would get. One might think, too, that the better she played the more satisfied she would be with her life, so she should simply strive to be as good a violinist as she can. But things are not that simple. Satisfaction with one's life depends on how closely one's accomplishments match one's aspirations, and so, were she to strive to be as good a violinist as she could, she might end up, as a result of setting such a high standard, less satisfied with her life than if she had set her sights somewhat lower. As William James (1842–1910) sagely put it, a person's self-esteem is equal to the ratio of his pretensions to his successes, and if his pretensions are too high, then his self-esteem will drop notwithstanding his successes.[1] To

---

[1] William James, *The Principles of Psychology*, 2 vols. (1890; reprinted New York: Dover Publications, 1950), vol. I, p. 310.

resolve her uncertainty, therefore, our violinist must weigh the pleasure of playing the violin well against the pain of not meeting the standard she sets and adjust that standard upward or downward until she has set her sights on a degree of excellence whose pursuit promises to yield more pleasure from playing the violin well and from a sense of accomplishment in doing so than the pursuit of some higher degree of excellence or the acceptance of a lower one.

No similar resolution of her uncertainty is possible, however, if she takes the perfectionist's account of happiness as her guide. Because the two elements of the concept of happiness are irreconcilable on a perfectionistic interpretation, they represent independent dimensions of happiness. Accordingly, our violinist, in trying to resolve her uncertainty, must treat how well she would play the violin as a separate measure of happiness from how satisfied she would be with her accomplishments. But to weigh how well she would play against how satisfied she would be with her accomplishments is to compare apples and oranges. The two are incommensurable. Consequently, it is not possible for her to determine what standard of virtuosity she should strive to achieve or whether, having set one, to adjust it upward or downward. Presumably, up to a point, the higher the standard she sets the more accomplished a violinist she will become, yet at the same time after a point, her level of accomplishment will fall increasingly short of the standard she sets and as a result her dissatisfaction will grow. Thus, relative to the contribution that excellence makes to happiness, on the perfectionist's account, she should set for herself the highest standard in the range of those whose pursuit makes her an increasingly excellent violinist, and relative to the contribution that satisfaction with her accomplishments makes, she should set for herself the lowest standard in the range of those whose pursuit initiates an increasingly wider gap between her accomplishments and her aspirations. But the former standard is not likely to coincide with the latter, and if they diverge, there is no basis on which she can decide between them or strike a compromise. On the perfectionist's account, there is no basis for balancing excellence against satisfaction in determining what standard to set.

The example brings out the difficulties that the disunity in the perfectionist's account of happiness creates. It well illustrates the indeterminacy that is produced in egoism when one gives its central concept a perfectionistic interpretation. That the hedonist's version of egoism is not similarly deficient recommends taking it as the theory's preferred formulation as long as no argument has settled the issue of whether human well-being consists of pleasure or excelling at things worth doing. For the rest of the chapter, therefore, let us put the perfectionist's version of egoism aside and assume the hedonist's version as the standard. Perfectionism will reappear in the next chapter as part of a different theory.

3. The primary argument for egoism

The fundamental principle of egoism identifies happiness as the highest good for an individual. Accordingly, egoism takes happiness to be the ultimate end of all right action. It is ultimate in the sense that it is pursued for its own sake and not for the sake of some other end. In addition, on this theory, it is uniquely ultimate. That is, in right action, happiness, and happiness alone, is pursued for its own sake. Any other end one pursues is pursued for the sake of happiness, either directly or indirectly. Any other end of right action, in other words, is an intermediate rather than an ultimate end. As such, it corresponds to an instrumental good. A college scholarship, for example, is an instrumental good. Winning such a scholarship is helpful to gaining the knowledge and understanding that higher education imparts. Hence, one seeks it for the sake of gaining such knowledge and understanding. One does not seek it for its own sake, for a college scholarship can have no value apart from the goods one can use it to attain. Similar points may then apply to knowledge and understanding. They, too, would be intermediate ends if they were sought for the sake of the greater enjoyment of arts and literature, science and technology, that they made possible. In this case, one would seek them for the sake of the pleasure or satisfaction their exercise brings. Alternatively, though, one might seek them for their own sake, in which case they would be ultimate rather than intermediate ends. Typically, then, on the hedonistic interpretation of happiness, knowledge and understanding count as instrumental goods. On the perfectionistic interpretation, they count as constituents of the highest good.

Few people would argue with the proposition that happiness is an ultimate end of right action. People generally regard their own happiness as something good in itself and not something they pursue for the sake of some other end. They also regard it as something that sometimes it is right to promote even though doing so results in frustrating somebody else's pursuits. Egoism, then, in taking happiness as an ultimate end of right action, squares with ordinary opinion. Where it goes beyond ordinary opinion is in its taking happiness to be the only ultimate end of right action. For many people would disagree. They think that what makes an action right, in some cases, is its being done for the sake of another's happiness rather than one's own. Thus, while they might agree with the proposition that one's own happiness is an ultimate end of right action, they would disagree with the proposition that it was uniquely ultimate. So the main burden of proof on a defender of egoism is to make a convincing case for this proposition. The success of any argument for egoism's fundamental principle largely rests on its meeting this burden.

The most important argument was made famous by Hobbes. It relies on a theory of human motivation that Hobbes put at the foundation of his moral and political thought. That theory concerns the springs of intentional action. To explain it, let us first distinguish, as Hobbes did, between intentional actions, like your drawing the blinds when night falls, and reflexive behavior, like your blinking when a light is suddenly shown in your eyes.[2] Intentional actions spring from motives. They are movements (or refrainings from movement) that you execute to achieve an end provided by some motive. Reflexive actions are automatic. They are movements that the activity of your nervous system produces without the interposition of some motive. The chief doctrine of Hobbes's theory is that the motive of every intentional action is at bottom the same. It is the desire to promote one's own interests. This is the doctrine of psychological egoism. The theory advances this doctrine as a basic truth about human nature and so a fundamental law of human psychology. Accordingly, every human motive is reducible to a self-interested desire. Fear, for instance, is at bottom the desire to avoid something that threatens to harm one. Anger is at bottom the desire to retaliate against an aggressor in the interest of deterring future aggression. Love is at bottom the desire to connect with another whose companionship brings one pleasure. And so forth. Successful reduction to self-interested desire of the great variety of motives that we commonly ascribe to people to explain their actions would thus complete Hobbes's theory and confirm its chief doctrine.

[2] Hobbes, *Leviathan*, ch. 6, par. 1.

The doctrine, if sound, furnishes a defender of egoism with a seemingly powerful argument for egoism's fundamental principle. In particular, if sound, it seems strongly to support the proposition a defender must establish to meet the main burden of proof on such arguments. Let us call this argument *the primary argument for egoism*. Intuitively, it draws on the thought that it makes no sense to prescribe for someone actions that best promote of some end unless he or she could have a motive to pursue that end. What would be the point? Hence, clearly, if it is a fact of human nature that at bottom the only motive people could ever have is the desire to promote their own interests, then the only end whose promotion it makes sense to prescribe as an ultimate end is a person's own interests, which is to say, his or her own happiness. Therefore, the only end whose promotion it makes sense for a fundamental principle of right action to prescribe is the actor's own happiness. And this, in effect, is the proposition the defender of egoism must establish.

The primary argument can be given a more explicit statement, one that makes clearer how it proceeds from its psychological premises to its ethical conclusions. On this more explicit statement, the argument's basic premiss is the doctrine of psychological egoism (that the motive of every intentional action is at bottom the desire to promote one's own interests). A second premiss is that if the basic motive of every intentional action is the same, then the end provided by that motive is the only ultimate end of every intentional action. From these two premisses, it follows that one's own interests, which is to say, one's own happiness, is the only ultimate end of every intentional action. And since all right actions are intentional actions – a third premiss – it further follows that the actor's own happiness is the only ultimate end of right action. Hence, the highest good for an individual is his or her own happiness. Hence, from the doctrine of psychological egoism one can, in a few, simple steps, arrive at the fundamental principle of egoism.

4. Psychological egoism

Plainly, the weight of this argument lies with its first premiss, the doctrine of psychological egoism. So the question to ask is: How plausible is it? Some thinkers have thought it was very plausible if not indisputable. Others have dismissed it as utterly preposterous. Given such a great disparity in opinions, one might suspect that the doctrine was understood differently by the different parties to the dispute. So we would do well to examine this possibility, considering first how it might be understood as plausible and whether, on such an understanding, the primary argument for egoism would still be cogent. Certainly, the doctrine would be plausible if all it meant were that a person's intentional actions always sprang from motives supplied by his own interests. After all, it would be hard to see how a person could be moved to pursue something if he had absolutely no interest in it and did not believe that failure to pursue it would lead to the loss of something he did have an interest in. But if the doctrine came to no more than that a person's own interests were the sole source of the motives of his or her intentional actions, then the primary argument would not be cogent. Specifically, its basic premiss would be too weak to support the proposition a defender of egoism must establish for the argument to meet the main burden of proof on arguments for egoism. The reason is that a person typically has interests in many things and people besides himself: his family, his friends, his neighborhood, his country, the associations and communities to which he belongs, his relationship to God, and so forth. These interests focus his thoughts and feelings on people and things other than himself, and accordingly the motives that they supply are motives to act for the sake of those people and things and not for his own sake.

Take, for example, the interest a person typically has in his family. Typically, a person regards his family's welfare as something that is important to him absolutely and not just in relation to his own happiness. So his interest in his family supplies a motive to promote their welfare for their sake alone. It follows, therefore, that their welfare, and not his own happiness, is the end this motive provides. Consequently, the ultimate end of the intentional actions that spring from this motive need not be his own happiness. It may be his family's welfare only and, indeed, will be if the actions spring from no other motive. And similar points follow about the motives that many of the other interests a person has in people and things besides himself supply. Plainly, then, if the doctrine of psychological egoism came to no more than that a person's interests were the sole source of the motives of all of his or her intentional actions, one could not infer from it that the ultimate end of every intentional action was the actor's own happiness. Yet without this inference the primary argument for egoism breaks down. Without it one cannot go on to infer that the ultimate end of every right action is the actor's own happiness, and this is the proposition a defender of egoism must establish to meet the main burden of proof on arguments for egoism.

It would thus appear that the doctrine, to be strong enough to support this proposition, must be understood to mean something more than that a person's intentional actions always spring from motives supplied by his own interests. It must also be understood to imply that none of the motives a person's interests supply him with has force independently of the motive to promote his own happiness. But now the question is whether the doctrine, on this understanding of it, is at all plausible. Is it at all plausible to think that none of our interests in people and things besides ourselves supplies us with motives whose force is independent of the motive to promote our own happiness? Is it plausible, for instance, to think that our interests in our friends and our family do not supply us with such motives? Admittedly, if these interests were like the interest an individual stockholder typically has in the companies in which she invests, then it would be plausible to think that they never supplied us with such motives. For in this case, they would derive entirely from the interest we have in our own happiness, just as the stockholder's interest derives entirely from her interest in her financial well-being. But for most of us the interests we have in our friends and our family are not like the interest of the typical individual stockholder in the companies in which she invests. They are not just interests in the utility of our friends' and our family's prosperity for our own happiness. Rather they are also interests in our friends' and family's welfare as something important to us in itself. For this reason it is implausible to deny that they supply us with motives whose force is independent of the motive to promote our own happiness. The doctrine, therefore, must be judged as similarly implausible when it is understood to exclude the possibility of such motives.

The upshot of this examination then is that the primary argument for egoism runs into serious difficulty once we consider how the doctrine of psychological egoism is best understood. In a word, the argument is caught in a bind. If the doctrine is understood in a way that makes it strong enough to support the proposition that the ultimate end of every intentional action is the actor's own happiness, then it is rendered implausible, and consequently the argument fizzles out from a faulty premise. If instead the doctrine is understood in a way that makes it plausible, then it is rendered too weak to support this proposition, and consequently the argument breaks down at its first inference. The question, then, is whether there is any way out of this bind. On balance, the most hopeful strategy is first to construe the doctrine as strong enough to support the proposition and then to argue for its plausibility. But successful pursuit of this strategy has yet to occur. Invariably, attempts to show that the doctrine is plausible, given the way it's being construed, fall short of explaining away (or explaining as wholly self-interested) the motives of friendship, paternal and filial love, civic pride, community spirit, religious devotion, human kindness and sympathy, and the like that sorely test its credibility.

5. An alternative argument for egoism

A variation on this strategy is to construct a new argument for egoism that proceeds along similar lines as the primary argument but with a different psychological doctrine as its basic premiss. The theory of human motivation that best fits this strategy is psychological hedonism. Its chief doctrine is that the motive of every intentional action is at bottom either a desire for pleasure or an aversion to pain. Psychological hedonism is one of the oldest and most influential theories of human motivation in the history of philosophy and psychology. The famous opening lines of Jeremy Bentham's great work, *An Introduction to the Principles of Morals and Legislation*, capture it succinctly: "Nature has placed mankind under the governance of two sovereign masters, pain and pleasure. It is for them alone to point out what we ought to do as well as to determine what we shall do."[3] Bentham (1748–1832) himself, we should note, did not use the theory to ground the fundamental principle of egoism. He thought it supported a different principle, and later we will find it instructive to see why. But many philosophers have thought that the theory does support egoism, and the argument they favor is worth examining to determine whether it makes a better case for egoism than the primary argument.

While the argument's basic premiss, the doctrine of psychological hedonism, is different from that of the primary argument, its second premiss is the same. In addition, the argument follows, at the beginning, the same pattern of inferences. So its first few steps parallel those of the earlier

---

[3] Bentham, *An Introduction to the Principles of Morals and Legislation*, ch. 1, par. 1.

argument. Thus its first two premisses combine to yield the proposition that the ultimate end of every intentional action is to experience pleasure or escape from pain. And from this proposition and the same third premiss as the primary argument's, which is that all right actions are intentional actions, it follows that the ultimate end of every right action is to experience pleasure or escape from pain. At this point, however, the two arguments diverge. Where the primary argument moves quickly to its final conclusion, the argument from psychological hedonism takes more steps. The reason for this difference is worth considering.

The primary argument moves quickly at this point to its conclusion thanks to an earlier simplification. The simplification is to equate the pursuit of one's interests with the pursuit of happiness. Yet, as our criticism of it makes clear, this equation masks a serious problem. Specifically, it masks an ambiguity in the doctrine of psychological egoism that, once detected, exposes the argument as having either a faulty premiss or an unsound inference. In the argument from psychological hedonism, by contrast, no corresponding simplification occurs. For the corresponding simplification would be to equate the pursuit of pleasure (and freedom from pain) with the pursuit of happiness, and this equation is clearly false. Imprudent and self-indulgent pursuits of pleasure are as sure a road to unhappiness as any. In other words, while the ultimate end of every right action is either pleasure or freedom from pain, it is not pleasure no matter how much pain one ends up suffering as a result or freedom from pain no matter how much pleasure one ends up having to forgo. The person who immerses himself in immediate pleasures heedless of future, deleterious consequences to his health and well-being is not acting rightly. The argument, then, includes an additional premiss whose point is to deny that such imprudent and self-indulgent actions are right actions.

This fourth premiss is that an act is right if the actor could not obtain, by some other action, more of what he is pursuing or less of what he is trying to escape from and if nothing else besides what he is pursuing or the absence of what he is trying to escape from is an ultimate end of his intentional actions. The premiss gives a formal condition on the rightness of an action within a teleological theory. As such, it represents a requirement of reason, specifically, in this case, a requirement of economic reason. If one is pursuing, as an ultimate end, something of which one can enjoy more or less, it is not rational to opt for less when one knows one can get more without additional cost. When this requirement is combined with the identification of one's experiencing pleasure or escaping from pain as the ultimate end of every right action, it follows that the only ultimate end of every right action is one's experiencing as much pleasure and as little pain as one can. In other words, given the hedonistic account of happiness, one's own happiness is the only ultimate end of every right action. It is, therefore, the highest good for an individual. Thus, using a somewhat more complicated argument than the primary argument, one can base the fundamental principle of egoism on the doctrine of psychological hedonism.

6. Psychological hedonism

Needless to say, this argument would be no more successful than the primary argument if the doctrine of psychological hedonism were as problematic as the doctrine of psychological egoism. So the main question is how well it holds up on examination. How plausible is it to think that the motive of every intentional action is at bottom either a desire for pleasure or an aversion to pain? This question might not seem to pose much of a challenge. Indeed, it is tempting to regard the doctrine as a plain truth. After all, since one can characterize any motive as either a kind of desire or a kind of aversion, the question amounts to asking about the plausibility of the thesis that every desire is a desire for pleasure and every aversion an aversion to pain. And this thesis may seem beyond dispute. No one, you might think, could have a desire that was not in essence a desire for pleasure or an aversion that was not in essence an aversion to pain, at least if 'pleasure' is taken as the general name of every sort of agreeable experience and 'pain' the general name of every sort of disagreeable one. As John Stuart Mill (1806–73) once wrote, "to desire anything except in proportion as the idea of it is pleasant is a physical and metaphysical impossibility."[4]

Yet though the doctrine may seem to be a plain truth, it is hardly such. What makes it seem plainly true is a common confusion. When you have a desire for something, you typically anticipate getting pleasure from it. Let us even suppose that you invariably anticipate such pleasure when you desire something. This supposition is certainly plausible, especially given the plausibility of supposing that when you desire something, you

---

[4] Mill, *Utilitarianism*, ch. 4, par. 10.

anticipate having the desire satisfied and that such satisfaction is itself a source of pleasure. Nonetheless, it does not follow that the pleasure you anticipate getting is always the true object of your desire. It may merely be a welcome extra. To be sure, sometimes a person may desire something, an apple, say, just for the pleasure of its taste, in which case the pleasure he anticipates is also the true object of his desire. But sometimes a person may desire an apple for its nutritional value, in which case, though he antici-pates the pleasure of its taste, this pleasure is not what he is after. So it is not the object of his desire. More important, still, is the observation that the pleasure you anticipate getting when you have a desire cannot be the object of that desire in the case in which the source of the pleasure is the satisfac-tion of the desire. The reason for this is internal to logic of desire. Your desire for something is satisfied when you get the thing you desire. Therefore, the object of your desire – the thing you desire – must be distinct from the satisfaction of the desire, since the satisfaction presupposes the object. But this means that the pleasure you get from the satisfaction of the desire cannot be the desire's object, since this pleasure, too, presupposes the object. The common confusion that makes the doctrine of psychological hedonism seem plainly true is due to a tacit and faulty assumption that the two are identical.

The observation that the object of a desire cannot be the pleasure one gets from the satisfaction of that desire is the key to a powerful criticism of psychological hedonism that Joseph Butler (1692–1752) first made in his sermons on human nature.[5] Butler used this observation to support a dis-tinction he drew between the general desire for one's own happiness, what he called self-love, and particular desires for food, clothing, riches, the welfare of one's children, the good opinion of one's fellows, and so forth, which he identified as particular appetites and passions. Because the sat-isfaction of one's particular desires is essential to happiness, Butler argued, self-love involves self-reflection. A person who seeks happiness necessarily reflects on how best to satisfy her particular desires. Thus, the pleasures of such satisfaction are the concerns of self-love; the most felicitous combina-tion of them over a whole life is its object. This point nicely fits with the important observation that the object of a desire cannot be the pleasure one gets from the satisfaction of that desire. Such pleasure, because it is

[5] Butler, *Fifteen Sermons Preached at the Rolls Chapel*, sermon xi.

essential to happiness, is obviously the object of a human desire, and Butler's point is that self-love is that desire, while the particular desires, whose satisfaction is the object of self-love, have different objects. In some cases, no doubt, these are experiences of sensory pleasure, like the taste of chocolate or the smell of roses. But in others they are not. Rather they are things such as wholesome food, well-made clothing, gems and other riches, the welfare of one's children, a good reputation, and the like. Defenders of psychological hedonism have to deny, of course, that these things are ever the true objects of particular desires. They have to maintain instead that all particular desires are desires for experiences of sensory pleasure (or the absence of sensory pain). But it is hard to see any grounds for so restricting the objects of particular desires. It is hard, that is, to see any grounds on which the doctrine of psychological hedonism can be sustained.

We can summarize Butler's criticism of the doctrine briefly. Happiness consists, in large part, of the pleasures that arise from the satisfaction of one's particular desires, and those desires are satisfied when one gets the things one desires. The desire for happiness is self-love. Its object is the pleasure that comes from satisfying one's particular desires. The objects of those desires are various, but in no case can the object of a particular desire be the pleasure one gets from its satisfaction, for such satisfaction presupposes a distinct object. If psychological hedonism were true, then the object of every particular desire would have to be the experience of a sensory pleasure (or the absence of a sensory pain), for it is the only thing consistent with both the doctrine of psychological hedonism and Butler's observation that the object of a particular desire cannot be the pleasure one gets from the desire's satisfaction (or the absence of the pain one experiences from the desire's frustration). But to restrict the objects of particular desires in this way appears arbitrary. To hold, for instance, that a person's desire for the welfare of his children must at bottom be, say, the desire for experiences of sensory pleasure that result from seeing his children flourish seems very far-fetched.

Butler's criticism, in bringing out the implausibility of psychological hedonism once the desire for happiness is distinguished from other desires, parallels our earlier criticism of the doctrine of psychological egoism. That criticism similarly showed, by distinguishing between a person's interest in his own happiness and his interests in people and things outside of himself, that the doctrine of psychological egoism is implausible when it is understood to be strong enough to support the proposition that the ultimate end of every intentional action is one's own happiness. On this understanding, the doctrine, as we saw, implies that none of the many external interests a person has, such as his interests in his family and friends, supplies him with a motive whose force is independent of the motive to promote his own happiness, and to deny that any of these interests supply such a motive is like denying that any of a person's particular desires has as its object something other than the experience of pleasure or the absence of pain. The denials in both cases are implausible.

This parallel between the two criticisms suggests, moreover, that the relation between a person's particular desires and his general desire for his own happiness, his self-love, from which Butler drew his criticism is a good model for understanding the relation between a person's external interests and his interest in his own happiness, his self-interest. Accordingly, the satisfaction of a person's external interests contributes importantly to his happiness, and his self-interest is thus partly an interest in the satisfaction of these external interests. The motives they supply can therefore be understood as distinct from the motive of self-interest. Attempts by defenders of psychological egoism to show the contrary, that the motivational force of the former must derive in every case from that of the latter, invariably fail. On a more plausible theory of human motivation, a person develops interests in people and things besides himself as he becomes, in growing up, increasingly engaged with people and things around him. At some point, perhaps very early in his development, he comes to reflect on these interests and the importance to him of their satisfaction and, in consequence, develops an interest in his own happiness. At the same time, that the development of his external interests precedes the development of his self-interest means that the motives they supply have force independently of the motive it supplies, and there is no reason to think that they lose their independent force with the development of self-interest and the incorporation into it of the external interests that supply these motives. The implausibility of psychological egoism, like the implausibility of psychological hedonism, can be traced, then, to a dubious view of the relation between the desire for happiness and the desires and interests whose satisfaction is essential to happiness.

The lesson in these criticisms is that no argument for egoism is likely to succeed if its premises deny the fundamental diversity of human motives.

The most plausible theories of human psychology affirm such diversity and, in consequence, affirm the possibility of more than one ultimate end of intentional action. Since each of these ends can be regarded as a candidate for the highest good, a direct argument for egoism must present reasons for regarding one's happiness as more desirable or worth pursuing than any of these other ends. It cannot, that is, consistently with the assumption of the fundamental diversity of human motives, preclude these other ends from even being considered on the grounds that at bottom the ultimate end of every intentional action is the same. It must instead make the case for egoism on the merits of having one's own happiness and not one of these alternatives be the ultimate end of one's actions. It must, in other words, make the case for its always being right to act on self-love and never right to suppress self-love in the interest of acting on some other motive that conflicts with it. The prevalence of self-love in human life and the difficulty of seeing a person's preferring the satisfaction of his own interests to the satisfaction of others' as unreasonable make clear why a person's own happiness is a leading candidate for the highest good and may also suggest how such an argument might go. At the same, it is hardly obvious that such an argument would succeed in the end. The burden of proving that one's own happiness is uniquely the ultimate end of right action remains a large obstacle. The important thing, though, is that, being consistent with the fundamental diversity of human motives, it would in this respect be an advance over the primary argument for egoism and the argument from psychological hedonism.

7. The Hobbesian program

Both the primary argument for egoism and the argument from psychological hedonism take the form of a proof of egoism's fundamental principle. Their failure can of course be an inspiration to search for a better argument of this form. Alternatively, though, one could drop the idea of finding such an argument and look instead for a less direct defense of egoism. Specifically, one could look for such a defense to the theory's program of grounding the basic standards of justice, honesty, kindness, charity, and the like in its fundamental principle. The thought here is that the success of this program would itself be an argument for accepting the theory, notwithstanding the difficulties of finding a proof of its fundamental principle.

Indeed, if it should turn out that there is no ethical theory whose funda-mental principle or principles are susceptible of such proof, then the suc-cess of this program could be a powerful and perhaps decisive argument for the theory. Many systems of thought are developed from postulates, which are the unproved "first truths" of a system and from which the system's major results are derived as theorems, and an important measure of the soundness of such systems is what propositions are derivable within it as theorems. To be sure, egoism lacks the rigor one expects of such systems. But this should not preclude it from being judged by the same measure of soundness. Consequently, if the theory's program of grounding basic stand-ards of right and wrong in its fundamental principle were successful, one could, by appealing to this measure, make a persuasive case for it.

The program received its definitive statement in Hobbes's *Leviathan*. In two crucial chapters of that work, Hobbes produced derivations of more than a dozen rules of right action, which he called laws of nature, and these derivations are a useful guide to carrying out what I shall call *the Hobbesian program,* the program of grounding what are commonly taken as the basic standards of right and wrong in egoism's fundamental principle.[6] Equally useful are the important reflections on the natural conditions of human life that Hobbes offered in the chapter immediately preceding his derivations.[7] Hobbes, in this earlier chapter, drew a very bleak picture of what human life would be like if men and women did not follow the laws of nature in their conduct toward each other. "Solitary, poor, nasty, brutish, and short" were the words he used to sum up his description.[8] The description, by itself, seems excessively harsh, but Hobbes supported it by showing how such harsh conditions would eventuate given a few natural facts – or what he took to be facts – about human beings and their habitat and given his hypothesis of conduct ungoverned by the principles of right action. His point was that, since the facts are unchangeable, human beings must govern their conduct by these principles to avoid the short and miserable life that would otherwise eventuate. He further thought that they needed rulers and a state to enforce the principles. But it is not necessary to go into his political theory to understand his derivations and so to use them as

---

[6] Hobbes, *Leviathan*, chs. 14 and 15.   [7] Ibid., ch. 13.

[8] Ibid., ch. 13, par. 9. Spelling in this and subsequent quotations from Hobbes's *Leviathan* changed to conform to modern English usage.

guides to carrying out the Hobbesian program. Grasping his point about everyone's needing to follow the standards he derived to avoid a short and miserable life should be sufficient. His derivations can then be understood as conditioned on the natural facts he adduced to support this point.

Three are crucial. First, there is the predominance, among the motives to which human beings are subject, of self-love and the desire for the necessities of life. For Hobbes, this fact was the germ of the theory of human motivation he put at the foundation of his moral and political thought, and thus one might, in view of our criticism of that theory, wonder whether he had really gotten hold of a fact in this case. But regardless of how Hobbes conceived of the predominance of self-love among human motives, it can be understood apart from the theory and thus seen to be both free of the theory's special problems and unlikely to excite controversy. For it should be uncontroversial – and this is the first fact – that in human beings self-love and the desire for the necessities of life tend to dominate the altruistic motives to which human beings are also subject, and their domination is greater the more socially distant are the potential beneficiaries of the altruism that the latter motives prompt. The second fact is that of scarcity in the necessities of life. The earth, Hobbes held, is not so hospitable a habitat for human beings that they can get the things they need to nourish themselves, protect themselves from the elements, maintain their health, care for their small children, and so forth without expending any effort or worrying about coming up short. Finally, the third fact is that of a certain equality among human beings. People are all equal, Hobbes said, in that they are all vulnerable to lethal attack and mortal injury. This is obviously a weak criterion of human equality, but Hobbes's derivations required nothing stronger. For convenience' sake, let us refer to these three facts as the facts of equality, scarcity, and predominating self-love.

Hobbes conditioned his derivations on these facts by showing that they define circumstances in which all human beings would be better off collectively if, in their conduct towards each other, they followed standards of the kind he derived than if they followed no such standards. His argument begins with the fact of scarcity. Thus, because of scarcity, people would be better off collectively if they got along with each other and worked together than if they isolated themselves from each other and tried to scrape by on their own. Such cooperation would be more beneficial for them both because it would reduce the friction and potential for conflict that competition for scarce goods inevitably creates and because it would, through collaborative enterprise, increase the overall supply of goods that human beings need to live a tolerable life. Unfortunately, because of predominating self-love, one cannot expect people to get along with each other or work together solely out of the goodness of their hearts. If they were naturally more motivated by kindness and generosity than by self-love and the desire for the necessities of life, then of course they could get along and work together without giving any thought to whether such conduct was in their self-interest. But since the opposite is true, they cannot. Hence, to gain the fruits of cooperation they must recognize and follow standards of conduct general adherence to which would enable them to get along and work together in ways that were mutually beneficial. Finally, then, because of equality, every human being is similarly situated with respect to these circumstances. Thus, no human being would be better off if people didn't get along or work together. The reason why should be clear. The greater hostility among people – the increased conflict that competition for scarce goods inevitably creates – significantly increases everyone's risk of being the victim of a lethal attack. Hence, everyone would be better off if they recognized and followed standards of conduct general adherence to which enabled them to get along and work together than if they ignored them.

While these considerations show that to live in circumstances in which people recognize and follow such standards is to everyone's advantage, it still remains an open question whether someone who lives in such circumstances always best promotes his happiness by adhering to these standards. The question remains open because it is possible for someone who lived in such circumstances to enjoy the benefits of people's recognizing and following standards general adherence to which enables them to get along and work together without following the standards himself. It is possible, that is, for someone to get a free ride, for a person could evade the standards without thereby affecting whether others continued to adhere to them, and if they did, then the benefits of their adherence would still be available to all, including him. This possibility plainly threatens the Hobbesian program, for if someone living in such circumstances could best promote his happiness by selectively rather than strictly adhering to these standards, then for that person, according to egoism, adhering to them is sometimes the wrong thing to do. The standards, in other words, would lack authority in practical thought that is backed by reason, since at these times following them is inconsistent with what reason requires, namely, promoting the highest good. The theory, therefore, would have fallen short of vindicating them as the standards of morality. Hence, to ground them in the theory's fundamental principle, one must further show that no one who lives in circumstances in which people, for the most part, strictly adhere to these standards could best promote his happiness by selectively rather strictly adhering to them. Finding an argument that shows this is a make-or-break challenge, so to speak, for the Hobbesian program. It is the challenge posed by the free-rider.

The challenge did not escape Hobbes. He dealt with it as part of his derivation of the natural law of justice, which he construed as prescribing that one keep one's word. For reasons having to do with his political theory, he took keeping one's word as the primary act of cooperation by which people reduce the conflict among themselves that competition for scarce goods inevitably creates. So in answering the challenge, he considered whether one could, in circumstances in which others strictly kept their word in their dealings with one, best promote one's happiness by selectively rather than strictly keeping one's word in one's dealings with them. His answer, though, can be easily adapted to answering the broader challenge to the entire Hobbesian program and not just to his derivation of the law of justice. Thus, on the Hobbesian program, every act of following standards general adherence to which enables people to get along and work together counts as an act of cooperation, no matter which particular standard is being followed. Accordingly, let us define *cooperation* as following such standards of conduct. The question to be considered, then, is whether one can, in circumstances in which others always cooperate with one, best promote one's happiness by selectively rather than strictly cooperating with them.

Hobbes's answer appeals to the risks and costs of being excluded from the cooperative arrangements that general adherence to the standards makes possible. The costs of such exclusion, Hobbes maintained, are enormous. They include not only one's being excluded from sharing in the surplus of goods that result from people's working together in collective enterprises but also one's becoming a target of their hostility and fair game for predatory invasions. In short, to be excluded from these arrangements is to be made a pariah, and the life of a pariah is wretched indeed. No benefits could be worth such a cost. It is of paramount importance, then, that one avoid incurring it. To do so, one must maintain the trust of others. Trust is what cements the relations among people on which cooperative arrangements for their mutual benefit depend. If one loses the trust of others, one's relations with them become ruptured. Cooperation with them breaks down. And since the way people come to trust each other is by their manifesting certain dispositions of character in their dealings with one another, a person could not reasonably expect to maintain the trust of others if he did not cultivate in himself these dispositions. Call these the dispositions of a cooperator. They include dispositions like justice, honesty, kindness, modesty, fair-mindedness, the willingness to compromise, *inter alia*, and to cultivate them in oneself requires that one cooperate strictly with others and forbear from cheating and bullying them when the opportunity for profiting by such actions arises. Selective cooperation, in other words, is inconsistent with cultivating in oneself the dispositions of character whose manifestation in one's dealings with others elicits and strengthens their trust. Hence, selectively cooperating with others without losing their trust would be possible only if one were able to fool them about one's character. And one cannot, Hobbes insisted, count on being able to do this.

Hobbes, it is important to note, did not deny that one could sometimes profit more by cheating others than by cooperating with them. He did not deny that a person might gain greater happiness by selectively rather than strictly cooperating with others. His point, rather, was that if one did gain greater happiness through selective cooperation, one would have gained it by luck and not solely by design. For success at cheating others, he argued, is contingent on their never coming to know that one is untrustworthy, which is to say, that one lacks the dispositions of a cooperator, and one cannot bank on their remaining ignorant of these deficits in one's character. Such ignorance depends on too many factors outside one's control. So selective cooperation, the willingness to cheat others when the opportunity for profiting by doing so arises, is a risky way of dealing with them. And given what one risks, the loss of others' trust, the consequent exclusion from cooperative arrangements, and the pariah status such exclusion entails, the greater happiness one might gain from cheating can hardly be worth this risk. Thus, strict cooperation with others, Hobbes concluded, is the wisest course for one to take in circumstances in which others are, for the most part, following the same course. This result, then, completes the defense of the Hobbesian program.

8. Troubles with the Hobbesian program's derivations

Hobbes's answer makes a strong case for cultivating in oneself the dispositions of a cooperator. At the same, one may still wonder how successful his answer is in showing that cheating someone is never the right thing to do in circumstances in which people, for the most part, are cooperating with each other. Clearly, if Hobbes's answer is that cheating is never the right thing to do in such circumstances because it always involves a risk of being found out that is too great to be worth whatever benefits one can get from cheating, then the answer is unsound. Its premiss about the riskiness of cheating is unrealistic. Granted, one seldom finds oneself in circumstances in which one can cheat and the risk of being discovered is negligible. But to assert that people never find themselves in such circumstances is a gross overstatement. Sometimes one finds a lost purse containing a huge wad of cash when nobody else is around. It is possible, though, to take Hobbes's answer to be based on a different premiss. One can take it to be based on the premiss that no one who cultivates in himself the dispositions of a cooperator can ever regard cheating, no matter how small the risk of being found out, as a more profitable course of action than cooperating. Hobbes's answer, then, if it is understood as based on this premiss, is that cheating is never the right thing to do because it is always inconsistent with one's having the dispositions of a cooperator. Either one has these dispositions, in which case cheating is not an option, or one does not have them, in which case the risk of being made a pariah if one fails to cultivate them in oneself is too great to be worth whatever benefits come from cheating. And this more sophisticated version of Hobbes's answer is not so clearly unsound.

Nevertheless, it is still open to criticism. A disposition of character is only a strong tendency to choose to act in certain ways. It is not a force that invariably produces such action in circumstances in which that sort of action is expected of someone who has the disposition. Consequently, a person's cheating on rare occasion would not necessarily imply that he lacked any of the dispositions of a cooperator. Suppose, then, a person who had cultivated in himself these dispositions found himself, unexpectedly, in circumstances in which cheating would add considerably to his wealth and the risk of being discovered was negligible. If the person could cheat in these circumstances and still have the dispositions of a cooperator, then, plainly, cheating would best promote his happiness. In retaining these dispositions, he would be at no greater risk of failing to manifest them in subsequent dealings with others than if he cooperated. He would be at no greater risk of being made a pariah. Cheating, therefore, would be the right thing for him to do in these circumstances, on the definition of right action that egoism endorses. Hence, this more sophisticated version of Hobbes's answer would also be unsound. It, too, would fail to show that cheating is never the right action in circumstances in which people, for the most part, are cooperating with each other. It, too, would be based on a faulty premiss, in this case the premiss that cheating is always inconsistent with having the dispositions of a cooperator.

A defender of this version of Hobbes's answer would no doubt object. Honesty, he would point out, is a disposition of character a person could not possess if he chose to cheat in these circumstances, and honesty is a paradigm of the kind of disposition whose manifestation in a person's dealings with others elicits and strengthens their trust. But this objection simply assumes what a defender of Hobbes's answer must show, for once the question of whether cheating is always inconsistent with possessing the dispositions of a cooperator surfaces, we can no longer assume that the only sort of dispositions that qualify as dispositions of a cooperator are virtues like honesty and justice. To be sure, on Hobbes's answer, one does well in cultivating these virtues in oneself. Manifesting them in one's dealings with others is certain to gain and maintain their trust, and one's happiness depends on this. But one would do even better if one cultivated in oneself dispositions that, on the one hand, were not so rigid as to keep one from taking advantage of circumstances in which cheating would bring large benefits and the risk of being discovered was negligible but, on the other, were sufficiently sensitive to the need to maintain others' trust as to qualify as the dispositions of a cooperator. Given that a person might cultivate such dispositions in himself, cheating need not always be inconsistent with being a cooperator.

But is it possible for someone to cultivate such dispositions in himself? Could someone be this flexible about following standards of conduct adherence to which he regards as important to achieving happiness? Consider, as an analogy, the dispositions of self-discipline. A person who is self-disciplined is able to keep to a regimen: a diet, a budget, a schedule, and so forth, yet at the same time she need not be so rigid about keeping to a diet, say, that if a once-in-a-lifetime opportunity to have a fabulous dinner prepared by a world-renowned chef came along, she would pass it up to keep to her diet. One can be self-disciplined and still flexible enough to make exceptions on those rare occasions when large benefits would be lost if one kept to the regimens one followed. Likewise, then, one could have the dispositions of a cooperator and still be flexible enough to cheat on those rare occasions when cheating brought large benefits without more than a negligible risk of discovery.

Perhaps, though, the dispositions of a cooperator are different from those of self-discipline. Perhaps no one who saw the importance of cooperation could at the same time be willing to cheat on rare occasions. This possibility would make sense if the importance of cooperation were different from that of a diet or a budget, if for instance it were important to the person for reasons other than its contribution to her happiness. But obviously this possibility is not one to which a defender of Hobbes's answer could appeal. On Hobbes's answer the cooperation of others is important to people because without it their lives would be miserable and short. So the analogy of the dispositions of a cooperator to those of self-discipline is apt. These are the dispositions that anyone clearheaded about the importance of cooperation would cultivate in himself.

The more sophisticated version of Hobbes's answer thus appears to be no sounder than the simpler one. It depends on the assumption that the paradigms of the dispositions of character whose manifestation in one's dealings with others elicits their trust are the traditional virtues like justice and honesty, and this assumption appears to be unwarranted. We have, it seems, no more reason to think that a person best promotes his happiness by cultivating in himself these traditional virtues than we have to think that he best promotes it by strictly following the standards general adherence to which enables people to get along and work together. The Hobbesian program of grounding these standards in the fundamental principle of egoism is equivalent to a program of showing that the fundamental principle endorses cultivating in oneself the traditional virtues like justice and honesty. One makes no progress, then, in trying to shore up the former by appealing to the latter. The Hobbesian program, therefore, in the absence of a better answer than Hobbes's to the challenge posed by the free-rider, falls short of vindicating these standards as the standards of morality.

9. Troubles with the Hobbesian program's scope

A second criticism of the program concerns its scope. Hobbes restricted his derivations of natural law to standards of conduct general adherence to which enabled people to get along with each other and work together. At the same time, he acknowledged other standards that he believed were derivable from natural facts about human existence and what a human being needs to live a tolerable life. These other standards concerned personal safety and health. Examples are standards of moderation in drinking intoxicating beverages and eating rich food. There are, however, still other commonly observed standards of conduct, and while some of these, like manners and etiquette, are essentially local and conventional, others, like standards of kindness toward nonhuman animals, appear not to be. An ethical theory can ignore the former, since being essentially local and conventional they do not represent standards whose authority in practical thought one could consider as being backed by reason rather than custom. But it cannot ignore the latter. If it excludes them from morality without explanation or a showing that they too, despite appearances, are essentially local and conventional, it is open to the criticism of being too restrictive. And egoism is open to just this criticism. Because it recognizes as standards of morality only standards conformity to which promotes the actor's own happiness, it excludes from morality standards that would otherwise seem perfectly good candidates for being standards whose authority in practical thought is backed by reason rather than custom.

One example will suffice. Consider the rule proscribing cruelty to nonhuman animals. This rule, unlike the one that proscribes cruelty to human beings, is not a standard one could hope to ground in the fundamental principle of egoism by applying the argument of the Hobbesian program. That argument applies to the rule proscribing cruelty to human beings since a person who is cruel to other human beings is not someone people will trust. But a person who is cruel to nonhuman animals is not similarly distrusted. One can speculate on the reasons why. One reason, presumably, is that, being less likely to identify with beasts than with our fellow humans, we are less likely to concern ourselves with being possible victims of a person's cruelty when it is inflicted on a nonhuman animal than when it is inflicted on another human being. But whatever the reasons, the fact is plain. Fox hunters who are indifferent to the pain and suffering of their quarry, cosmetics researchers who subject the laboratory animals on which they test new products to unconscionable physical torment, breeders of gamecocks who stage cock fights for the fun of watching two birds fitted with metal spurs bloody each other till one succumbs do not find themselves losing the trust of others because of these activities. Egoism, then, cannot recur to the Hobbesian program to establish the rule proscribing cruelty to nonhuman animals as a standard of morality. Nor does there appear to be any other secure basis on which the theory could establish this. Cruelty to nonhuman animals, it would seem, is not necessarily contrary to achieving happiness. Egoism, for this reason, appears too restrictive in what standards it can recognize as part of morality.

10. Thrasymachus' challenge again

Over and above the particular problems that beset the Hobbesian program, there remains to be reckoned with the challenge to the very project of ethical theory that Thrasymachus' moral skepticism represents. It challenges the project of ethical theory by denying the existence of the standards that ethical theory takes as its object, the standards of morality. It denies, that is, that there are any universal standards of conduct whose authority in practical thought derives from reason rather than custom. This challenge, as we noted earlier, is particularly sharp in the case of egoism, since Thrasymachus, too, thinks that one's own happiness or well-being is the highest good one can achieve. But because he also thinks that some people are superior to others, he rejects the idea of a set of universal standards of conduct whose authority every human being, through an exercise of reason, would recognize. Thus, his challenge differs importantly from the challenge to egoism posed by the free-rider. Anyone could be a successful free-rider. Anyone could evade standards that others are following and thereby reap the benefits of their cooperative behavior while avoiding the costs of cooperation. But not just anyone, on Thrasymachus' view, can successfully flout the standards of justice in the imperious way he applauds. Rather, in his view, such conduct is reserved for the few whose superiority in power enables them to practice such injustice with impunity. What is more, the question of the risk of their being discovered is not an issue for him. As far as he is concerned, they can practice injustice openly, for overawing power and not stealth is the key to their success. Answering the challenge his skepticism represents, then, does not require making the risk of discovery real. It requires, instead, arguing against Thrasymachus' exceptionalism about those whom he regards as superior human beings.

The argument answering the challenge becomes evident once one puts Thrasymachus' exceptionalism in the terms of the Hobbesian program. Accordingly, Thrasymachus' view is that some people are so powerful that they can achieve happiness even if no one trusts them. In other words, none of them needs to manifest the dispositions of a cooperator in his dealings with others to get them to cooperate with him. Fear of his power alone is sufficient, Thrasymachus must have supposed, for securing their cooperation. And he must have further supposed that because of this tyrant's power, the tyrant has nothing to fear from others and so cooperation with them is unnecessary. Clearly, these two suppositions amount to a denial of the fact of equality on which Hobbes's derivations are conditioned. Thus, the argument answering Thrasymachus' challenge consists in showing that these suppositions are inconsistent with this fact. In short, it is that no one is so powerful as to be invulnerable to lethal attack and mortal injury. Because human beings are all equal in this respect, even powerful tyrants have something to fear from others. For them to practice injustice on the grand scale Thrasymachus imagined is for them to act in ways that, however powerful they are, increase the risk of their being the victim of lethal attack, and an increase in this risk is not worth the benefits of the injustices they practice. These tyrants, too, have reason to cultivate in themselves the dispositions of a cooperator.

An admirer of Thrasymachus' position could dispute this, of course. But to rebut it he would have to do more than give examples of happy tyrants who greatly enriched themselves at the expense of their subjects, lived long lives, and died of natural causes. For the same point applies here as the one Hobbes made in answering the challenge posed by the free-rider. Because success alone may be due to luck, one cannot simply just give examples of successful tyrants to rebut the argument. Thus to rebut it our admirer of Thrasymachus would also have to show that their escaping from a premature and violent death was to be expected from the provisions for safety they made, that owing to these provisions they could count on being safe from such violence despite their odious conduct. And it is far from certain that he can show this. Citing the tyrants' power in terms, say, of the weaponry and soldiery at their command or the wealth they could draw on would not show it. Such power alone does not provide the necessary assurance. There is also the tyrants' need of the loyalty of their lieutenants, and for any tyrant who practices injustice on a grand scale retaining this loyalty over the long run is surely a chancy thing. Here at any rate is the weak point in the admirer's rebuttal. Even powerful tyrants have something to fear, and the less attention they give to manifesting the dispositions of a cooperator the more their lives are ruled by fear. In view of the fact of equality on which Hobbes conditioned his derivations, a defender of egoism, then, has a reasonable, if not conclusive, answer to the challenge that Thrasymachus' skepticism represents.

When Glaucon restates Thrasymachus' position, he replaces the tyrant who practices injustice with impunity with a shepherd-turned-criminal, Gyges, whose ability to commit crimes with impunity is due to his having the power, thanks to a magical ring, to make himself invisible at will. The switch is not inconsequential. Thrasymachus bases his moral skepticism on his demographic distinction between the powerful and the weak, and with the switch of examples this distinction is lost. What replaces it is a distinction between people who have magical powers and the rest of us, and this new distinction cannot serve as a basis for moral skepticism. The upshot is that Glaucon, by switching examples, replaces the challenge that Thrasymachus' skepticism represents with a different one. It is the one posed by the free-rider. For Gyges is the ultimate free-rider. Yet Plato does not mean this example to be a disproof of egoism. His point is not to show that, on the definition of right action that egoism endorses, criminal action is the right thing to do if you have a magical ring that enables you to make yourself invisible at will. His point, rather, is to question the relation that egoism supposes right action bears to the highest good. When the highest good is identified with a life filled with pleasure unspoiled by pain, right action is understood as instrumental to producing pleasure and escaping from pain. Plato's view is that the relation right action bears to the highest good is different. It is such that one could not even imagine someone's achieving the highest good without living according to the standards of right action. To hold this view, however, requires that one make right action inseparable in conception from the highest good and therefore reject hedonism as the theory of human well-being. Plato did both in constructing a theory on which the development and exercise of the traditional virtues is integral to realizing the highest good. It is this theory that we shall take up next.

3   Eudaimonism

1. Egoism v. eudaimonism

Eudaimonism was the dominant theory in ancient Greek ethics. The name derives from the Greek word 'eudaimonia,' which is often translated 'happiness' but is sometimes translated 'flourishing.' Many scholars in fact prefer the latter translation because they believe it better captures the concern of the ancient Greeks with the idea of living well. This preference suggests that a useful way of distinguishing between eudaimonism and egoism is to observe, when formulating their fundamental principles, the distinction between well-being and happiness that we drew in the last chapter. Accordingly, the fundamental principle of eudaimonism is that the highest good for each person is his or her well-being; the fundamental principle of egoism remains, as before, that the highest good for a person is his or her happiness. Admittedly, this way of distinguishing between the two theories would be theoretically pointless if the determinants of how happy a person was were the same as the determinants of how high a level of well-being the person had achieved. Thus, in particular, when hedonism is the favored theory of well-being, this way of distinguishing between eudaimonism and egoism comes to nothing. It fails in this case to capture any real difference between them. For when hedonism is the favored theory of well-being, determinations of how happy a person is exactly match the determinations of how high a level of well-being a person has achieved.

Matters are different, however, when perfectionism is the favored theory of well-being. In this case, one can capture a real difference between eudaimonism and egoism by distinguishing one from the other according as its fundamental principle takes a person's well-being or his happiness to be the highest good. For on a perfectionist conception of well-being, determinations of how happy a person is do not match the determinations of how high a level of well-being a person has achieved. The determinants are not the same, as our example in the last chapter of the aspiring violinist shows. Hence, when one takes perfectionism as the favored theory of well-being, this way of distinguishing between eudaimonism and egoism has theoretical significance, and accordingly one can treat the former as a separate object of study. Plato's ethics is its original form. To answer the challenge put to Socrates by Glaucon and Adeimantus, Plato argued for perfectionism as an advance over hedonism in the theory of well-being. He thus, in effect, showed us how to fix eudaimonism as a distinct ethical theory from egoism.

Nonetheless, you might still wonder whether it made sense to draw this distinction. You might wonder, specifically, whether it made sense to define 'egoism' so narrowly that it applied only to a theory whose fundamental principle took a person's happiness, rather than his or her well-being, as the highest good for that person. Granted, there is a real difference between eudaimonism and egoism on this way of distinguishing between them, but you might still wonder whether this difference was too small to warrant treating the former as a separate theory. Why isn't a theory that identifies a person's highest good with his well-being also egoistic? It would be, after all, as we noted earlier, if hedonism were the correct theory of well-being. So why is it not also egoistic if perfectionism is the correct theory of well-being?

The answer comes from the pivotal point in Plato's rejection of hedonism. Plato rejects egoism and turns to perfectionism when he hits upon the idea of a noninstrumental relation between right action and the highest good. If eudaimonism could not accommodate this idea, then we would learn nothing from treating eudaimonism as a distinct theory from egoism. Doing so would yield no significant results apart from those that were directly due to the difference between perfectionism and hedonism. In that case, we might just as well define 'egoism' more broadly to include eudaimonism and then distinguish between the latter's hedonistic and perfectionistic versions. But because eudaimonism can accommodate Plato's idea, it is possible to elaborate it in a way that represents right action as action worth doing for its own sake and, indeed, as a constituent of the highest good. For this reason it is appropriate to treat it as a distinct theory from egoism and therefore to define 'egoism' narrowly so as to exclude it.

Specifically, it is appropriate to do so because our idea of egoism is that of a theory whose conception of the highest good is consistent with the possibility of someone's realizing it by being a free-rider. Accordingly, a theory on which right action is a constituent of the highest good does not fit this idea. The reason is clear. If right action is a constituent of the highest good, no one can realize the highest good by being a free-rider. The incorporation of Plato's idea into a perfectionistic account of well-being thus yields a form of eudaimonism that, because it avoids the challenge free-riders pose for egoism, offers theoretical possibilities beyond the scope of egoism. It is no surprise, then, that this specific form of eudaimonism, owing to its being, unlike the other forms, differentiable from egoism, has come to be identified with the general theory.

2. The Platonic form of eudaimonism

Plato embedded his idea in the problem that Glaucon and Adeimantus put to Socrates when they restated Thrasymachus' position. The problem was to show conclusively that a person who practices justice gains, from acting justly, benefits that he could not otherwise get and that surpass any that he could get by appearing to be just without really being so. Conventional wisdom, Glaucon pointed out, does not commend practicing justice as a way of acting towards others that is salutary and worthwhile in its own right. Rather it says that the reason one practices justice is to gain a reputation for being a just person, for such a reputation secures the trust of others and thereby brings opportunities from which people known to be unjust are typically excluded. Yet if the benefits of such a reputation were the sole reason a person had for being just, then he could gain them merely by appearing to be just when he really wasn't, provided, of course, that his appearance was convincing. Glaucon makes this point with his example of Gyges' ring. The example, moreover, not only illustrates this specific point but also makes clear the more general one that appearing to be just can be at least as profitable as really being just so long as practicing justice brings a person no benefit that he cannot gain in some other way. In other words, appearing to be just can be at least as profitable as really being just so long as practicing justice is never more than a means to the benefits it brings.

To solve the problem, then, that Glaucon and Adeimantus put to Socrates requires showing that practicing justice is constitutive of living well and not merely a means to it. That is, it requires showing that practicing justice is an essential ingredient in the achievement of a durable state of well-being. Plato, one could say, set a problem for himself whose solution required a theory on which a person's well-being included among its integral parts his being just and thus having the disposition to act justly. Such a state, on any theory that solved this problem, could not be a state that the exercise of that disposition was merely instrumental in producing. Plato thus set terms for a form of eudaimonism whose theoretical possibilities outstripped those of egoism.

Generally speaking, every form of eudaimonism affirms the ideal of the wise pursuit of well-being. If one takes hedonism as the favored theory of well-being, then one obtains a form of eudaimonism that affirms the ideal of the wise pursuit of pleasure and freedom from pain. This form, as we noted above, is indistinguishable from egoism when one makes the same assumption about hedonism's being the favored theory of well-being. Correspondingly, then, egoism, on this assumption, affirms the very same ideal. By contrast, if one takes perfectionism as the favored theory of well-being, then one obtains a form of eudaimonism that affirms the ideal of the wise pursuit of excellence in the service of ends whose achievement makes life worth living. Or put more simply, since wisdom is itself an excellence and since it entails the adoption of ends whose achievement makes life worth living, the ideal this form of eudaimonism affirms is that of the wise pursuit of excellence. This is plainly a different ideal from the one implicit in egoism. While one can pursue happiness and excellence at the same time, achieving the one is not the same as achieving the other. Our example of the aspiring violinist who is uncertain about how high to set her sights makes this clear.

Moreover, if one takes the Platonic form of eudaimonism as the best representative of those forms that assume perfectionism as the favored theory of well-being, then the ideal the form affirms is that of the wise pursuit of intellectual and moral excellence. For on the Platonic form excellence consists in wisdom in the choice of ends as well as means to achieving those ends and also in such dispositions as justice, honesty, and courage, which keep one's choices from straying from right action. This ideal differs even more starkly from the ideal that egoism affirms. Because a person's happiness can be more reliably secured if she does not aspire always to do what is most just or courageous, it takes luck to achieve both. Someone, aware of this fact, who aspires to intellectual and moral excellence gives up any aspiration to happiness. The study of eudaimonism, then, when it focuses on the Platonic form of the theory, departs significantly from the study of egoism.

Whether the Platonic form is the soundest form is, to be sure, another matter. It is to this question that we now turn.

3. Perfectionist objections to hedonism

The choice between different forms of eudaimonism depends, in the first place, on whether to favor hedonism or perfectionism as the sounder theory of well-being. The question comes down to whether the highest good consists in one's experiencing maximal pleasure and freedom from pain in life or in one's achieving the greatest degree of excellence in life. It comes down to whether there is more reason to affirm pleasure or excellence as the ultimate end of one's actions. In other words, would a life that is filled with as much pleasure and as little pain as possible be the best life one could live, or would the best life be one in which one achieved excellence, to the greatest degree possible, in pursuits whose undertaking make life worth living? Pleasure is no doubt among the first things, if not the very first thing, a person considers to be the highest good. Likewise hedonism is among the oldest theories of well-being, if not the oldest. The theory has a prominent place, for instance, in the *Protagoras*, one of Plato's early dialogues, and it was also advocated in Plato's time by other followers of Socrates.[1] Excellence, by contrast, does not so quickly recommend itself as the highest good, especially since many of the excellences one first thinks of are gifts and skills, like agility and intelligence, efficiency and technical facility, that seem worth having, not for their own sake, but because of the advantages having them brings. Nevertheless, perfectionism, too, goes back to Plato. It arises out of his critique of hedonism. Hedonism may be the oldest theory of well-being, but opposition to it is virtually as old, and from this opposition, thanks to Plato's genius, a powerful alternative emerged.

The main objection to hedonism is that to regard pleasure and freedom from pain as the highest good for a human being is to regard the life of human beings as no different in kind from the life of other animals capable of experiencing pleasure and pain. J. S. Mill, in his discussion of hedonism, put the objection directly when he wrote:

> Now such a theory of life excites in many minds, and among them in some of the most estimable in feeling and purpose, inveterate dislike. To suppose

---

[1] Aristippus of Cyrene (435–356 BC).

that life has (as they express it) no higher end than pleasure – no better and nobler object of desire and pursuit – they designate as utterly mean and groveling; as a doctrine worthy only of swine, to whom the followers of Epicurus were, at a very early period, contemptuously likened; and modern holders of the doctrine are occasionally made the subject of equally polite comparisons by its German, French, and English assailants.[2]

Mill, it should be said, wrote as a defender of hedonism and not as a critic. His statement of the objection occurs as a prelude to his answering it. But before we consider his peculiar answer, let us press the objection further and in a direction that more clearly encompasses Plato's alternative.

Experiences of pleasure may be more or less intense and more or less long-lasting. When one considers examples, common ones include gratification of a strong appetite and the kind of feelings that go with relief from physical stress or discomfort, the kind of feelings that relaxing in a comfortable chair or a warm bath produces. Such pleasures are not unique to human life. Cats, too, can have strong appetites and experience intense pleasure from their gratification, and though they do not like warm baths, they do enjoy curling up in comfortable chairs. Similar observations apply to cows, pigs, moose, otters, and rats. Hence, so the objection goes, if the best life a human being can live is a life that is filled with pleasures of varying intensity and duration and free of all but perhaps the most transitory and bearable pains, then that person's highest good would seem to be no different from a cat's highest good or a cow's. By taking pleasure and freedom from pain as the sole elements of well-being, hedonism would seem to have reduced human well-being to animal well-being and therefore to have denied that it consists in anything special to human existence. Except for the possibility that our distinctively human powers and capabilities enable us to experience more intense pleasures and longer-lasting ones than other animals, hedonism offers us no reason to prefer being human to being a cow. Yet a bovine life, however much pleasure and little pain it might contain, surely lacks many of things that make human life worth living. Contrary to hedonism, then, so it appears, there is more to *human* well-being than pleasure and freedom from pain.

The same conclusion, moreover, appears to follow from a further objection. Thus, on the account of human well-being that hedonism endorses, a

---

[2] Mill, *Utilitarianism*, ch. 2, par. 3.

person could not only live a good life by spending it gratifying his appetites and relaxing in stress-free circumstances, but his life could also be made better by his enlarging and then gratifying his appetites and by his finding increasingly snug circumstances in which to relax. In the end, it would seem, the best life for a human being, according to hedonism, could be realized by a person's gorging himself on rich foods, downing large quantities of thirst-quenching beverages, copulating in as many ways and with as many partners as his enlarged sexual cravings demand, and spending the in-between times bathing, sleeping, and lounging around on plush sofas or in gently swaying hammocks while peacefully listening to soothing music. Such an indulgent life, however, is not the picture of human well-being, for the trajectory it represents is that of descent into a kind of mindless bliss. Its terminus would be a life in which one became solely a receptor of pleasure-giving and nutritive substances, perhaps delivered intravenously, and in which the days were passed entirely listlessly in a drug-induced state of continuous pleasure. Call this the life of total passivity. It may not represent, on hedonism's account of well-being, realization of the highest good. It is possible that the highest good is realized in a life in which some pleasures are not drug-induced and in which the pursuit of pleasure is not entirely passive. But hedonism's account of well-being cannot rule out a priori the possibility that the life of total passivity does represent the best life for a human being. For this reason the account appears misconceived. Specifically, it appears to yield an inapt conception of human well-being.

Plato, too, believed that hedonism's account of well-being would be seen as misconceived when its endorsement of a life consisting of constant gratification of larger and larger appetites was pushed to the limit. Such a life, according to Plato, was destined to end in madness. As a person's appetites grew ever larger, Plato argued, his or her personality would become progressively disordered. The end results were a derangement of the mind, like that experienced in dreams, and a breakdown of self-control, like that exemplified by the most impulse-driven maniacs. To make this argument, though, Plato had to draw on his own conception of the human personality and the perfectionist theory of well-being it supports. Hence, as a criticism of hedonism, his argument is too closely tied to this rival account of well-being to be telling. Criticisms that are independent of rival accounts are more effective. Nevertheless, Plato's criticism is important in the way it sets the perfectionist account to which it is tied against hedonism. The opposition between the two illuminates the traditional themes of the perfectionist tradition that he began.

Thus, according to Plato, one achieves the highest good through the development of a well-ordered personality. One achieves it, that is, by cultivating and preserving in oneself the best arrangement of the various traits and powers that constitute one's personality. In so doing one realizes the best life one can live as a human being. In such a life, the constituent parts of one's personality work together harmoniously. These are, for Plato, following his famous tripartite division of the soul, reason, spirit, and appetite, and harmonious cooperation among them results when reason, with the help of the emotional energy Plato identified as spirit, regulates and constrains the appetites. Plato argued for this thesis from an analogy he drew between the constitution of a man's or woman's personality and the constitution of a city, a city being the primary political society or state in Plato's time. Accordingly, Plato observed, just as in the best-governed city the wisest men and women, with the help of an auxiliary martial force, rule over a compliant and prosperous proletariat, so too in the best-governed soul, reason, the seat of intelligence and knowledge, with the help of spirit, regulates and constrains the appetites. And from a similar comparison between poorly governed cities and dysfunctional individuals, Plato inferred that disharmony in the soul resulted when a person's appetites, aided by spirit, became the ruling forces in his personality. The ascendancy of the appetites corresponds to a decline in the influence of reason, and this decline brings a loss of coherent thought and a breakdown in self-control. Hedonism, therefore, Plato maintained, insofar as it takes gratification of the appetites as the chief source of the highest good, advances a specious account of human well-being.

4. Epicurus' answer

A defender of hedonism has no trouble answering Plato's criticism directly. Since madness is bound to bring more pain and less pleasure than sanity, the best human life, on the hedonist account, cannot tend toward madness. Hedonism, too, counsels that one discipline one's appetites. The grounds of this advice are that the pleasures of gratifying appetites without restraint are impure and their impurity, which is to say, the painful consequences of such gratification, reduces the value of the experiences to something less than its cost, as measured by the amount of pain one later endures. Severe stomach cramps that follow overeating is an obvious example. A defender of hedonism, then, can maintain, in answer to Plato, that the way to achieve the highest good, on the hedonist account of it, is to balance the value of the available pleasures against their cost and to seek those that either have the least impurity or exceed in value to a greater extent than others the cost in pain that experiencing them entails. This answer represents the wise pursuit of pleasure and freedom from pain, which is the ideal implicit in hedonistic eudaimonism, and in practice this pursuit may differ marginally, if at all, from the pursuit of a well-ordered personality that Plato recommended. Indeed, the leading defender of hedonism among ancient Greek philosophers, Epicurus, maintained as a central theme of his ethics that the wise pursuit of pleasure and freedom from pain entailed avoiding exciting pleasures because of their impurities. One should seek, instead, according to Epicurus, quieter, contemplative pleasures, and the life of contemplative pleasure that he recommended closely matches the life of philosophy that Plato extolled.[3]

Epicurus' defense of hedonism thus answers Plato's criticism. It does so by showing that in practice the wise pursuit of pleasure does not lead to a life spent feeding one's appetites. Instead, it leads to a life spent in the cultivation of one's intellectual powers and their contemplative exercise. In practice, then, on this Epicurean defense, hedonism promotes a kind of life organized around distinctively human powers and aspirations, and such a life is not open to Plato's criticism. Yet showing that hedonism in practice promotes such a life as the best life for human beings is not the same thing as showing that the theory can conceive of no other life as being better. In particular, it is not the same thing as showing that, as a matter of principle, hedonism rejects the life of total passivity as the best life for human beings or denies that the best human life may be no better than the best bovine life. Consequently, a defense of hedonism, like Epicurus', that appeals to the consequences of hedonistic practice does not shield the theory from criticisms of its conception of human well-being, for the conception may still be in error even if, owing to the actual contingencies of human life, the theory works out well in practice. Plato maintained that it failed disastrously in practice, that it led to wantonness and ultimately to madness,

---

[3] See Epicurus, "Principle Doctrines."

and a defender of hedonism can answer Plato's charge, as Epicurus did. But to answer criticisms that target hedonism's conception of human well-being, a different kind of defense is needed.

5. Mill's defense of hedonism

Mill's defense is of this kind. Hedonism, he declared, when properly understood, does not conceive of human well-being as comparable to the well-being of other animals. Rather it elevates human well-being above that of every other animal. To support this view, Mill first distinguished the kinds of pleasure that only human beings are capable of experiencing and then argued for the superiority of these to the kinds the experience of which is common to both humans and other animals. His argument for the superiority of the former depends on a novel thesis he put forward about the factors determining the intrinsic value of an experience of pleasure. On the standard account of these factors, they are all quantitative: one estimates a pleasure's intrinsic value by gauging its intensity and duration, which are, in principle, measurable in units of force and time. Mill's thesis, by contrast, was that the quality of a pleasure, as well as these quantitative factors, determined its intrinsic value. "It would be absurd," Mill wrote, "that while in estimating all other things quality is considered as well as quantity, the estimation of pleasure should be supposed to depend on quantity alone."[4] And he further held that the experiences of pleasure of which only human beings were capable so far exceeded in quality the experiences of pleasure common to both humans and other animals as to make considerations of intensity and duration inconsequential when one was estimating their intrinsic value. As he put the point himself, they have "a superiority in quality so far outweighing quantity as to render it, in comparison, of small account."[5] From this point and his novel thesis, hedonism's elevation of human well-being above that of every other animal follows immediately.

It follows, too, that hedonism does not require a conception of human well-being on which a life spent gratifying one's appetites could, in principle, be the best life for human beings. Quite the contrary, Mill maintained, hedonism could avail itself of a conception of human well-being on which

---

[4] Mill, *Utilitarianism*, ch. 2, par. 4.   [5] Ibid., ch. 2, par. 5.

such a life was necessarily worse than a life in which one found pleasure in the exercise of such distinctively human powers as reason, imagination, and moral sentiment. Such pleasure, Mill argued, had greater intrinsic value than the pleasure of gratifying one's appetites. Its intrinsic value was greater because the pleasure was qualitatively superior to that of gratifying one's appetites and because the difference in quality was sufficiently great as to make considerations of quantity of little account. Hence, Mill concluded, a life enriched by the pleasure one gets from successfully engaging in activities that draw on one's distinctively human powers was necessarily better than one in which the pleasure of gratifying one's appetites predominates.

In effect, then, Mill's defense of hedonism is an attempt to disarm the criticism of hedonism that perfectionism inspires. His revision of hedonism to include quality as one of the factors that determine the intrinsic value of an experience of pleasure enables the theory to grade the kinds of pleasure human beings are capable of experiencing independently of their intensity and duration and to place such value on experiences of high-grade pleasure in comparison with experiences of low-grade pleasure as to make the contribution to human well-being of the latter of little consequence, regardless of their intensity and duration. Mill's defense, if successful, could thus save hedonism from having, in principle, to allow that a life in which experiences of low-grade pleasure predominated could be the best life for human beings. Indeed if, as Mill maintained, high-grade pleasures were the pleasures one derived from exercising the abilities and strengths that counted as human excellences, then the defense would seem to allow hedonism to endorse as the best life for human beings the very same life as the one perfectionism endorsed. Hence, if the defense were successful, the opposition between hedonism and perfectionism would become merely abstract and the issue between them moot.

To be sure, whether the defense is successful depends on the soundness of Mill's thesis that quality, along with intensity and duration, is a factor determining the intrinsic value of experiences of pleasure. It depends, too, on the truth of his identifying high-grade pleasures with the pleasures one derives from exercising distinctively human powers and low-grade pleasures with the gratification of animal appetite. Why, after all, should one think that the one kind of pleasure is qualitatively any better, as a kind of pleasure, than the other? Mill answered this question directly. The ultimate test, he declared, of whether one kind of pleasure is qualitatively better than another is the preferences of those who have experienced both kinds and are capable of appreciating either. If such experts in pleasure clearly prefer one kind over the other, then, according to Mill, their preferences prove beyond doubt that the kind they prefer is qualitatively better. "Of two pleasures," he wrote, "if there be one to which all or almost all who have experience of both give a decided preference, irrespective of any feeling of moral obligation to prefer it, that is the more desirable pleasure."[6] And he went on to state that people who have experienced and can appreciate both the kind of pleasure that humans derive from the exercise of their higher human powers and the kind that comes from gratification of their animal appetites have a clear preference for the former over the latter. In Mill's words, "[I]t is an unquestionable fact that those who are equally acquainted with and equally capable of appreciating and enjoying both do give a most marked preference to the manner of existence which employs their higher faculties."[7]

How convincing is this answer? To be convinced one must first agree with Mill about the ultimate test of whether one kind of pleasure is superior in quality to another, and agreement about this test is hardly a given. To the contrary, some of Mill's sharpest critics – notably G. E. Moore (1873–1958) – have rejected it.[8] Suppose Mill were right, Moore argued, and those who had experienced and could appreciate each of two kinds of pleasure had a marked preference for one kind over the other; then these experts would have to find the kind they preferred more desirable than the other. But for one kind of pleasure to be more desirable than another it must either be more pleasurable, in which case the quantity of the pleasure, not the quality, determines its desirability, or have some property besides its pleasantness that positively contributes to its being desirable and that the other kind lacks, in which case pleasure and freedom from pain are not the only determinants of desirability. Hence, Mill's view must fail since, on his view, neither of these alternatives is possible. The first requires giving up the thesis that quality as well quantity is a factor determining the intrinsic value of pleasure. The second requires giving up hedonism. Moore's objection, though, falls short of being a refutation. One can resist it. (Couldn't one pleasure's being more pleasurable than another be a qualitative and not a quantitative difference? Couldn't it be

---

[6] Ibid.   [7] Ibid., ch. 2, par. 6.
[8] See G. E. Moore, *Principia Ethica* (Cambridge: Cambridge University Press, 1903), pp. 77–81.

like one argument's being more subtle than another?) Still, even if one agrees with Mill and accepts his test, one has reason not to be convinced by his answer. For the answer rests on an unwarranted assumption.

The assumption is implicit in the test itself. To take the preferences of those who have experienced and can appreciate each of two kinds of pleasure as the ultimate test of whether one kind is superior in quality to the other is to assume that the object of these experts' preferences is pleasure and not, say, the things or activities from which they derive pleasure. An analogy should make this clear. We regard the preferences of those who know wines as proof of which merlots, say, are superior because we think such experts are better able, in virtue of their experience and knowledge, to discriminate among different grades of wine. Likewise, we regard the preferences of those who know the voice as proof of which sopranos have superior voices because we think such experts are better able, in virtue of their experience and knowledge, to discriminate among different qualities of voice. In either case, we take the preferences as reliable indicators of expert judgment about the wine's or the voice's quality, and there is no better proof of the quality of a wine or voice than such judgment. Yet the preferences count as proof only because their objects are the taste of the wine, rather than, say, its viscosity, or the sound of the voice rather than the movements of the mouth out of which it comes. If their objects were different, then they would not reliably indicate expert judgment about which wine or voice was superior in quality. The same, then, must be true of the preferences to which Mill appeals as proof of the superior quality of a pleasure. They, too, would not reliably indicate expert judgment about which kind of pleasure was superior if their object were not that pleasure but the things or activities that are its source. They would not, therefore, count as proof of the superior quality of pleasure of that kind.

Mill, then, must be assuming that the object of the preferences to which he appeals is the pleasure of exercising higher human faculties and not the faculties themselves or the activities that employ them. But on what basis can he make this assumption? He thinks it is "an unquestionable fact," as we saw, that people who know both this kind of pleasure and the kind that comes from gratification of animal appetite "give a most marked preference for the manner of existence that employs the higher faculties,"[9] yet such

---

[9] Mill, *Utilitarianism*, ch. 2, par. 6.

people could have this preference without also preferring the pleasure they get from exercising those faculties. Indeed, Mill appears to accept this point when he writes:

> Few human creatures would consent to be changed into any of the lower animals for a promise of the fullest allowance of a beast's pleasures; no intelligent human being would consent to be a fool, no instructed person would be an ignoramus, no person of feeling and conscience would be selfish and base, even though they should be persuaded that the fool, the dunce, or the rascal is better satisfied with his lot than they are with theirs. They would not resign what they possess more than he for the most complete satisfaction of all the desires which they have in common with him.[10]

And again, when he declares, several sentences later:

> It is better to be a human being dissatisfied than a pig satisfied; better to be Socrates dissatisfied than a fool satisfied. And if the fool, or the pig, are of a different opinion, it is because they only know their side of the question. The other party to the comparison knows both sides.[11]

These remarks, far from supporting his assumption, accent our uncertainty about it. The preferences they describe appear to be preferences for a life that employs the higher faculties despite its being less pleasurable than a life employing only the lower ones. They appear, that is, to fit a perfectionistic outlook rather than a hedonistic one. So what could Mill's reason be for thinking his assumption was consistent with this description?

The answer can only be Mill's belief that every preference is at bottom a preference for pleasure. It can only be, in other words, the doctrine of psychological hedonism, to which Mill, as we noted in the last chapter, firmly adhered. Plainly, if this doctrine were true, then Socrates' preference for the philosophical life, despite its being less satisfying than a fool's, would have to be a preference for the pleasures distinctive of that life. But it is equally plain that if the doctrine were false, there would be no reason to think Socrates' preference was a preference for pleasure. On its face, after all, it is a preference for living a life befitting a rational being, even when such a life brings less pleasure than one suited to fools. So to justify taking it as at bottom a preference for pleasure, one needs to assert

---

[10] Ibid.   [11] Ibid.

some basic principle of psychology according to which the real object of such preferences is different from their manifest object. And in this case the principle would have to be the doctrine of psychological hedonism. More generally, then, one must assert this principle to justify the assumption that the object of the preferences for a life requiring the exercise of higher human faculties that all whom Mill cites as experts in the matter display is the pleasure of exercising those faculties. In other words, the assumption implicit in Mill's test for the qualitative superiority of one kind of pleasure over another is based on the doctrine of psychological hedonism. Working backwards, then, from this result one can see that Mill's defense of hedonism is itself built on his presumption of this doctrine. It is built on his fundamental belief that pleasure is the ultimate object of every preference.

One can see, too, how, if the doctrine of psychological hedonism were true, Mill's defense would succeed in disarming the criticisms of hedonism that perfectionism inspires. The problem, however, is that the doctrine is not obviously true and is, in fact, open to serious doubt. Certainly perfectionists would reject it as a principle of psychology. Echoing Butler, they would insist that the pursuit of excellence is the pursuit of excellence, and not another thing. Mill's defense of hedonism, therefore, succeeds only by presupposing a principle that its opponents would reject, and not unreasonably. Its success is, in a word, hollow. Nor are perfectionists the only ones who regard the doctrine as false. The difficulty of sustaining it that Butler's criticisms show has persuaded many other thinkers as well that it is false. Nonetheless, it remains a perennial of moral philosophy, which continues to attract new believers while retaining its stalwarts, and they may still look hopefully to Mill's defense for a way to escape the main objections to hedonism's conception of human well-being. Yet given the difficulty of sustaining the doctrine, they might just as well plump directly for that conception. In any event, as long as the main objections to the conception remain unanswered, the opposing conception supplied by perfectionism should seem more promising. Being a conception that has no trouble distinguishing human from bovine well-being or excluding a priori the possibility of the life of total passivity's being the best human life, it avoids the embarrassments of the hedonistic conception. For this reason at least, it appears to yield the sounder form of eudaimonism.

6. Plato's ethics

Let us continue to take Plato's ethics as the touchstone for this form of eudaimonism. Recall, from our earlier account, that Plato developed his ethics from three related theses. First, the highest good for a human being is achieved through the development of a well-ordered personality. Second, in such a personality, the constituent parts, reason, spirit, and appetite, work together harmoniously. And third, this harmony of mind or soul results when reason, with the help of the emotional energy of spirit, regulates and constrains appetite. Plato placed reason at the helm of the well-ordered personality because, as he put it, good governance requires knowledge of what things benefit and harm the governed, and reason is the seat of all knowledge. This knowledge, then, that good governance requires is the same as wisdom. Accordingly, wisdom is the virtue a person possesses when reason excels in its capacity as the ruling part of the soul. Further, it consists both in the knowledge of what things are worthwhile in themselves and in the knowledge of how best to achieve them given one's circumstances. This knowledge is the most important kind a person can have, though of course it is not the only kind. Other kinds fall into the category of technical expertise, the special knowledge that artisans and technicians, such as builders and navigators, have. Such knowledge equips its possessors with the command of their specific occupations that is necessary to be successful in them. In our examples these are the activities of building houses and moving ships across the sea. Wisdom, by contrast, equips its possessors with the self-command necessary to be successful in the much more general activities of living a life and leading a community.

Wisdom is the first virtue in Plato's ethics. On his theory, because one's highest good is the perfection that one achieves through the development of a well-ordered personality, and because such perfection results from reason's excelling in its governance of one's soul, it results from wisdom. To be sure, these points alone do not distinguish Plato's conception of wisdom from conceptions that hedonistic forms of eudaimonism could advance. Epicurus, too, could hold that wisdom was the first virtue, for he, too, took wisdom to be general knowledge of what things benefit and harm one and thought that one achieved the highest good by acquiring such knowledge and putting it into practice. What distinguishes Plato's conception from Epicurus' is the special object of the knowledge that Plato identified with wisdom. Where Epicurus took the object of the knowledge he identified with wisdom to be pleasure and its sources, Plato took it to be the idea of perfection itself. Consequently, while a wise person, on a theory like Epicurus', regards his wisdom and the other virtues that follow from it as useful to the achievement of the highest good, he does not regard them as constitutive of that good. By contrast, on Plato's theory, since wisdom and the other virtues are themselves perfections, they exemplify the very idea that is the object of wisdom, and hence are regarded by the wise person as constitutive of the highest good. That good, in other words, on Plato's theory, not only is achieved through wisdom but also contains wisdom and the other virtues as integral parts. Such is the consequence of Plato's taking perfection rather than pleasure as the highest good.

The wise person, according to Plato, both comprehends and finds compelling the idea of perfection. He is like a master craftsman or accomplished artist whose knowledge of his craft or art and corresponding grasp of perfection in its exercise guide him toward the production of as perfect an artifact, composition, or performance as he can create. Wisdom, therefore, for Plato, is knowledge of perfection itself and how it applies to the conduct of a human life and also to the life of a city. In the latter case, a city displays wisdom when its rulers have such knowledge and apply it in governing the community of people of which their city consists. Such excellence in statecraft thus consists in the rule of philosophers and its acceptance by their auxiliaries and the working men and women who make up the majority of the city's population. And Plato, then, following his analogy between the city and the soul, identifies wisdom in the individual with the rule of reason and its acceptance by spirit and appetite when reason has attained the requisite knowledge. Wisdom is thus exemplified in a well-ordered personality by the excellence of reason, having attained knowledge of perfection, in governing how one conducts one's life.

By the same token, Plato identifies the other virtues exemplified in a well-ordered personality by their place in the operations of its three constituent parts. He identifies courage, for instance, with the workings of spirit under the guidance of reason. Courage, on Plato's view, consists in spirit's working to supply the confidence and strength of character one needs to follow reason's direction when one is faced with threats from which a person of lesser mettle would shrink. This view nicely matches the traditional view of courage as the power to stand up to threats when pursuing goods of greater value than that of safety from those threats, which the easily frightened are prone to seek. Spirit, as Plato understands it, is like the flight–fight mechanism that ethologists attribute to animals in explaining their responses to predators and rivals: an inherited mechanism that when properly trained and brought under the command of reason enables its possessor to stand fast in defense of important goods when he is threatened with their loss and to persevere in their pursuit despite the dangers that the pursuit involves. Similarly, the virtue of moderation, Plato points out, is exemplified in the well-ordered personality by appetite's subordination to reason. Traditionally, moderation is the power to resist strong desires, like those for rich food, intoxicating drink, and carnal pleasure, whose indulgence would bring one more harm than good, and again Plato's identification of this virtue with appetite's submission to reason nicely matches this traditional view.

Of course, the virtue that is of special interest to Plato is justice. He finds this virtue, too, in the well-ordered personality. But the question is where, since unlike the other three virtues, wisdom, courage and moderation, justice is not particularly associated with the workings of any one of the soul's constituent parts. Recognizing this, Plato again looks to his analogy between the constitution of a well-governed city and that of a well-ordered personality. The strategy makes good sense if one accepts the analogy. For justice must exist in the well-governed city. No well-governed city, after all, could also be unjust. Further, what makes a city well-governed, Plato observes, is the fidelity of each of its constituent parts to fulfilling its proper role. So justice, according to Plato, as an excellence of a city and, and indeed of any political community, consists in the community's parts each playing its proper role in harmony with the others. Correspondingly, Plato then argues, justice as a personal virtue consists in the constituent parts of the soul each playing its proper role in harmony with the others. Justice, there-fore, is exemplified in a well-ordered personality, just as it is exemplified in a well-governed city. And once one locates its source in the latter, one can see it in the former as well.

We have now arrived at Plato's solution to the *Republic*'s core problem. It offers not only a very congenial picture of the best life for human beings but, even more important, reassurance that such a life is possible only for those who live justly. Crooks and bullies, Plato tells us, necessarily live inferior lives, for having turned to injustice to achieve their ends, they have abandoned the possibility of achieving the highest good and settled instead for something much cheaper. This is unquestionably an elegant and inspiring solution. It shows not only that justice, being integral to a well-ordered personality, is good in itself and not merely good as a means to something else, but also that justice, because it is necessary to achieving the highest good, is superior in value to whatever good one can achieve through injustice. Thus it speaks directly to the challenge that Glaucon and Adeimantus put to Socrates.

Nonetheless, the solution is open to a powerful objection. The analogy between a well-governed city and a well-ordered soul on which it depends does not get Plato all the way to the conclusions he needs to answer successfully Glaucon and Adeimantus' challenge. It fails because, though it supports attributing justice to the well-ordered soul, the attribution it supports is only of justice in the relations among the soul's constituent parts and not of justice in the way an individual whose soul is well-ordered acts toward others. One can see this, once one recognizes the limits on what the analogy implies. Specifically, the justice it supports attributing to a well-ordered soul must be like the justice that is necessarily found in a well-governed city on account of its being well-governed, and the latter consists in justice among the members of the city in their conduct toward each other. In particular, it is realized in government by those who are equipped to rule, helped in their efforts by auxiliary forces, and obeyed by the members of the city's economically productive class, who, knowing the wisdom of their rulers, willingly accept their authority. Correspondingly, the justice that one may attribute to a well-ordered soul on the basis of this analogy consists in justice among the soul's constituent parts in their relations to each other. It is realized, that is, in the rule of reason, when reason through education is equipped to rule and when its rule is backed by the workings of spirit and unchallenged by appetite. The existence of such justice in the soul, however, does not imply that someone whose soul is just in this way will act justly towards others. Nothing, for instance, in this characterization of justice as a personal virtue implies that one whose soul is well-ordered is certain upon finding a purse containing a huge wad of cash to try to return it, and the cash, to its owner.

The gap in Plato's argument is due to Plato's having failed to take note of two different areas of political life in which a city can exhibit justice. First, it can exhibit justice in its domestic or internal affairs. It exhibits such justice when the relations among its members are wholly just. A well-governed city necessarily exhibits such justice, for it cannot be true of a city that it is well-governed if the relations among its members are unjust. Second, a city can exhibit justice in its foreign or external affairs. It exhibits such justice when its conduct toward other cities is just, when, for instance, it fully complies with the trade agreements it has entered into with them and does not seek unfair advantage by cheating on those agreements. Such justice, though it may, as a rule, be observed by well-governed cities, is not necessarily observed by them. That a city is well-governed, in other words, is no guarantee of its being just in its foreign or external affairs. For its being well-governed means that each member keeps to his or her proper role and does not cause any internal strife by trespassing on other members' roles, and a city that behaves unjustly toward other cities may nevertheless have achieved such civic harmony. Plato's error, then, consists in his conflating civic justice in domestic affairs with civic justice in foreign affairs, for his analogy between a soul and a city allows him to attribute the analog of the former to a well-ordered soul but not the analog of the latter. Yet it is the analog of the latter that a well-ordered soul must have for possession of such a soul to imply that one is just in one's conduct towards others. It is the analog of the latter, that is, that a well-ordered soul must have if Plato's account of it as the highest human good is to yield a successful answer to Glaucon and Adeimantus' challenge.

Though Plato's solution to the *Republic*'s core problem falls short of answering Glaucon and Adeimantus, it contains an important insight that suggests other, possibly more promising solutions. The insight is implicit in Plato's account of the motives behind unjust action. On a plausible reconstruction of that account, Plato proceeds on the unstated assumption that injustice is never an ultimate end of a person's actions. Consequently, when injustice is done, it is done either as a means to some other end, as embezzlement is a means to enrichment, or as a side effect of an action whose intended effect is different, as depriving others of their fair share is a side effect of grabbing things one wants before anyone else can take them. In either case, the motive behind the act, Plato thought, is an unmet need such as an appetite in need of gratification or a fear in need of removal. People, in other words, are moved to act unjustly by needy states, states that demand satisfaction or relief. When such states are the dominant motives in a person's life, then that person is ruled by his appetites and fears, and his life consists in striving for gratification of the former and escape from the latter. The striving is ceaseless, short of death, though it may occasionally be punctuated by temporary states of satiation and repose. Thus the ends that give shape and direction to this life of ceaseless striving are never more than temporarily achieved. In such a life, situations recommending injustice as the expedient course of action occur repeatedly, yet whether one chooses expedience and so acts unjustly or resists and so acts justly makes little difference in the long run. The life is unfulfilling in either case. Such is the fate of the person in whom appetite and its correlative fears dictate his ends.

Plato's way out of this quandary is to find in our personalities a source of ends that, unlike those whose source is appetite and its correlative fears, are permanently achievable. These are the ends of perfection. Their source is reason. With the proper education of reason, Plato held, a person can come to understand perfection in itself, to know its many forms, beauty, truth, goodness, and justice among others, and to commit himself deeply to realizing them in his life. Such a person would then live a life in which the ends of perfection dominated those whose source was appetite and its correlative fears. The former ends and not the latter, that is, would shape and give direction to his life. Accordingly, such a person would be ruled by reason rather than appetite, and his life would consist in contemplative and creative activities through which he could realize perfection. Such a life, Plato believed, would be complete and fulfilling. In particular, it would lack the bottomless privations characteristic of life lived under the rule of appetite. And being free of those privations, people who lived such lives would never see their situations as recommending injustice as the expedient course of action. They would always act justly as a matter of course. The reason why, Plato thought, is that the realization of perfection entails the development of a well-ordered personality and therefore, by analogy to the well-governed city, the instantiation of justice as an integral aspect of one's personality. Of course, as we saw, this argument of Plato's fails. The analogy does not imply that people who have developed a well-ordered personality will act justly towards others. But the general ideas leading to it, that people whose lives were complete and fulfilling would not be liable to the motives from which unjust actions towards others spring and that such lives are possible only if shaped and directed by ends whose achievement can be permanent and so by ends that are distinct from those of appetite and its correlative fears, are nonetheless promising. To see whether they can yield a sound solution to the *Republic*'s core problem, however, we must look to a different account of human personality from Plato's.

7. Rationalism v. naturalism

Plato's ethics initiated the great tradition of rationalism in the theory of moral psychology. Its central themes are the fundamental opposition between reason and appetite (likewise reason and passion) and the supremacy of reason in any well-functioning and upright personality. In this tradition human motives are divided into two kinds: the motives that the powers of rational thought and action produce and the motives that come from animal appetite and brute emotion. Adherents to the tradition then characterize human life as a site of struggle between motives of the former kind and motives of the latter and as lived well only when the former prevail over the latter. The nearly universal struggle to curb an appetite for sweets and the now familiar struggle to suppress a desire to get back at some inconsiderate driver would be typical examples. Each arises from an immediate, seemingly instinctive attraction or impulse, to which, knowing of the harmful effects of eating too many sweets or the dangers of petty tit-for-tat behavior, one responds with resistance, and this resistance, on the rationalist tradition, represents the force of reason. Accordingly, such struggles are seen as revealing a basic division in human personality between its rational and irrational parts and indicating the need for the former to control and rule the latter. The ideal rationalist resolution thus consists in reason's mastering appetite and passion and so in the subordination of the latter to the rule of the former. In all of these ideas and themes rationalism has followed Plato's lead.

Its chief opponent in the theory of moral psychology has been naturalism. This is because in the rationalist tradition, again beginning with Plato, reason is seen as operating independently of the forces of nature. In the naturalist tradition, by contrast, the operations of reason are understood to be natural phenomena explicable, like other natural phenomena, by the forces and conditions of nature. The foremost point of disagreement between the two traditions, then, is over what I will call the doctrine of the independence of reason, which rationalists affirm and naturalists deny. Other points of disagreement follow from this one, at least when rationalists, as they have commonly done, interpret this doctrine as having certain metaphysical implications. Thus rationalists and naturalists have traditionally disagreed over the nature of death and the possibility of the immortality of the soul, for rationalists have commonly interpreted the doctrine of the independence of reason as implying that the human soul, in virtue of its being the seat of reason, can exist outside of the natural world and therefore independently of the human body it inhabits. And when so interpreted, the doctrine supports a conception of death as consisting in the separation of the soul from the body and the consequent belief in the possibility of the soul's being immune to the destructive forces of nature. Naturalists, by contrast, having denied the doctrine of the independence of reason, find nothing in the mental activities and processes of human life to imply that any part of the human soul exists outside of nature or that it enjoys an immunity from nature's destructive forces. According to naturalism, these activities and processes are themselves activities and processes of life. They are no different in this respect from respiratory activities and processes. Hence, they cease when life itself ceases, if not before, and death consequently, as naturalists conceive of it, consists in their permanent cessation.

These disputes show the metaphysical depths of the traditional opposition between rationalism and naturalism. At the surface, however, the disputes between the two traditions concern matters of psychology alone. Above all, they concern the possibility of reason's being a source of motives that can conflict with the motives that come from animal appetite and brute emotion. Naturalists deny that it can. They deny, that is, that the operations of reason can ever generate motives. The powers of reason, they maintain, do not include the power to initiate action. Thus they deny that when, knowing of the harmful effects of eating too many sweets, say, we resist the attraction of after-dinner chocolates, our resistance represents the force of reason. What it represents instead, they argue, is the fear of pain and disability that, owing to our foreseeing the pain and disability caused by eating too many sweets, moves us to resist the temptation. And they trace this fear to its origins in the aversion to pain and the instinct for self-preservation that human beings, like other sentient animals, have inherited as part of their motivational constitution. In this way they exclude reason from being a source of motives. On naturalist theories of moral psychology, reason contributes to the formation of motives, not by originating them, but by providing the intelligence necessary to guide actions motivated by fear and aversion, desire and inclination, away from objects of the former and toward objects of the latter. It serves, in other words, as a pilot of action only, and not as an engine. Hence, in direct opposition to the rationalist idea of the conflict between reason and appetite or reason and passion, naturalists maintain that all conflicts of motives are conflicts among appetites and passions. Some of these motives, being informed by foresight and knowledge, are more conducive to one's well-being and to the promotion of the highest good than others, and what rationalists take to be conflicts between reason and appetite or reason and passion are therefore, on naturalists' theories, conflicts between these enlightened motives and motives that are uninformed by foresight and knowledge.

We might, then, look to this naturalist tradition for the nonplatonic account of human personality that we seek in considering whether Plato's ideas about the motives of injustice can yield a sound, eudaimonist solution to the *Republic*'s core problem. To see whether they can, let us first configure Plato's ideas to fit these naturalist accounts. In particular, we need to replace Plato's account of the human personality as divided into rational and irrational parts that can produce conflicting motives with an account of human personality on which our rational powers do not include the power to produce motives. That is, instead of working with conceptions of reason and appetite as being separate sources of motivation that can oppose each other, we must work with conceptions of them as being separate capacities with different functions, cognitive in the case of reason, motivational in the case of appetite, that work together more or less coordinately in the production of human action. Accordingly, appetite supplies motivational energy that powers human action, and reason directs that energy and so guides the movements it powers. Such direction and guidance come about through the greater understanding of what a good life consists in and how best to achieve it that reason provides. What makes for a well-ordered personality, then, on this naturalist account, is the harmonious coordination of reason's cognitive functions with appetite's motivational functions. When one's judgments about what activities and experiences one ought to pursue perfectly fit the ends one is motivated to pursue, then reason and appetite are working together harmoniously. Specifically, when one's judgments of the relative importance of some activity or experience to advancing one's well-being matches the strength of one's motivation to engage in that activity or pursue that experience, then one's personality is well-ordered. We can thus define, on the naturalist account, an ideal of a well-ordered personality that corresponds to the one to which Plato's argument appeals.

At the same time, we must keep in mind how it departs from the ideal to which Plato's argument appeals. Plato, recall, makes the development of a well-ordered personality dependent on one's attaining knowledge of perfection. He identifies such knowledge with wisdom and maintains that to attain it, reason must undergo a rigorous education in the disciplines whose mastery is necessary to understanding perfection in all of its forms. Once this education is successful, on Plato's account, the rational part of the soul will have achieved supremacy over the soul's other parts and will, with the aid of spirit, rule appetite. The personality will be well ordered. On the naturalist account, by contrast, development of a well-ordered personality depends not only on the attainment of wisdom but also on the acquisition of the self-command necessary to act in accordance with the deliverances of wisdom. Hence, in addition to the education of reason, by which one acquires wisdom, appetite, too, on this account, must be conditioned so that the ends toward which it moves one and the strength of one's desire to realize those ends match what wisdom determines are the activities worth doing and the experiences worth pursuing. To achieve harmonious coordination of reason's cognitive functions with appetite's motivational functions requires, in other words, training the latter so as to enable one to enact the wisdom that results from the education of the former. Only then will one acquire, in addition to wisdom, the excellences of courage, moderation, and justice, among others. A well-ordered personality, on the naturalist account, unlike Plato's, does not, then, result from the successful education of reason alone.

By the same token, one cannot, on the naturalist account, unlike Plato's, assume that the proper education of reason guarantees the acquisition of the ends whose pursuit makes for a complete and fulfilling life. Plato can make this assumption because reason, on his account, is the source of such ends by virtue of being the source of the motives whose dominance over the motives of appetite is the essence of a well-ordered personality. But on the naturalist account, because reason is not the source of such motives or indeed any motives, one cannot assume that it is the source of such ends. What the ends are whose pursuit makes for a complete and fulfilling life is itself a question for naturalists. They cannot, that is, attribute such ends to reason without argument. Further, for naturalists who propound perfectionist theories of human well-being, the question of what the ends are whose pursuit makes for a complete and fulfilling life is a question of what activities in life are worth doing for their own sake. We must therefore find an answer to this question before we can determine whether the accounts of human personality that such naturalists put forward offer a solution to the *Republic*'s core problem.

8. Aristotle's naturalism

This naturalist program goes back to Aristotle (384–322 BC). After Plato, Aristotle is the most important exponent of perfectionism in the theory of well-being. He is also, after Plato, the most important exponent of the specific form of eudaimonism that Plato originated. Like Plato, Aristotle identifies human well-being (eudaimonia) with the ideal of living a complete and fulfilling life. It is complete, Aristotle says, in the sense that one could not make it a better life through the addition of some further good, and it is fulfilling in the sense that one aims to live such a life for its own sake and not for the sake of some other good. In short, such a life lacks nothing that could improve it and is wholly satisfying in itself. It thus fits Plato's ideal of a life lived in pursuit of ends that are permanently achievable. But unlike Plato, Aristotle does not identify these ends with perfection itself. He takes ethics to be a study of the good for human beings without supposing that it proceeds from a study of goodness or perfection generally. Thus, while he agrees with Plato about the completeness and self-sufficiency of the best human life, he differs from Plato in thinking that knowledge of what such a life consists in requires attention to the nature of our humanity and to the sort of life that is distinctive of our species and not, as Plato thought, to some abstract idea of perfection by which everything that is good in itself is measured. And while Aristotle also shares Plato's general view that the best human life is the life of rational thought and activity, he bases this view on decidedly different considerations from those on which Plato based it.

Specifically, Aristotle bases it on considerations of biology. That is, he develops the view by considering human beings as living things. As such, he holds, humans have a distinctive form of life. Accordingly, determining what makes for a good human life requires first defining its distinctive form, just as one would first define, say, what the distinctive form of literature a novel is before determining what makes for a good novel or the distinctive form of meal a buffet luncheon is before determining what makes for a good buffet luncheon. And the way Aristotle defines the form of life distinctive of humankind, or indeed of any animal species, is to identify those powers that are special to that species and then to make the exercise of those powers definitive of that form of life. From such a definition it follows that the best life for the members of the species entails full development of those powers and excelling in activities that display their exercise.

Consider, as an illustration of this approach, how one would determine what makes for the best life for eagles. To answer this question requires first defining the form of life distinctive of eagles, which means identifying the eagle's special powers. These include, not only the power of flight, but also, in particular, the power to glide for great distances high above the ground. Further, they include remarkable visual powers, specifically, the power to see faraway objects clearly and distinctly. Accordingly, the form of life distinctive of eagles includes such activities as dwelling on high cliffs or other eyries, soaring over large tracts of land, and homing in on prey with great accuracy. The best life for an eagle therefore entails living in this way and excelling at these activities. Eagles that live in other ways necessarily have worse lives, for they have lives in which their distinctive powers are either dormant or exercised weakly and defectively. Eagles that live in captivity, for instance, whose wings are clipped and whose nests are near to the ground, however well-fed, disease-free and lovingly cared for they may be, live markedly worse lives than those that thrive in their natural habitat. For such eagles never exercise the powers that are the special gifts of their species. Indeed, their existence, when regarded in this light, seems sad. Though they are eagles, their lives seem stunted by comparison with the form of life that we readily identify as an eagle's.

For Aristotle the same sort of consideration applies in defining the form of life distinctive of humankind and determining, in consequence, what is the best life for human beings. Unsurprisingly, Aristotle singles out reason as the power special to human beings whose exercise defines the form of life distinctive of our species. So the best life for human beings, Aristotle maintains, is a life in which one's rational powers are fully developed and in which one excels in activities that display their exercise. Men and women who never develop their powers of reason or whose lives lack opportunities for exercising them, people who cannot without assistance deal with the complex circumstances that are common to life in all but perhaps the most primitive human societies or who work long hours in mindless, repetitive tasks, do not have as good lives as those whose rational powers are fully developed and whose occupations and avocations afford plenty of opportunity for their exercise. The former, on Aristotle's view, have a sadder existence in comparison to the latter, just as eagles who live in captivity have lives that pale in comparison to those of their conspecifics who live in the wild. This is not to say, of course, that their lives are less pleasurable, though it would be astonishing if they weren't. For Aristotle's theory of well-being, remember, is that of perfectionism and not hedonism. It is to say, then, that their lives fall significantly short of the perfectionist ideal of human well-being as compared to the lives of the latter.

To be sure, to characterize the best life for human beings as a life in which one's rational powers are fully developed and in which one excels in activities that display their exercise is not yet to identify ultimate ends in life whose pursuit makes for a complete and fulfilling life. A great many different kinds of life fit this characterization, for the range of human activities excellence in which requires the exercise of one's rational powers is indefinitely large. What is more, plenty of these activities have ends whose pursuit would not make for a complete and fulfilling life if they were one's ultimate ends in life. A life spent in pursuit of fame, the life of the publicity seeker, for instance, though it would require the exercise of rational powers, would not be complete and fulfilling if fame were its dominant end, for it is in the very nature of fame to die out over time in the absence of renewed efforts at gaining publicity. Hence, this characterization of the best life for human beings is not sufficient for determining the ends whose pursuit makes for a complete and fulfilling life. Aristotle, therefore, since he meant his view of the best life for human beings to be one of a life that is complete and fulfilling, must have thought there was more in the considerations of biology on which he based this view than we have so far allowed.

In fact, Aristotle did think there was more. His view, which he expressed in an important passage in his *Nicomachean Ethics*, is that the very point of human life is to exercise reason.[12] Rational activity for its own sake,

---

[12] Aristotle, *Nicomachean Ethics*, bk. I, ch. 7, 1097b22–1098a20.

Aristotle held, is therefore the end whose pursuit makes for the best life for human beings when one excels in that activity. This conclusion, he thought, follows from analogy. Just as the point of being a flute player is to play the flute and the point of being a sculptor is to make sculptures, so too there is a point of being human. Or as Aristotle put it, in drawing a second analogy, just as eyes have a natural function and hands have a natural function, so too in nature the whole of man has a function. And to understand what that function is, one must determine the powers and capabilities that distinguish humankind from other animal species. Aristotle, as we noted before, took these to be the powers of reason. Hence, for him the same considerations that lead to defining the form of life distinctive of humankind also determine what humankind's function is. On his view, then, the best life for human beings is a life in which one fulfills that function, and such a life would be one whose point and final end is rational activity. Such a life, if it displayed excellence in the activities to which it was devoted, would necessarily be complete and fulfilling, for a life in which one fulfilled one's function as a human being and achieved excellence in doing so would be one that was wholly satisfying in itself and lacked nothing that could make it better.

How are we to understand this argument of Aristotle's? Its meaning is not immediately clear, and the obscurity is undoubtedly due to the distance between the biological notions of the ancient Greeks and the notions of modern biology with which we are familiar. Still, the analogies on which Aristotle bases his thesis that human beings have a distinctive function in virtue of being human offer some clue to understanding his argument. Consider, then, his appeal to flute players and sculptors. To be either, one must engage in the activity that is distinctive of their art. When flute players or sculptors engage in this activity they function as flute players or sculptors, as the case may be, and this functioning defines their function. So too, Aristotle must be arguing, when a man engages in the activity that is distinctive of his species, he functions as a human being, and this functioning defines his function. To function as a human being, according to Aristotle, is to engage in rational activity, for reason is the power that distinguishes human beings from other animals. Looking and listening, smelling and tasting, by contrast, are activities that both humans and other animals engage in. Consequently, one functions as a sentient animal, and not particularly as a human being, when one looks at things, listens to things, smells them, or tastes them. The sensory powers one exercises in these activities are not peculiar to human beings. Likewise one functions merely as a living thing, and not specially as a human being or even as a sentient animal, when one drinks, eats, and sleeps, for such nutritive and metabolic activities are common to both plants and animals. And because Aristotle expressly draws these contrasts, one can assume that he means to distinguish between activity whose very point is the exercise of reason and activities whose point is the exercise of these other powers. Hence, what he means to show by this argument is not that only some of the ends whose pursuit requires the exercise of reason are ends whose pursuit can make for a complete and fulfilling life. Rather, he means to show that any set of ends whose pursuit requires the exercise of reason are ends whose pursuit can make for a complete and fulfilling life if the point of pursuing them is ultimately to develop and exercise one's reason, which is to say, to live a life in which one functions as a human being, and to achieve excellence in so functioning.

Let us call this the broad interpretation of Aristotle's function argument. It is broad because the argument, on this interpretation, is not meant to narrow the range of ends around whose pursuit a life that has the form distinctive of humankind must be organized to be the best life for a human being. Rather it is meant to establish that a certain view and attitude toward those pursuits is necessary to living a complete and fulfilling life. A person's life becomes organized around the pursuit of certain ends long before he comes to reflect on the meaningfulness of pursuing them. Success in life consists in his achieving those ends, so achieving them, he may naturally think, on first reflection, is what makes their pursuit meaningful. Later, though, if the pursuit of these ends calls for the development and exercise of his rational powers, he may come to see that his having such ends has created for him a life whose form is distinctively human and so to regard the activity that qualifies it as distinctively human as what makes their pursuit meaningful. He will have come, in other words, from seeing and valuing these pursuits as means to success in life to seeing them as consisting in activity whose point is the exercise of reason essential to it and whose value therefore lies in his excelling in such rational activity. He will thus have come to have the view and attitude toward the pursuits around which his life is organized that, on the broad interpretation of Aristotle's function argument, is necessary for his life to be complete and fulfilling, for only then will the point of these pursuits have become for him the development and exercise of his rational powers so as to excel in his functioning as a human being. Only then will he be living a life that meets Aristotle's definition of the best life for a human being: the life consisting in activity of human thought and action in accordance with virtue. And with this definition, Aristotle comes to the final conclusion of his function argument.

9. A problem in Aristotle's program

At this juncture, however, Aristotle's naturalist program runs into trouble. The trouble occurs because Aristotle takes human virtue to consist in the capabilities and dispositions whose exercise corresponds to excellence in human functioning, and he identifies these with all the standard virtues, wisdom, courage, moderation, justice, honesty, generosity, and the like. In short, he believes that excellence in human functioning consists in activities that call for the exercise of these standard virtues. Yet his function argument, on the broad interpretation of it, is too broad to support this belief.

The reason is that the argument, on this broad interpretation, does not exclude any life that has the form distinctive of humankind from being the best life for human beings on account of the ends around whose pursuit it is organized. Even a life spent in pursuit of fame is consistent with being the best life for a human being, for it is conceivable, however implausible as a matter of human psychology, that a person who spent his life in pursuit of fame could see his pursuits as affording him opportunity to exercise his rational powers and therefore take the point of the activity that his pursuit of fame consisted in to be the development and exercise of those powers so as to excel in his functioning as a human being. So too, a life spent swindling others, the life of a con artist, as it were, is, as far as Aristotle's function argument goes, on its broad interpretation, consistent with the best life for human beings, for it, too, is a life success in which requires the development and exercise of one's rational powers. And it is therefore conceivable, however implausible as a matter of human psychology, that a person who spent his life swindling others could regard the pursuits around which he had organized his life as affording him opportunity to exercise his rational powers and therefore take the point of the activity that the pursuit of a good con consisted in to be the development and exercise of those powers.

Clearly, though, such a life is inconsistent with a person's having the virtues of justice and honesty. Hence, the function argument, on its broad interpretation, does not support Aristotle's belief that functioning well as a human being consists in activities that call for the exercise of all the standard virtues, including, in particular, justice and honesty.

To support Aristotle's belief, then, the function argument has to be given a different interpretation. Specifically, one has to interpret it as being meant to narrow the range of ends around whose pursuit a life that has the form distinctive of humankind must be organized to be the best life for human beings. And to interpret the argument in this narrower way means taking Aristotle as holding that some forms of rational activity are, by virtue of their forms, better suited to realizing excellence in human functioning than others. On one such narrower interpretation, for instance, Aristotle holds that the pursuit of truth and knowledge elicits the development and exercise of one's rational powers to a higher degree of perfection than the pursuit of fame, wealth, public service, triumph in battle, or artistry in any art or craft. Accordingly, the best life for human beings would be a life which was organized around the pursuit of truth and knowledge and in which one excelled in the activities essential to discovering truth and advancing knowledge, which is to say, science and philosophy, research and scholarship.

Plainly, such an interpretation of Aristotle's function argument, and indeed any interpretation of it as being meant to narrow the range of ends around whose pursuit a life that has the form distinctive of humankind must be organized to be the best life for human beings, depends on attributing to Aristotle a conception of our rational powers on the basis of which one can distinguish some forms of rational activity from others as truer or more exemplary exercises of those powers. For otherwise one could not interpret him as holding that some forms of rational activity were, just by virtue of their forms, better suited than others to realizing excellence in human functioning. Yet it is difficult to see how one could justify drawing such a distinction among forms of rational activity. And if one cannot, then the function argument must fail to exclude from being the best life for human beings a life that is organized around ends whose pursuit is inconsistent with having all the standard virtues.

The problem with justifying such a distinction is this. Human intelligence comprises a number of different capacities for productive thinking.

These include capacities for conceptual and logical thought, for invention, for creative synthesis of sensory experiences, for empathic understanding, and more. A conception of our rational powers that can serve as the basis for distinguishing some forms of rational activity from others as truer or more exemplary exercises of reason must be one that either limits reason to some one or few of these capacities or, though it comprehends all of them, sharply distinguishes each from the others. Yet clearly, if the latter is the conception of our rational powers that is attributed to Aristotle on the narrower interpretation of his function argument, then the argument must also include a premiss to the effect that, though the exercise of any of these capacities is an exercise of reason, the exercise of some is a truer or more exemplary exercise of reason than the exercise of others. And such a premiss would be very hard to justify. To elevate any of these capacities above the others as a capacity whose exercise represents a purer or more perfect form of reason, when one takes the exercise of each to be an exercise of reason, would seem merely to reflect some arbitrary preference for one form of rational activity over others.

Suppose, then, that the former is the conception of our rational powers that is attributed to Aristotle on the narrower interpretation of his function argument. It follows that our rational powers, on this second version of the interpretation, include some but not all of the capacities for productive thinking that human intelligence comprises. Consequently, the conception can serve as the basis for distinguishing some forms of rational activity from others as being truer or more exemplary exercises of reason, for one can use it to distinguish the elements of the activity that are due to exercises of reason from the elements that are due to exercises of other capacities that human intelligence comprises. Accordingly, one form of rational activity is a truer or more exemplary exercise of reason than another the greater the contribution of the powers of reason to that activity relative to the contributions of these other capacities. But now what had appeared, on the first version of the narrower interpretation, to be an arbitrary preference for one form of rational activity over others reappears, on this second version, as an arbitrary preference for one form of human functioning over others. After all, if some of the capacities for productive thinking that human intelligence comprises are distinct from our rational powers, then Aristotle has to justify excluding their exercise from humankind's distinctive function, and it is hard to see how he could. Since there appears to be no basis for taking only our rational powers as what distinguishes humankind from other animal species, when human intelligence is understood to comprise other capacities for productive thinking, there appears to be no basis for taking the exercise of reason to be humankind's function to the exclusion of these other capacities.

The upshot is that Aristotle's function argument, on either version of the narrower interpretation, does not support taking the exercise of any of the capacities for productive thinking that human intelligence comprises as more excellent or perfect kinds of human functioning than the exercise of any other. Hence, it does not support taking one life as better for human beings than another because pursuit of the ends around which the former is organized is more conducive to the exercise of some one of these capacities than pursuit of the ends around which the latter is organized, given that pursuit of the ends around which the latter is organized is more conducive to the exercise of a different capacity among those that human intelligence comprises. The argument does not, for instance, support taking a life devoted to the pursuit of truth and knowledge as a better life than a life devoted to music, painting, cooking, or some other fine or practical art. While the former life is presumably organized around ends whose pursuit is more conducive to the exercise of the capacity for conceptual and logical thinking than pursuit of the ends around which the latter is organized, nothing in the argument supports taking the exercise of that capacity as a more excellent or perfect kind of human functioning than the exercise of the capacity for synthesis of sensory experience, the capacity to whose exercise pursuit of the ends around which the latter life is organized is more conducive. And similarly for a life organized around ends whose pursuit is most conducive to exercising the capacity for invention: the life devoted to solving practical problems, making new tools, or organizing cooperative enterprises. Indeed, the same holds even for a life that is organized around ends whose pursuit is most conducive to exercising the capacity for seeing absurdity and incongruity, the life devoted to comedy, parody, mime, or other forms of humorous entertainment and commentary.

In sum, Aristotle's function argument, if interpreted as meant to limit the range of ends around whose pursuit a life that has the form distinctive of humankind must be organized to be the best life for human beings, is too weak to establish such limits. And failing this, the argument cannot reach the conclusion that Aristotle intended. His function argument notwithstanding, a man could live a complete and wholly satisfactory life, a life in which he fulfilled humankind's function and achieved excellence in doing so, yet the thought and action to which he devoted his life need not be in accordance with all the standard virtues, justice and honesty in particular.

10. Prospects for contemporary eudaimonism

Like Plato, Aristotle too believed that people whose lives were complete and fulfilling would not be liable to the motives from which unjust and dishonest actions spring. Whether or not he agreed with Plato in seeing these motives as needy states, he did regard them as states of excessive appetite and passion that dispose one to seek more than one's due. As such, they are dysfunctional states. To act under their influence is to act badly, which is to say, defectively as a human being. Consequently, to live a life in which one fulfills one's function as a human being and achieves excellence in doing so is to live a life free of these dispositions. Justice, Aristotle thought, is therefore among the virtues someone who lived a complete and fulfilling life would possess, for no one could excel in functioning as a human being if he were liable to such excessive appetites and passions. The argument on which Aristotle relied for this conclusion collapses, however, as we have seen. Nothing in it, on its broad interpretation, excludes the possibility of one's acting unjustly from different appetites or passions, in particular, appetites or passions that are consistent with one's fulfilling one's function as a human being and achieving excellence in doing so, and any narrower interpretation of the argument one gives so as to exclude this possibility rests ultimately on an arbitrary preference for some forms of human functioning over others. Hence, Aristotle's naturalist program, too, falls short of sustaining Plato's idea that people whose lives were complete and fulfilling would not be liable to the motives from which unjust actions towards others spring.

Nonetheless, it is important to note that the failure of Plato's and Aristotle's programs to sustain this idea does not show that the idea itself is bankrupt. To the contrary, the idea may still represent an important insight into human nature. If it does, though, it may take empirical studies of human lives to confirm this. Both Plato and Aristotle undertook to establish its truth through a study of the very meaning of human well-being. They undertook, that is, a quintessentially philosophical study. The lesson of the failures of these studies to show that being just and honest in one's dealings with others is necessary to living a good life may well be that a different kind of study is required to vindicate Plato's idea. Its vindication, for instance, may require a study of the lives of particular people who have lived well and whose success in life encompasses the development and exercise of their distinctively human powers and capabilities. Ideally, it would be a study that was designed to show whether such people were significantly less susceptible to the kinds of motives from which unjust and dishonest actions spring than others. But more realistically, one might have to settle for a study designed to determine whether those kinds of motive occurred less frequently in the lives of such people than in the lives of people who have lived less well, either because of a lack in development or exercise of their distinctively human powers and capabilities or because of a lack of success in life despite the development and exercise of these powers and capabilities. In any case, the studies would follow the research protocols of the social sciences, and their result would be the statistical generalizations characteristic of findings in those disciplines and not the universal and necessary truths that are the object of philosophical study.

So we can be sure that such results would not satisfy Glaucon and Adeimantus. They want Socrates to demonstrate a universal and necessary incompatibility between being unjust and living a good life. Showing a significant lack of susceptibility to the motives from which unjust actions spring in those who live good lives could only seem to them a poor substitute. They have challenged Socrates to give a philosophical defense of justice, and such a defense must deliver stronger results than generalizations representing susceptibilities and tendencies. Yet we must consider the possibility that their challenge asks too much from a philosophical study. We must consider, that is, the possibility that the form of eudaimonism Plato originated and Aristotle remodeled is not fully defensible within philosophy. Perhaps, then, in the end, the best defense of their theory follows Aristotle's program up to the point of defining, by reference to the special powers and capabilities of human beings, human life's distinctive form and subsequently characterizing the best life for human beings as one that is complete and fulfilling by virtue of the realization of these powers and capabilities. Having reached this point, however, this proposed defense of their theory abandons the effort to demonstrate that possession and exercise of the virtue of justice is necessary in all cases to living a good human life and appeals instead to contingencies of human life that would seem to make highly improbable the absence of this virtue in people who have, through the realization of their special human powers and capabilities, achieved a complete and fulfilling life. Such a defense is not, to be sure, a solution to the core problem of Plato's *Republic*. But it does offer some hope of refuge from the anxieties about the truth of Thrasymachus' nihilism that lead Glaucon and Adeimantus to press their challenge on Socrates.

4 Utilitarianism

1. Impartiality

Both egoism and eudaimonism share an outlook of self-concern. They both identify the perspective from which a person judges what ought to be done as that of someone concerned with how best to promote his own good. On either theory, then, the highest good for a person is that person's own good, whether this be his own happiness or his own well-being. Hence, on either theory, ethical considerations are understood to have the backing of reason insofar as they help to advance this good.

The self-concerned outlook prevailed in ancient ethics, for eudaimonism was its dominant theory. Modern ethics, by contrast, has been marked by a shift away from this outlook. Eudaimonism no longer dominates the field, and while egoism has continued to have supporters throughout the modern period, theories that presuppose a different outlook from that of self-concern have eclipsed it. These later theories do not identify the perspective from which a person judges what ought to be done as that of someone concerned with how best to advance his own good. Nor do they explain reason's backing of ethical considerations by showing how those consider-ations help to advance that good. To explain this backing modern moral philosophers have supposed, instead, that ethical considerations speak to some other element in human personality than concern about one's own good. Some philosophers have placed this element within the powers of reason themselves and supposed that we have a special rational capacity for knowing our duty. Such philosophers typically support deontological theo-ries of ethics. Others have pointed to our benevolent dispositions toward our fellow man and other members of the animal kingdom as the element to which ethical considerations speak. These philosophers typically endorse utilitarianism, which is the theory that, in its classical form, takes the highest good to be the good of humankind or the good of sentient animals generally. A third group synthesizes the chief themes of the first two. Specifically, they endorse utilitarianism on the grounds that reason dictates the pursuit of the good of humankind or the good of sentient animals generally. Thus, like the first group, these philosophers also identify reason as the element in human personality to which ethical considerations speak. Utilitarianism is the subject of the present chapter.[1] We will turn to deontological theories in the following chapter.

Utilitarianism, like egoism and eudaimonism, is a teleological theory. The prescriptions it grounds are judgments of what one ought to do in the sense of what one would be well-advised to do in view of one's ends and interests. The end in view of which utilitarianism grounds the prescriptions of ethics is the general good, understood either as the good of humankind or, more comprehensively, the good of all animals capable of experiences with which human beings can sympathize. To simplify our exposition, though, let us assume the less comprehensive of these ends as the one on which utilitarianism grounds the prescriptions of ethics. The good of humankind, then, on our simplified exposition of utilitarianism, is the ultimate end of ethics and thus the highest good for human beings. Acts are right or wrong according as they further or impede the achievement of this end. To be more exact, on the most careful formulation of the utilitarian standard of right and wrong, an act is right if it furthers the achievement of this end as well as, if not better than, any other act one could do in the circumstances one faces. An act is wrong if it fails to further the achievement of this end or furthers it less well than some other act one could do in those circumstances. This standard is commonly known as the Principle of Utility or, in keeping with the utilitarian tradition that looks to Jeremy Bentham as its founder and John Stuart Mill as its most eminent defender, the Greatest Happiness Principle. On a formulation of the principle as a

---

[1] The division of utilitarian theorists into two groups, those who identify general benevolence as the element in human personality to which ethical considerations speak and those who identify reason as that element, captures a trend in the development of utilitarian ethics. Classical utilitarians like Mill tend to belong to the first group. Since Henry Sidgwick (1838–1900), who originated and developed, in his masterwork, *The Methods of Ethics*, 7th edn. (London: Macmillan and Co., 1907), the idea of synthesizing the chief themes of rationalist deontology and classical utilitarianism, utilitarians have gravitated toward the second. The exposition of utilitarianism in this chapter is consistent with the views of either group.

prescription, in accordance with this Benthamite tradition, it runs: *So act as to bring about as much happiness in the world as you can in the circumstances you face.*

Bentham's formulation of the Principle of Utility as a prescription about the promotion of happiness reflects his acceptance of hedonism as the correct theory of well-being. The formulation is thus characteristic of classical utilitarian theory. But it is not required of all versions of the theory. The principle, in other words, is not wedded to hedonism. One could also formulate it in a way that reflected acceptance of perfectionism as the correct theory of well-being. Or one could formulate it in a way that reflected acceptance of some mixed theory. To put the point generally, the Principle of Utility does not presuppose any specific theory of either well-being or happiness. It prescribes that one act so as to bring about as much good overall in the world as one can, and how one conceives of that good, whether one conceives of it as happiness or well-being, and whether one defines it hedonistically, perfectionistically, or as some combination of the two, determines a specific version of utilitarianism but is otherwise unnecessary to its study. We can therefore, in pursuing the study, leave aside questions about the substantive nature of this good.

At the same time, we do need to specify the procedure by which the overall good an act brings about is calculated. Following Bentham's model of a hedonic calculus, let us take this procedure to consist in one's first assessing the amounts of good and evil the act brings about in the lives of everyone it affects and then separately totaling all the good it brings about and all the evil. Finally, one subtracts the latter total from the former. One thus arrives at the net balance of good over evil that the act produces. If one defines the overall good hedonistically, then the net balance of good over evil one arrives at results from subtracting the total amount of pain the act produces from the total amount of pleasure. And if one defines the overall good perfectionistically, then the net balance of good over evil one arrives at results from subtracting the degree and extent of the deficiencies in human activity the act produces from the degree and extent of the excellences in human activity it produces. To apply the Principle of Utility, then, one canvasses the different actions a person can take in the circumstances he faces, calculates for each the projected net balance of good over evil it would produce, and then identifies the right action, the action the person ought to do, as the one that will produce the greatest net balance of good over evil. Accordingly, one could state the Principle of Utility as prescribing that one so act, in the circumstances one faces, as to produce as great a net balance of good over evil as one can.

On Bentham's hedonic calculus, experiences of pleasure and pain figure in the overall good an act brings about according to how intense they are and how long they last. That is, one measures how much pleasure or how much pain an experience of either consists of along two dimensions of the experience, intensity and duration, and the resultant quantity of pleasure or quantity of pain one attributes to the experience translates directly into the amount of good or evil the experience represents. Thus, it is implicit in Bentham's calculus that experiences of pleasure and pain contribute, positively or negatively, to the overall good an act brings about regardless of whose experiences they are. Equally intense and long-lasting experiences of pleasure contribute equally to the overall good whether they are yours, mine, or some stranger's, and similarly for equally intense and long-lasting experiences of pain. The calculus is therefore, in a word, impartial among all of the people whose experiences of pleasure and pain figure in the calculation of the overall good that an act brings about. And this impartiality is implicit in every utilitarian procedure for calculating this good.

Thus utilitarianism, by virtue of this procedure, entails an impartial outlook toward all of humankind. For the procedure requires that you consider, when calculating the overall good that an act brings about, everyone whose life the act affects for good or ill and include in the calculation all benefits and harms each receives or will receive as a result of the act. Further, it requires that you treat a benefit or a harm to someone as adding or subtracting the same amount of good to the overall good the act brings about regardless of who the person benefited or harmed is. In particular, it does not matter whether this person is yourself, a friend, or a stranger. Clearly, then, utilitarianism rejects the outlook of self-concern common to egoism and eudaimonism. It rejects as well outlooks that are likewise partial to some people or biased against others. It therefore rejects clannish and chauvinistic outlooks and, indeed, any outlook that involves favoritism toward one group over another. To act as the Principle of Utility prescribes means that one regard the good of others as equally important as one's own good or the good of one's friends, family, countrymen, or the like. Bentham's dictum "Everyone to count for one, no one to count for more than one" expresses this utilitarian ideal of impartiality succinctly.

The ideal, as we've seen, is inseparable from the utilitarian procedure for calculating the overall good that an act brings about. Yet it is not the sole ideal that utilitarianism endorses. Since utilitarianism's orientation is toward benefiting humankind, we should understand its ideal of impartiality as belonging to the grander ideal of a life devoted to making the world a better place. Moreover, "being," in Mill's words, "a direct emanation from [the Principle of Utility]," the ideal of impartiality belongs to this grander ideal as an integral part and not merely as an add-on.[2] It emanates directly from the Principle of Utility, for to take the good of humankind as the highest good means treating all parts of that good, which is to say, the well-being of each and every human being, as equally important. Failure to do so would make about as much sense as treating one's well-being on Tuesdays and Thursdays as more important to advancing one's own good than one's well-being on the other days of the week. Differential treatment in either case, whether it is favoritism toward some people because of who they are or favoritism toward some times in one's life because of the days of the week in which they occur, is wholly arbitrary. And to incorporate it into one's procedure for determining how best to advance the good of humankind or one's own good, as the case may be, is likely to make things worse, not better. Hence, the complete ideal of human life that utilitarianism endorses is that of a life of impartial service to making the world a better place.

This is, without question, a morally admirable ideal. Its similarity to the Christian ideals of universal love and unconditional charity toward all is unmistakable. "In the golden rule of Jesus of Nazareth," Mill wrote, "we read the complete spirit of the ethics of utility. To do as you would be done by, and to love your neighbor as yourself, constitute the ideal perfection of utilitarian morality."[3] Jesus, as we know, set very demanding ideals for human beings, and the utilitarian ideal is no less demanding. The question, then, is how one could realize it in a human life. The difficulty of living up to Christian ideals is a central theme of Christianity and one of the chief lessons of the religion's teachings. Much, in fact, has been written in criticism as well as in praise of Christian ethics on account of this theme. The difficulties of realizing the utilitarian ideal are, if anything, even more pronounced and similarly the basis of much criticism.

---

[2] Mill, *Utilitarianism*, ch. 5, par. 36.   [3] Ibid., ch. 2, par. 16.

2. Two problems

One immediate difficulty of realizing the utilitarian ideal is due to the very impartiality that is built into the procedure for applying the Principle of Utility and that separates utilitarianism from egoism and eudaimonism. This impartiality, as we noted, consists in treating everyone's interests as equally important and so, in particular, in treating one's own interests or the interests of one's friends and close kin as no more important than the interests of mere acquaintances and strangers. And while the idea of treating one's own interests as no more important than the interests of a stranger has obvious moral appeal in the humility and solidarity with humanity it expresses, the idea of regarding the interests of one's friends as no more important than the interests of some stranger hardly seems similarly inspiring. Quite the contrary, it seems to contradict what it means to be someone's friend. By the same token, if you found someone who regularly treated the interests of his or her spouse as no more important than those of a stranger, you would ordinarily take this as a sign of a marriage gone bad and not of a person exercising moral virtue. Defenders of utilitarianism who have bitten the bullet, so to speak, and declared, as the early utilitarian William Godwin (1756–1836) did, that if he were to happen upon a burning building in which an important public official and his valet were trapped, he would first save the official even if the valet were his son, have simply seemed out of touch with human life rather than wise in the ways of morality.

This is not, of course, to say that there are no circumstances in which doing the right thing requires treating the interests of one's friends, one's spouse, or one's children as no more important than the interests of mere acquaintances and strangers. One who has assumed the responsibilities of a judge, a magistrate, or an administrator of government services, for example, and acts rightly in carrying them out, acts impartially, and this means that he or she, in fulfilling these responsibilities, treats the interests of friends and close kin as no more important than the interests of mere acquaintances and strangers. But we expect such impartiality of judges, magistrates, and government administrators because of the public offices they hold. We do not similarly expect it of private individuals as they go about their daily lives. Utilitarianism, however, by making such impartiality the rule in everyday decisions about what to do would appear to expect people always to act as if they were carrying out the responsibilities of a public official. And such expectations, if they truly represent the perspective on life utilitarianism recommends, threaten the theory's credibility.

A second difficulty of realizing the utilitarian ideal arises when one tries to fit adherence to standards of justice and honesty into a life lived in pursuit of this ideal. Admittedly, this might not at first seem to be much of a difficulty. After all, just and honest actions are actions that typically promote the well-being of others. Indeed, this feature of them is what led Thrasymachus to dismiss as foolish and weak people who adhered to standards of justice and honesty when they could ignore them with impunity. Just and honest actions therefore, because they seem to be actions contributing to the good of humankind by virtue of serving the interests of those on their receiving end, may seem to fit easily into a life lived in pursuit of the utilitarian ideal. Yet problems emerge nevertheless when one tries to square adherence to these standards with faithfully following the Principle of Utility in the conduct of one's life. These problems emerge because in some situations, so it seems, one can bring about a greater net balance of good over evil by acting unjustly or dishonestly than one could bring about through just and honest actions.

Our example of finding a lost purse containing a huge wad of cash nicely illustrates this point. Although you might initially think that to follow the Principle of Utility in this situation required returning the purse along with the cash to its owner, a little reflection should lead you to the opposite conclusion. For you need to consider, when applying the Principle of Utility, every act you could do in this situation, and while more overall good might come from returning the purse and cash to their owner than keeping the cash for yourself and discarding the purse, there are doubtless other acts you could do that would bring about even more overall good than either of these. A huge wad of cash, after all, can be used to do a lot of good for people who urgently need help or whose lives are so impoverished as to lack many of the basic necessities of a decent life. So to apply the Principle of Utility you would need to consider whether giving the cash to some charitable organization whose programs help such people would in fact bring about more overall good than returning it to its owner.

To get down to cases, suppose it is evident from your examining the contents of the purse that the owner is a well-to-do dentist who lives in a fashionable suburb, or suppose on looking at her driver's license you recognize her name as that of a prominent and wealthy member of the community, you should then confidently conclude that the loss she will suffer, if you do not return the cash to her, will be more than offset by the great good that would come from giving it to Save the Children or Second Harvest. Calculating with respect to each of these acts the good and evil that it is likely to bring about should lead you to see that the net balance of good over evil of the former is significantly less than that of the latter. Following the Principle of Utility in this situation appears, then, to require that you act dishonestly. The Principle, in other words, when applied to the situation, yields a prescription that directly conflicts with what basic standards of honesty prescribe. Such a conflict is plainly a serious problem for the theory.

The problem, moreover, goes beyond the conflict. For the example also shows that the theory treats considerations of justice and honesty in a way that is foreign to even an elementary understanding of how these consider-ations figure in deliberations about what to do. When you find a lost purse containing a huge wad of cash, you come into possession of another person's property without their consent. Recognizing that the purse and its contents belong to someone else, you realize, even on an elementary understanding of property, that you are not free to dispose of them as you see fit, that to do so would be to transgress the limits that another's being the owner of this purse places on your conduct, and that such a transgression would be an act of dishonesty. Yet this fact about the purse and its practical implications do not seem to register anywhere in the procedure for applying the Principle of Utility to the situation you face. For on this procedure, you regard every act that you can do in the situation as an option until you determine that it will bring about less good overall than some other act you can do. Consequently, until you make such a determination about some act, you are to regard yourself as free to do it. That the purse is not yours but someone else's does not then, it would seem, enter into your thoughts as restricting what actions you may consider doing. The dishonesty of disposing of the cash in the purse without its owner's consent would therefore appear, on this procedure for applying the Principle of Utility, never in itself to figure in your deliberations as a consideration that bears on whether the act is right or wrong. Hence, the conflict between the prescription that results from applying the Principle and the prescription that basic standards of honesty yield signifies an even deeper problem in the theory than that its prescriptions can conflict with those that basic standards of justice and honesty yield.

3. Consequentialism

The source of this problem is utilitarianism's supposition that at the foundation of ethics is a single standard of right and wrong, the Principle of Utility or Greatest Happiness Principle, that prescribes optimal promotion of the highest good. As a result of this supposition, the theory defines right action strictly by its consequences for good or ill in comparison with the consequences for good or ill of the other actions the agent can do in the circumstances, and similarly for its definition of wrong action. In other words, according to utilitarianism, the sole determinants of whether an act is right or wrong are the consequences of that action for good or ill in comparison with the consequences of the other actions available to the agent in the circumstances of his action, and therefore the only considerations that bear on whether an action is right or wrong are these consequences. Considerations of honesty and justice, by contrast, encompass other things besides the consequences of actions for good or ill. They encompass as well relations to past actions and present circumstances. The dishonesty of spending or giving away cash that one knows belongs to someone else and that one possesses without its owner's consent is not a matter of the consequences for good or ill of the action. It is rather a matter of the action's circumstances (viz., that the cash belongs to someone else) and the absence of certain past actions (viz., that the owner never consented to one's disposing of her cash as one sees fit). Similarly, the dishonesty of telling a lie is not a matter of the consequences of saying something one knows to be false to someone but rather a matter of circumstances (viz., that what one said to this person is false and that one said it with the intention of deceiving him). A theory that excludes such factors from being determinants of right and wrong actions, a theory that restricts the determinants of right and wrong actions to an action's consequences either absolutely or in comparison with the consequences of other actions, exemplifies consequentialism. And the difficulty for utilitarianism that our example of your finding a lost purse containing a huge wad of cash illustrates is due to the consequentialism of the theory.

   Standards of justice and honesty include many of the basic rules of social conduct, rules that prohibit or require certain conduct because of present circumstances or past actions and that we learn at an early age. Among them are the rules that prohibit our taking what belongs to others without their consent and that require our telling the truth. At first, because children have limited experience of the social world and abbreviated development of their capacities for self-restraint, these rules are taught as unbreakable. In time, however, as children venture out from their homes and families into the wider social world of schools, churches, clubs, work, and community affairs, they acquire a more complex understanding of these rules and greater confidence in their judgment about how to apply them. The rigidity of our early obedience to them relaxes somewhat as we learn about exceptions and about how to incorporate considerations of the consequences of our actions into our judgments about how the rules apply to our circumstances. Sometimes, as we learn, the consequences of obedience to one of these rules may be so bad that avoiding those consequences justifies our disobeying the rule: when emergencies occur – when the neighbor in the apartment across the hall slices off his thumb with a carving knife and you are his only hope for getting quickly to the hospital – your breaking a promise to visit a lonely aunt or your taking your roommate's car without his permission is justified. Nonetheless, we still understand the rules of justice and honesty as placing limits on our conduct, even though we also understand that those limits can be justifiably crossed in extreme circumstances. That is, leaving aside such emergencies and other crises, we continue to understand the rules as excluding from the range of actions open to us actions that would break the rules and so to regard these actions as not among our options, notwithstanding their having better consequences than the consequences that will result from our obeying the rules. Accordingly, we continue to understand the rules as binding upon us.

Consequentialism, in contrast, abandons this understanding of the rules of justice and honesty as binding. It invites us not only to take the consequences of an action as the sole determinants of whether it is right or wrong but also to see every action we can perform as, in principle, among our options until such time as it is determined that its consequences would be worse than the consequences of some other action open to us. It thus opposes directly our common understanding of the rules of justice and honesty as excluding from the range of actions open to us those that would break these rules. According to consequentialism, the rules of justice and honesty do not set barriers to our conduct but rather represent good, though less than surefire guides to what actions will have the best consequences in the circumstances we face. Definitions of 'right' and 'wrong' that exemplify consequentialism remove from those words the import they ordinarily have as terms for actions that respect or violate limits on conduct that moral standards impose, and this loss is most apparent in the way theories that incorporate such definitions render the rules of justice and honesty.

4. Mill's restatement of utilitarianism

Mill was keenly aware of these problems. The second, in particular, was the source of the popular criticism of utilitarianism that it was a philosophy of expediency and as such the enemy of justice. The criticism seemed well targeted when leveled at Bentham's statement of the theory, and Mill, in his famous short work, *Utilitarianism*, set out to restate Bentham's ideas so as to avoid this criticism. Specifically, he recognized the embarrassing prescriptions the theory yields when one takes its supposition that the Principle of Utility is the foundation of ethics to mean that one should apply the Principle directly to one's circumstances when determining what one ought to do. To avoid these embarrassing results, then, it is necessary to deny that utilitarianism requires that one apply the Principle directly to one's circumstances. To say that it is the fundamental principle of morality, Mill argued, is not to say that the theory recognizes no other moral principles. "It is a strange notion," he wrote, "that the acknowledgement of a first principle is inconsistent with the admission of secondary ones."[4] To the contrary, like other systems of ethics, utilitarianism, too, recognizes secondary principles whose use is necessary to achieving the end that the fundamental principle prescribes. "Whatever we adopt as the fundamental principle of morality," Mill declared, "we require subordinate principles to apply it by; the impossibility of doing without them being common to all systems, can afford no argument against any one in particular."[5]

   Hence, on Mill's restatement of utilitarianism, the theory recognizes a plurality of moral principles that are subordinate to the Principle of Utility. They are subordinate in the sense that their validity is due to their importance to people's achieving the end that the Principle of Utility prescribes, to their achieving, that is, the greatest overall good for humankind. To achieve this end, Mill held, it is necessary for people to accept and follow

---

[4] Ibid., ch. 2, par. 24.   [5] Ibid.

these subordinate principles. Accordingly, he refers to them as "corollaries from the Principle of Utility" and remarks that they represent the collective wisdom of humankind concerning what actions best promote its end.[6] "There is no difficulty," Mill observed, "in proving any ethical standard whatever to work ill if we suppose universal idiocy to be conjoined with it; but on any hypothesis short of that mankind must by this time have acquired positive beliefs as to the effects of some actions on their happiness; and the beliefs which have thus come down are the rules of morality for the multitude."[7] On Mill's theory, then, people, when determining what they ought to do, should consult these rules of morality and apply them directly to their circumstances, for by doing so they will best fulfill morality's fundamental principle. Of course, Mill conceded, these rules of morality are not immutable. They change as the conditions of human life change and as people gain greater wisdom about the world and how it works. "But to consider the rules of morality as improvable," Mill cautioned, "is one thing; to pass over the intermediate generalization[s] entirely and endeavor to test each individual action directly by the first principle is another,"[8] and utilitarianism's critics, he maintained, have misrepresented the theory in supposing that it requires the latter.

Mill's restatement of utilitarianism thus removes the Principle of Utility from directly determining whether an act is right or wrong. As a result, the version of the theory Mill presented does not define right action strictly by the action's consequences for good or ill in comparison with the consequences for good or ill of the other actions that the agent can perform in the circumstances he faces; and similarly for its definition of wrong action. Instead, the theory appeals to principles subordinate to the Principle of Utility, the rules of morality, in defining right and wrong. That is, on Mill's version of the theory, an action is right if it conforms to the rules of morality and wrong if it violates them, where the rules of morality are those principles that wisdom has shown to be the principles human beings must observe and follow if they are to secure and promote the general good. Since the basic standards of justice and honesty are among these principles, this version of the theory does not yield prescriptions that conflict with what the basic standards of justice and honesty prescribe. It does not, in particular, tell you that the right thing to do when you find a lost purse

[6] Ibid.   [7] Ibid.   [8] Ibid.

containing a huge wad of cash is to give the cash to a charitable organization that will use it to bring about more good for humankind overall than could possibly result from returning the cash to its owner. Rather it tells you to consult the rules of morality and apply them directly to the situation, and since the basic standards of justice and honesty are the applicable rules in these circumstances, it tells you that the right thing to do is to return the purse and the cash to its owner. By interposing a set of secondary principles between the primary principle, the Principle of Utility, and the circumstances of action Mill was therefore able to formulate a version of utilitarianism on which neither right nor wrong action is determined by direct calculation of the action's consequences and those of its alternatives in the manner that Bentham had prescribed.

Yet Mill was careful, in presenting this version of utilitarianism, not to deny that the consequences of an action can ever determine its moral quality or that circumstances can arise in which, because of grave consequences that following some moral rule would have, the right thing to do is to act contrary to it. Even the rule requiring that one tell the truth, Mill observed, "admits of possible exceptions … the chief of which is when the withholding of some fact (as of information from a malefactor, or of bad news from a person dangerously ill) would save an individual (especially an individual other than oneself) from great and unmerited evil, and when the withholding can only be effected by denial."[9] Further, Mill proposed, these exceptions, like the rules themselves, are generalizations whose validity is due to the importance to achieving the general good for humankind of their being recognized and followed. The same wisdom, that is, that has shown what rules human beings must follow to achieve the end that the Principle of Utility prescribes also teaches us about the special circumstances in which one must set a rule aside for the same purpose. The Principle of Utility, in other words, on Mill's restatement of utilitarianism, not only determines the rules of morality but carves out their exceptions as well. These exceptions are therefore part of the system of rules by which the Principle of Utility is applied, just as tax exemptions are part of the tax code. And by understanding exceptions to the rules of morality in this way Mill was able to acknowledge them consistently with his program of removing the Principle of Utility from directly determining whether an act is right or wrong.

---

[9] Ibid., ch. 2, par. 23.

In fact, according to Mill, the only times when one must consult the Principle of Utility directly to determine what act ought to be done are when two or more of the secondary principles apply to one's circumstances and yield conflicting prescriptions.[10] Suppose, for example, that you have been taken into another's confidence and have given him assurances that you will keep his secret. You would then find yourself in conflictual circumstances of the sort Mill had in mind if someone were to ask you a direct question to which you could not respond truthfully without betraying that confidence. In these circumstances, some method of resolving the conflict, some method of determining whether the right thing to do is to keep the secret or respond truthfully, is necessary, and one of the virtues of utilitarianism, Mill argued, as compared with the traditional systems of ethics that recognize a plurality of moral rules but treat each as having independent authority, is that it contains a method for resolving these conflicts. Its method consists in one's directly consulting the Principle of Utility to determine which act of complying with the rules best achieves the end on which they are all founded, for by determining which act best achieves this end, one determines which rule should have precedence in the circumstances one faces. In other words, although one directly consults the Principle of Utility to determine what act ought to be done, the act's being right is still a matter of its being prescribed by the rules of morality. Hence, even in these circumstances, Mill's endorsement of direct appeal to the Principle of Utility is fully compatible with his thesis that appeal to subordinate principles is necessary to determining whether an act is right or wrong. His acknowledgment of the propriety of directly appealing to the fundamental principle of morality to resolve conflicts between prescriptions that can arise when two or more of the secondary principles apply to one's circumstances is therefore consistent with his denying that one ever determines, on the utilitarian system, whether an act is right or wrong by applying the Principle of Utility directly, which is to say, independently of any of the principles subordinate to it.

Mill's argument shows, then, how one can, by restating utilitarianism so that the Principle of Utility never decides questions of right and wrong independently of its subordinate principles, assert the Principle as the fundamental principle of morality without being committed to the

---

[10] Ibid., ch. 2, par. 25.

embarrassing prescriptions that threaten the credibility of the theory as Bentham stated it. In addition, it articulates a version of utilitarianism that escapes the first problem that we noted in Bentham's version, the problem of misplaced impartiality. By limiting the role of the Principle of Utility so that it does not decide questions of right and wrong independently of other principles, Mill's version avoids the necessity of always treating everyone's interests, whether they are the interests of close friends or complete strangers, as equally important when determining what one ought to do. Such impartiality, as we saw, is inherent in Bentham's version by virtue of its being built into his procedure for applying the Principle of Utility to the circumstances of action. Hence, the problem arises for this version because questions of right and wrong, on Bentham's statement of the theory, are decided in every case by directly applying the Principle of Utility in accordance with this procedure. On Mill's restatement of utilitarianism, by contrast, impartiality is a feature of the subordinate principles and their exceptions in virtue of their being corollaries to the Principle of Utility. Accordingly, one acts consistently with the utilitarian ideal and, in particular, the ideal of impartiality it implies so long as one's actions conform to these principles as qualified by their exceptions. And just as the subordinate principles include basic standards of justice and honesty, they include as well principles that make possible friendship and close ties among the members of a family, for such personal relations are among the most important elements of human well-being. That is, the principles permit one, as one goes about one's daily life, to treat the interests of friends and family as more important than those of mere acquaintances and strangers insofar as such partiality is necessary to sustaining these personal relations. On Mill's version of utilitarianism, therefore, favoring one's friends and loved ones, because their interests matter to one more than the interests of acquaintances and strangers, need not and typically does not put one at odds with the utilitarian ideal.

5. An inconsistency in Mill's restatement

Mill's restatement of utilitarianism shows how one can formulate the theory to avoid the embarrassing prescriptions to act unjustly and dishonestly that Bentham's statement of it entails. Yet the question remains whether it also preserves our understanding of the basic standards of justice and honesty as placing limits on our conduct. How can Mill's explanation of these standards as principles subordinate to the Principle of Utility square with our understanding of them as binding? Plainly, it can do so only if one can understand Mill's restatement as incorporating a suitable conception of these principles. Not any conception will do. Mill himself seems not to have recognized this, for he shifts in his several discussions of them between different conceptions. In particular, while it is certain that he saw these principles as indispensable to the utilitarian system of ethics, it is uncertain whether he saw their indispensability as due exclusively to inescapable limits on human powers of discernment, foresight, and calculation or also to the necessity for the enjoyment of certain essentials of human well-being of there being rules with which people generally comply. And depending on which of these ways one sees their indispensability a different conception of them is implied. Thus correcting Mill's inconsistency in his discussion of these subordinate principles will make clear which conception of them he needs if his restatement of utilitarianism is to preserve our understanding of the basic standards of justice and honesty as placing limits on our conduct.

Mill's inconsistency is due to his running together at least two different kinds of rule that exist in human life. Some rules, such as "See your dentist twice a year" and "Don't put off till tomorrow what you can do today," embody lessons about avoiding trouble and achieving success. Others, such as "Do not butt in line" and "A wedding ring is worn on the ring finger of the left hand," regulate conduct within practices and institutions like queues and marriage. Games with a long tradition of play offer good examples of both kinds. Consider chess. The rules that define how the game is played are the ones you will naturally think of first. These are the rules that determine where each of the pieces is placed at the beginning of the game, which player moves first, how each piece can be moved, how it can be captured, what counts as winning, and so forth. "No two pieces can occupy the same square at the same time" is a rule that governs the movement of all pieces. "Kings move one square at a time in any direction" is the rule for the movement of kings. Further, there is a somewhat complicated rule for the special coordinate movement of kings and rooks called castling.[11] Let us call

---

[11] The rule is: If the king and either rook occupy the squares on which they were placed at the beginning of the game and neither has ever been moved from that square and if

all such rules the institutional rules of chess. In addition, there are what I'll call strategic rules that good chess players know and follow. "Control the center of the board" and "Castle early" are examples of strategic rules that apply to the early stages of the game. Following the first of these improves your chances of putting your opponent on the defensive and ultimately checkmating your opponent's king. Following the second makes your own king less vulnerable to attack by your opponent's pieces and so to being checkmated. These strategic rules, in other words, embody lessons about how to achieve victory and avoid defeat that experience at playing the game has taught.

One important difference between these two kinds of rule is this. Institutional rules regulate conduct within some practice or institution categorically in the sense that any act that breaks an institutional rule is a wrong act within the practice or institution of which the rule is a part. Take games again as the paradigm of a practice. The institutional rules of a game regulate its play categorically in the sense that any violation of them is necessarily a wrong move and as such is immediately nullified and may also be subject to a sanction. The game's institutional rules thus place limits on what a player can do in playing the game. They can be said, then, to be binding. Strategic rules, by contrast, do not apply categorically. To break one of them is not necessarily to do something wrong. Indeed, it may even be the best act one could do in the situation. In a game, for instance, sometimes one makes a better move by breaking some strategic rule than by following it. Strategic rules, in other words, do not place limits on what one can do within the game. They are not binding. Rather they are guides that good players generally follow because even the best players cannot calculate all the possible consequences of each potential move they could make at a given point in the game. And since the reason for following a strategic rule is that experience has taught that doing so generally improves one's chances of winning, one has no reason to follow the rule in the occasional situation in which one can see that making a move breaking the rule will improve one's chances of winning even more than if one made a move that followed it. Bridge players who are familiar with the chapter "Defensive

there is no piece between them on the rank that contains the squares they occupy, then one can move the king two squares along that rank in the direction of the rook and then move the rook to the square on the other side of the king that is next to the square the king now occupies.

Rules – And When to Break Them" in the popular instructional guide 5 *Weeks to Winning Bridge* by Sheinwold will understand this point immediately.[12]

Mill's shift between different conceptions of the principles subordinate to the Principle of Utility consists in his sometimes treating these principles as strategic rules and sometimes treating them as institutional rules. When, for example, Mill deals with the objection that utilitarianism is woefully impractical because people generally lack the knowledge and cognitive capacities necessary to do the calculations that following the Principle of Utility requires, he treats them as strategic rules. They are, he says, like the principles of any practical art, grounded in the experience of the art's practitioners and usable as guides that represent more reliable calculations of what act will bring about the most good overall in the circumstances than a fresh calculation made without regard to the experience of those who have faced similar circumstances. On the other hand, when he deals with the objection that utilitarianism is the enemy of justice because it ultimately calls for expediency, he treats them as institutional rules. They include, he says, the rules of morality, and it is in the nature of such rules to define duties that are inescapable and backed by punitive sanctions. The rules of justice, in particular, Mill maintains, establish a regime of individual rights in human affairs necessary to preserving peace among human beings and developing their social feelings, and the great benefits of this regime establish them as principles subordinate to the Principle of Utility and justify their absolute obligation. "The moral rules which forbid mankind to hurt one another," Mill wrote, " . . . are more vital to human well-being than any maxims, however important, which only point out the best mode of managing some department of human affairs. They have also the peculiarity that they are the main element in determining the whole of the social feelings of mankind. It is their observance which alone preserves peace among human beings."[13]

It should be clear that if Mill's restatement of utilitarianism is to preserve our understanding of the basic standards of justice and honesty as placing limits on our conduct, then the principles subordinate to the Principle of

---

[12] Alfred Sheinwold, *5 Weeks to Winning Bridge*, rev. edn. (New York: Pocket Books, 1964), pp. 388–406.
[13] Mill, *Utilitarianism*, ch. 5, par. 33.

Utility to which Mill appeals must be conceived of as institutional rules and not as strategic ones. In other words, the way to fix Mill's inconsistency is to take as the correct conception of these principles the conception he advanced in answering the objection to utilitarianism that it is the enemy of justice. On this conception, because the principles subordinate to the Principle of Utility are part of certain practices and institutions, because they are institutional rules, they apply categorically to the conduct they regulate. To break them is necessarily to do something wrong within the practice or institution of which they are a part. It is to transgress the limits they place on the conduct they regulate. And because the practices and institutions of which they are a part are the right practices and institutions for human beings collectively to have, as judged by the fundamental principle of morality (i.e., the Principle of Utility), breaking these principles is wrong absolutely. It therefore follows that if the basic standards of justice and honesty can be shown to be part of practices and institutions that, as judged by the Principle of Utility, are the right practices and institutions for human beings collectively to have, which is to say, the practices and institutions the maintenance of which brings about the greatest good for humankind, then Mill's restatement will have succeeded in incorporating the basic standards of justice and honesty into the utilitarian system of ethics and at the same time preserved our understanding of these standards as placing limits on conduct.

6. Rule utilitarianism

The version of utilitarianism that we have recovered from Mill's restatement of the theory is now commonly called *rule utilitarianism*. It is so-called because on this version rules are what one evaluates by consulting the Principle of Utility. Individual acts are then determined to be right or wrong by the rules that, according to these evaluations, are the right rules for human beings to follow. In contrast, the version that originates with Bentham is commonly called *act utilitarianism* because on Bentham's version one applies the Principle of Utility directly to individual acts to determine whether they are right or wrong. The advantages of rule utilitarianism over act utilitarianism are, as we've seen, that rule utilitarianism avoids the embarrassing prescriptions that act utilitarianism yields and that it squares with our understanding of the basic standards of justice and honesty as placing limits on our conduct.

These advantages do not come without a cost, however. Rule utilitarianism, by interposing a set of moral rules between the Principle of Utility and the circumstances of action and making right and wrong action a matter of compliance with and violation of these rules, creates a problem of explaining why it is reasonable for a person to act rightly in circumstances in which his performing a different action would better promote the general good. It creates a problem, that is, of explaining why it is reasonable to act rightly in circumstances in which act utilitarianism would determine that the action was wrong. And the theory's sharpest critics have exploited this problem in pressing what is the most serious objection to the theory. It is an objection that seems to put the theory in the untenable position of being either an unsatisfactory form of utilitarianism or an unsatisfactory form of deontology.

The problem is evident when one considers someone who faces circumstances in which, to comply with the secondary moral rules, he must forbear from doing the act that in those circumstances would best promote the general good. Our example of your finding a purse containing a huge wad of cash suggests such circumstances, for one can easily imagine how in these circumstances your returning the purse and the cash to their owner would bring about less good in the world than your donating the cash to some worthy charity. Suppose, then, that this is so and that secondary moral rules nonetheless require you to return the purse and the cash to their owner. According to rule utilitarianism, therefore, you act rightly if you do so and wrongly if you do not. You act rightly because returning the purse and the cash to their owner is required by the right rules, and they are the right rules because general compliance with them is more conducive to promoting the good of humankind than general compliance with any of their alternatives. So it is natural to think that the point of following these rules is to promote the general good. Yet if this were the point of following the rules, then you would be choosing to comply with them for the purpose of promoting the good of humankind in circumstances in which you could better fulfill this purpose by violating them. You would have more reason, in other words, to violate the rules by donating the cash to a worthy charity than to comply with them by returning the purse and the cash to their owner. Hence, the question: why would it be reasonable to comply with the rules in such circumstances? And failure to find a satisfactory answer would mean that the theory could not explain why, on its account of right and wrong action, it was always reasonable to act rightly.

The problem, it is important to realize, is not with Mill's observation about the necessity of certain practices and institutions for the enjoyment of peace, security, individual liberty, and other essentials of human well-being. Nor is it with the companion thesis about the necessity of general acceptance of and compliance with the rules of these crucial practices and institutions for the maintenance of their effectiveness. Bentham, too, recognized that such practices and institutions must be in place in human society and their rules generally accepted and followed if human beings are to have tolerably decent lives. These observations are commonplace in utilitarianism. Consequently, no form of the theory, neither act utilitarianism nor rule utilitarianism, treats violations of the rules these crucial practices and institutions comprise lightly. On either form, because compliance upholds these practices and institutions and violation undermines them, the presumption in any situation will be that one acts rightly in following the rules and wrongly in breaking them. The reason should be clear. To weaken the authority of the practices and institutions is to jeopardize people's enjoyment of the essential human goods they make possible, and a violation of the rules of these practices and institutions weakens their authority inasmuch as it weakens the violator's own disposition to follow the rules and, if made known to others, has a similar effect on them. Hence, in view of the threat to the general good that violation of the rules creates, the presumption that such violation is wrong is substantial.

On act utilitarianism, this presumption is reflected in the weight that is given, in the procedure for applying the Principle of Utility, to harms that would result from weakening the authority of these practices and institutions. Accordingly, for a violation of their rules to be justified the good that it brings about must not only be so great as to overmatch whatever distinct harms it causes specific individuals to suffer but also be so great as to overmatch the presumed harms that result from its weakening this authority. On rule utilitarianism, by contrast, the presumption is reflected in the inviolability of the rules in all circumstances except for those in which a violation is necessary in order to comply with some other rule. Accordingly, for the violation to be justified in such circumstances the rule with which one complies must take precedence over the rule one violates, where precedence is determined by directly applying the Principle of Utility to those circumstances. The difference, therefore, between act utilitarianism and rule utilitarianism does not consist in whether the theory recognizes practices and institutions whose existence is crucial to human beings' enjoying a tolerably decent life. Both recognize such practices and recognize, too, the importance of people's generally accepting and following the rules the practices comprise. The difference consists, rather, in how those rules figure in the theory's procedure for determining whether an act is right or wrong. In act utilitarianism they figure as factors in the calculation of the overall good an act could bring about in the circumstances one faces, factors that have weight in view of the harms that violation of these rules would cause. In rule utilitarianism, they figure as authoritative constraints on the range of actions that one is permitted to do in those circumstances. And it is their figuring as authoritative constraints that generates the problem the theory has in explaining why it is reasonable to comply with these rules when one could promote greater good overall for human beings by violating them.

It generates the problem because, as authoritative constraints, the rules override all other factors one might consider in determining what it is right to do. Their authority, in other words, excludes consideration of any act outside of what the rules permit. In particular, it excludes any act that might bring about more good overall for human beings than any of the acts the rules permit. To do such an act would be to act against the authority of the rules, and on the rule utilitarian theory such disobedience is the mark of wrongdoing. At the same time, the rules derive their authority solely from the Principle of Utility. What makes them authoritative, in other words, is that general acceptance of and compliance with them is more conducive to promoting the good of humankind than general acceptance of and compliance with any of the alternatives. But if the ultimate authority is the Principle of Utility, if what makes its subordinate rules authoritative is their being conducive to promoting the general good, then it is hard to see on what grounds an act that best realizes the Principle, which is to say, an act that brings about the most good overall for humankind, could ever be understood as disobedient of that authority. If the sole basis for the authority of the rules is their conduciveness to promoting the general good and being subject to their authority is what makes it reasonable to follow them, then it is hard to see why one should regard them as authoritative and so reasonable to follow in circumstances in which breaking them would be more conducive to promoting the general good. Obedience to them in such circumstances appears merely to be blind.

In light of this problem, it is hard to resist the conclusion that rule utilitarianism is an unsustainable compromise. Insofar as it aims to capture the understanding of moral rules as authoritative constraints on conduct that is characteristic of deontology, it fails to give an adequate account of that authority. And insofar as it aims to adhere to the logic of utilitarianism, it falls short of being completely faithful to that logic.

7. Act utilitarianism revisited

Might there be a way of saving act utilitarianism from the embarrassing prescriptions it yields? There is no way of excising these prescriptions from the theory, to be sure. But perhaps one can sideline them instead. The most sophisticated defenses of act utilitarianism take this tack. The cornerstone of these defenses is the distinction between the evaluation of an action as right or wrong and the evaluation of the motives behind an action as sterling or corrupt. Defenders of utilitarianism from Mill forward have invoked this distinction to correct common mistakes about the theory that result from failure to appreciate its consequentialist character. "He who saves a fellow creature from drowning," Mill wrote, "does what is morally right, whether his motive be duty or the hope of being paid for his trouble."[14] The action's being right, Mill is saying, is a separate matter from its being done from a sterling or corrupt motive. And conversely an action's being done from a sterling motive is no guarantee of its being right; nor would its being done from a corrupt motive guarantee that it would be wrong. The point is well made in the old chestnut about the road to hell being paved with good intentions. With this point in mind and bearing in mind as well that act utilitarianism identifies acting rightly with acting in accordance with the Principle of Utility, it should be clear that someone who can be relied on to act rightly is not necessarily someone who consistently makes efforts to follow the Principle of Utility. He may, instead, act from different motives. More exactly, his personality or character may reflect values and goals whose achievement requires his following principles other than the Principle of Utility. In short, even though act utilitarianism identifies acting rightly with acting in accordance with the Principle of Utility, to be a reliable performer of right actions may nonetheless

---

[14] Ibid., ch. 2, par. 18.

require one's following principles other than the Principle of Utility. And because of this possibility, the embarrassing prescriptions that result from applying the Principle of Utility to situations like that of finding a lost purse containing a huge wad of cash may not be as problematic for act utilitarianism as they initially seem. Or so the sophisticated defenders of the theory whose argument we are now considering maintain.

Their argument consists of several steps. The first is to separate, as we have just done, questions about what are the right actions to do from questions about what are the right motives from which to act. While the theory's answers to questions of the former kind are in each case the action that would conform to the Principle of Utility in the circumstances the agent faces, the theory's answers to questions of the latter kind are the motives indicative of those traits of character that make a person the most reliable performer of right actions that he could be. The argument's second step, then, is to point out, in view of this separation of questions, the possibility that the most reliable performers of right action, in virtue of the traits of character that qualify them as such, do not directly apply the Principle of Utility in deciding how to act in the circumstances they face. This possibility should be evident, for it should be evident that a person who develops such traits may come, as a result, to pursue and live by goals and values whose realization requires his following principles other than the Principle of Utility. From this observation it follows that the theory's answers to questions about right actions may not always correspond to the decisions about what it is right to do that the most reliable performers of right actions make. And if the answers that do not correspond to their decisions include the embarrassing prescriptions the theory yields, then the most reliable performers of right actions would neither affirm nor act on those prescriptions. The prescriptions, in other words, would have no uptake in their lives. They would neither be regarded by such people as sound advice nor correspond to judgments about what to do that such people reached when deciding what to do. Thus, insofar as implementing the theory involved giving people the right motives from which to act and so making them the most reliable performers of right action they could be, it is possible that the embarrassing prescriptions the theory yields represent merely theoretical truths. At the final step of the argument, therefore, one observes that the embarrassing prescriptions might have no practical import within the theory and that they would, in that event, cease to be a serious problem for it.

Of course, to turn this argument into a successful defense of act utilitarianism, defenders of the theory must do more than point to the possibility that the most reliable performers of right action would apply other principles than the Principle of Utility in deciding how to act. They must also show that this possibility is a strong one. They must show, in other words, that there is strong reason to believe that the most reliable performers of right action would directly apply other principles than the Principle of Utility in deciding how to act and, in particular, that they would apply the basic standards of justice and honesty in making such decisions. Otherwise their defense would fall short of rendering plausible its crucial idea that the most reliable performers of right actions would not follow principles that yielded embarrassing prescriptions for the theory. It would fall short, that is, of proving what it must prove to nullify the practical import of those prescriptions. And failure to achieve this result would then mean that the prescriptions continued to represent a serious problem for the theory. It is reasonable to suppose, however, that defenders of act utilitarianism can achieve this result. For there does appear to be strong reason to believe that the most reliable performers of right action would follow principles that did not yield any of these prescriptions.

Mill's points about the indispensability of secondary principles to carrying out the Principle of Utility suggest why. Recall, in particular, his point that because of inescapable limits on human powers of foresight, discernment, and calculation, it is necessary for people to use secondary principles to achieve the end that the Principle of Utility prescribes. Even the most powerful human minds, Mill would say, are liable to some misperception, misjudgment, and miscalculation when applying the Principle of Utility directly to circumstances in which it is not obvious what the best course of action is. They, like those of us with less powerful minds, are therefore more likely to determine the best course of action in such circumstances by using generalizations reflecting the collective wisdom of people who have found themselves in similar circumstances. Consider, as an apt illustration, the difference between the way a great chess player like Gary Kasparov determines his moves and how Deep Blue, the powerful chess-playing computer that once defeated him in match play, determines its moves. Kasparov, owing to the limits on his powers of foresight, judgment, and calculation, necessarily makes his decisions by using good strategic rules of chess, the game's secondary principles, as it were, to analyze complex positions and determine the best moves in them. Deep Blue, by contrast, because it is not similarly limited in its powers of computation, can compute an enormous number of possible outcomes for each of the moves it can make in a given complex position and can also retain, without loss, its memory of these possibilities. Consequently, it can analyze such positions far more extensively than can Kasparov, and accordingly it can determine the best moves to make by direct calculation of which move has the highest probability of having outcomes that will lead to victory. Plainly, if the most reliable performers of right action, as defined by the Principle of Utility, were like Deep Blue, they, too, would directly calculate which course of action is likely to produce the most good. They would not, then, use secondary principles to determine the best action. But because they are, like Kasparov, human thinkers, there is strong reason to believe, instead, that they would apply secondary principles to make such determinations.

Further, it is reasonable to believe, in view of Mill's other point about the indispensability of secondary principles to the utilitarian system of ethics, that the secondary principles they would apply would include the basic standards of justice and honesty. Mill's other point, you will recall, is that the enjoyment of certain essentials of human well-being like peace, security, and liberty requires that all those who live together in some society generally accept and comply with the basic standards of justice and honesty, so it stands to reason that following such standards is necessary to bringing about the most good overall for humankind. Hence, it stands to reason that the most reliable performers of right action would include such standards among the secondary principles they apply in determining what it is right to do. Surely it would be odd, given the importance of the general acceptance of and compliance with such standards to the good of humankind, to discover that the most reliable performers of right action applied different standards.

8. Is act utilitarianism self-refuting?

Let us grant, then, that defenders of act utilitarianism could succeed in saving the theory from the embarrassing prescriptions it yields if their initial argument for seeing how these prescriptions might lack practical import within the theory were cogent. Accordingly, we are granting that the most reliable performers of right action, as defined by the Principle of

Utility, would directly apply other principles in determining what it was right to do in the circumstances they faced and that these other principles would include the basic standards of justice and honesty. These concessions allow us to narrow the question of the success of these defenders' efforts to save act utilitarianism to that of whether their initial argument, the argument that raises the possibility that the embarrassing prescriptions the theory yields would have no practical import, is cogent. Could it truly be said of these prescriptions that they lacked practical import within the theory despite their being consequences of the Principle of Utility? Or would such a statement be false or even incoherent?

The statement would clearly be false, of course, if it were assumed that the most reliable performers of right action believed the Principle of Utility to be the fundamental principle of morality. For if they believed this, they would then regard themselves as following other principles only because doing so made them more reliable adherents to the Principle of Utility and not because these other principles were basic determinants of right action. They would therefore understand these principles, the basic standards of justice and honesty, in particular, as strategic rules and not as rules that placed limits on their conduct. Consequently, they could not ignore a prescription to act dishonestly when they found themselves in situations in which they were confident that they could bring about more overall good by dishonest action than honest action. They could no more ignore such a prescription than Kasparov, analyzing a position in the middle of some game, could ignore a conclusion he reached by direct calculation of the position's possibilities that a particular move available to him would lead to certain victory. Even if he saw that the move broke some strategic rule of chess, this would not dissuade him from making the move, for strategic rules are not binding. And if he were confident of his analysis and reasoning in this case, then it is the move he would make. By the same token, the most reliable performers of right action would not be dissuaded from doing actions that, by their own lights, were certain to bring about the most good overall, even if they knew that such actions would violate basic standards of justice and honesty. For the standards, when understood as strategic rules, are not binding. If, having found a lost purse containing a huge wad of cash, they were confident of their calculation that donating the cash to a worthy charity would bring about more good overall than returning it to its owner, then they would treat the prescription to donate the cash as dispositive. Hence, the embarrassing prescriptions the theory yields would, at least in some cases, have practical import for them.

So our sophisticated defenders of act utilitarianism must assume that the most reliable performers of right action do not believe the Principle of Utility to be the fundamental principle of morality. They must assume, then, that the most reliable performers of right action regard other principles than the Principle of Utility as the basic determinants of right action. Asked what determines whether an action is right or wrong, a reliable performer of right action will answer by citing these other principles, including, in particular, the basic standards of justice and honesty. And he will, at the same time, deny that what makes an act right is its bringing about as much good for humankind overall as any other act that he could perform in the circumstances. Hence, the theory, on this defense of it, requires the advocacy and teaching of a different ethical theory for the purpose of developing in people the traits of character that will make them the most reliable performers of right action they can be. For people must be kept ignorant of what truly makes some actions right and others wrong if they are to develop these traits. The theory therefore requires, as a condition of its implementation, that people be kept from believing that the Principle of Utility is the fundamental principle of morality. On this defense of act utilitarianism, the theory calls for its own suppression.

This is a paradoxical result, to be sure. Indeed some critics of act utilitarianism once thought it showed that the theory was self-refuting. But the theory would be self-refuting only if morality was essentially public, and it would be hard to argue against act utilitarianism on the basis of this thesis without begging the question. For although many philosophers hold conceptions of morality on which its principles are analogous to the laws of a society and so are essentially public, defenders of act utilitarianism do not. Rather they maintain a conception of morality on which the question of whether to make a principle of morality public – whether to advocate or to teach it – is a question about what action to take with regard to making such principles public, and like all such questions, it is answerable on the utilitarian theory according to the consequences of the alternatives open to one. Thus, whether to make the Principle of Utility public is a question to which one can apply the principle itself, and the answer, needless to say, depends on whether publicity or obscurity best promotes the general good. That suppressing rather than publicizing the principle could turn out to be the action that best promotes the general good and therefore that the principle might require its own suppression may seem paradoxical. But the theory explains away the paradox when it makes clear that one can treat the principle like any truth and ask whether propagating knowledge of it is more conducive to the general good than keeping knowledge of it secret. Hence, the defense of the theory we are presently considering can withstand this criticism.

9. When act utilitarianism ceases to be an ethical theory

The defense contains a deeper problem, however. Its initial argument, the argument on which we are focusing, severs the very connection between right action and reasonable action that it is the business of ethical theories to explain. The connection is straightforward. Every ethical theory presupposes some notion of a competent moral agent, a person whose values and judgment are sound, and of such agents it assumes that when they act rightly, they act reasonably and conversely. A successful explanation of the connection is thus a vindication of right action as reasonable action. Were it otherwise, were the theory to employ a notion of a competent moral agent that failed to meet this condition, then the theory in answering questions of how such agents ought to act would sometimes be caught between giving answers advising that they act unreasonably in order to act rightly and giving answers advising that they act wrongly lest they act unreasonably. The theory would then have failed to vindicate right action as reasonable action. It would have failed as a practical discipline. When sophisticated defenders of act utilitarianism suppose that the theory takes the most reliable performers of right action as competent moral agents, they suppose, as a result, that the theory allows, as a possibility, that those people whose values and judgment are sound are people who do not follow the Principle of Utility as the fundamental standard of right and wrong action but follow other principles instead. Consequently, it is possible that the theory, on their defense of it, must sometimes in answering questions of how such people ought to act advise either that they act wrongly or that they act unreasonably. For it is possible that sometimes the most reliable performers of right action can act rightly only if they act contrary to their principles, and it would not be reasonable for someone to go against his principles if the values those principles reflected were sound. Thus in supposing that the theory takes the most reliable performers of right action as competent moral agents, our sophisticated defenders of act utilitarianism sever the connection between right action and reasonable action, and in doing so they render the theory incapable of vindicating right action as reasonable action.

In effect, this defense of act utilitarianism treats the theory as one that is not the product of a practical discipline. That it does so is clear from its having severed the connection between right action and reasonable action, for severance of the connection means that its being right to do some act does not imply that morally competent agents have good and sufficient reason to do the act. The upshot of the defense, then, is that it puts act utilitarianism out of the business of ethical theory and into a different line of work.

5   The moral law

1. Two theories of moral law

Teleological conceptions of morality originated in ancient Greek philosophy. The major systems of ethics among the ancient Greeks, those of Plato and Aristotle, in particular, were teleological. So too were those of Epicurus and other thinkers who founded important schools of philosophy in the period that came after Plato and Aristotle. Deontological conceptions, by contrast, have a different origin. They derive from an ideal of universal divine law that Christianity drew from the Judaic materials from which it sprang. Christianity, to be sure, drew from the ancient Greeks as well. Its identification of universal divine laws with the laws of nature, for instance, comes from the Stoics, chiefly through Cicero (106–43 BC). But the ideas in Christianity that yielded deontological conceptions are found in its understanding of divine laws as the laws of a supreme ruler that bind his subjects to obey him in the way that a covenant with him would bind them. These juristic ideas, which originated in Mosaic law, are the original frame for deontological conceptions. The principal text that inspired them is Paul's statement in Romans: "When Gentiles who have not the law do by nature what the law requires, they are a law to themselves even though they do not have the law. They show that what the law requires is written on their hearts, while their conscience also bears witness and their conflicting thoughts accuse and perhaps excuse them."[1]

The core thought of this passage is that human beings, simply by virtue of being human, have an innate capacity to know right from wrong and to be moved through their consciences, the seat of that knowledge, to do what is right and to forbear doing what is wrong. This knowledge is the knowledge of the requirements of law, and these requirements are written "on [our]

---

[1] Romans 2.14–15 (Revised Standard Version).

hearts," as Paul says. Their being so written means that we can have knowledge of them through reflection on what is in our hearts. For this reason none of us needs to be familiar with any holy book to have this knowledge. Exercising one's rational and reflective powers is sufficient. There is, therefore, a distinction to which Paul alludes, between knowing the law through scripture and knowing it through reason and reflection. The former is knowledge through revelation, and the latter is knowledge through reason. Ironically, then, this central tenet of Christian thought makes recourse to the Bible or any other religious text unnecessary for having knowledge of right and wrong.

Knowledge of right and wrong is thus, according to core Christian belief, knowledge of the requirements of moral law. But how can one know the requirements of such law without recourse to a text in which that law is written? How can one use reason apart from consulting such a text to discover this law? One answer is through the study of nature itself and, more specifically, human nature. If the laws in question are laws of nature, then the study of how they regulate human life, its growth and development, its maintenance in a healthy and thriving state, and its eventual decline and expiration will yield an understanding of how one ought to live. On this answer, one achieves the highest good by living according to nature. In Christian thought, the laws of nature are God's directives for realizing this good, for nature, being the work of God, is the realization of his goodness. That goodness guarantees harmony in how all the parts of nature work together. And since the laws of nature are what give harmony to the universe God has created, it stands to reason that men and women, being part of this creation, achieve goodness in their lives by living as nature (which is to say, God) intended. This is to say that men and women achieve goodness by guiding their conduct by the laws that manifest these intentions. This answer, however, plainly entails a teleological conception of ethics and not a deontological one. Indeed, the conception it entails was the dominant conception of the Middle Ages. To arrive at a deontological conception we must consider a different answer, one that emerged in the seventeenth century among a more lawyerly group of Christian thinkers.

This second answer, the deontologists' answer, derives from God's being the supreme ruler of the universe as well as its creator. To conceive of God as the supreme ruler of the universe is to understand him as sovereign over humankind. That is, being God's subjects, human beings are required to obey him. This obedience not only is required by God's sovereignty but also makes sense, given the natural conditions of human life. For humans, while naturally sociable creatures, nonetheless have difficulties in those conditions sustaining society. To do so we need rules that we recognize and obey in common, yet we would not recognize and obey such rules in common if we did not mutually accept them as having authority over the conduct of our lives. This mutual acceptance of the rules' authority follows immediately when God is understood to have issued them. His sovereignty over humankind entails it.

The difficulties that human beings in their natural state have in sustaining human societies are due to the conflicts that inevitably arise among people who are largely concerned with promoting their own interests and those of their loved ones. This is not to say that the natural conditions of human life are so harsh and the self-seeking of men and women so single-minded as to pit each of them against every other in a struggle for survival. One need not, that is, suppose such harshness and self-seeking as Hobbes supposed. Such a supposition was important to Hobbes's ethics because it supplied the basis on which he could derive moral laws from a fundamental principle of egoism. But an understanding of moral laws as rules God issues directly to men so that they can live together peaceably, because it does not rest on egoism, does not require suppositions like those Hobbes made about the natural conditions of human life. It would be enough to suppose that the conditions produced quarrels and created frictions among people that made their living together in society precarious. Rules restraining people from engaging in conduct that provokes or aggravates quarrels and rules requiring conduct that reduces friction, if they command sufficient obedience, make collective life more peaceable and less precarious. Hence, from an understanding of God as supreme ruler of the universe and of human beings as sociable creatures who nonetheless need some order imposed on their lives to live together peaceably, one can directly infer the idea of God's having given men and women laws general obedience to which establishes that order.

Implicit in this idea is the thought of there being in human society a moral order that is independent of the society's positive laws and customs. Every human society, according to this thought, instantiates this order, even if the society's positive laws and customs are contrary to it. Indeed, what determines the justness and rightness of those laws and customs is the degree to which they conform to the moral order that God's laws constitute. Appeals by Christian social reformers to higher law to justify their disobedience to positive law – the appeals to higher law of nineteenth-century American abolitionists, for example, to justify their violation of laws regulating slaveholding – reflect this thought. It is possible, then, to conceive of human society as existing prior to positive law and social custom, prior to government and culture. This conception goes hand in glove with an inquiry into the standards of right and wrong that looks to the natural conditions of human life for evidence of those standards. The hypothesis of a human society existing prior to government and culture leaves those conditions in place as the sole factors in determining the rules that create order in a society. Hence, one can discover what the moral law requires by reasoning from this hypothesis. In other words, one can have knowledge of the moral law by reflecting on what rules human beings, in the absence of government or culture, would need to obey in common to live peaceably together in society. The second answer thus follows from this hypothesis.

The critical difference between the two answers lies, then, in how each conceives of the relation between knowledge of what the moral law requires and knowledge of the actions one must do to achieve the highest good. The first answer, the answer of the scholastics, asserts that there is an intimate relation between the two types of knowledge. On the scholastics' answer, moral laws are laws of nature, and as such they give harmony to the universe that God created. They give harmony both to the universe as a whole and to the functioning of each thing that inhabits it. This harmony is the laws' distinctive contribution to the goodness of God's creation. Something therefore works well when it works in accordance with the laws that regulate the functioning of things of its kind. The moral law regulates the functioning of human personality, since human psychology is a phenomenon of nature. Consequently knowledge of the moral law is knowledge of how to live well as a human being. It is knowledge of how to achieve the highest good for human beings.

By contrast, the second answer, the answer of the deontologists, asserts that the two types of knowledge are separate. On the deontologists' answer, God imposes moral laws on men and women. The imposition is necessary because the natural desires and emotions of human beings are divided between the self-regarding and the social, and the conflicts among people due to the former prevent the agreement among them due to the latter from being sufficient to sustain a society. In short, human beings, while social creatures, are not like bees. They are only partly driven by their social instincts, and these instincts do not dominate the self-regarding ones. To the contrary, if anything, the reverse is true. As a result, external restraints on the self-regarding desires and emotions of human beings are necessary for sustaining a society. Moral laws supply those restraints. They are in this sense external to nature. Obedience to them is required because of God's sovereignty and not because of their pointing the way to achieve the ultimate end of human action. Indeed, sometimes obedience necessitates curtailing one's pursuit of the ultimate ends that are implied by one's self-regarding desires. Knowledge of the moral laws, therefore, on the deontologists' answer, is a separate matter from knowledge of the highest good. The one does not depend, not even implicitly, on the other.

The ideal contained in the deontologists' answer is that of one's living in fellowship with others as one's equals under the rule of law. This ideal corresponds to the notion we considered earlier of a moral order that is independent of a society's positive law and customs, its government and culture. The rule of law itself is of course an ideal. It is the ideal of a community whose members, to the last man or woman, are subject to its laws. No member stands above them or is exempt from their authority. But the ideal implicit in the deontologists' answer goes further. It also includes the ideal of equality under the law: that all men and women are equally subjects of the law and equally protected by it. In the case at hand, this means that all are equally subject to and protected by God's rule. The relation between him, as their sovereign, and them, as his subjects, is the same no matter who the subject is. In particular, no subject holds a higher rank than any other in his or her relation to God. None enjoys privileges that others lack. It follows, then, that all distinctions of rank among human beings, like those of nobility and commoner, aristocrat and plebeian, lord and vassal, have no basis in the moral order that God's law constitutes. They are, in all instances, artifacts of the positive laws and customs in the societies in which those ranks are recognized. And the same is true of regimes of male supremacy, white supremacy, or the supremacy of one ethnic group over another that have arisen throughout history in different civilizations. All such regimes are contrary to the norms of equality that are contained in this ideal. Thus the ideal that the deontologists' answer contains is one that implies a community in which everyone bears the same basic duties towards one another and towards the community as a whole and in which even the humblest member is accorded the same respect as a duty-bearing member of the community as any of its more powerful members.

2. Divine command theory

The deontologists' answer is based on a version of divine command theory. In its most general form, divine command theory is the theory that identifies right actions with actions that God has commanded and wrong actions with actions that God has forbidden. The principal idea is that compliance with God's will is what makes an act right and noncompliance with his will is what makes it wrong, and God's commands express his will. In the version of the theory on which the deontologists' answer is based, those commands are understood as laws that God, as the supreme ruler of the universe, addresses to humankind. This understanding corresponds to the modern conception of laws as the commands that a sovereign addresses to his subjects. Hobbes's definition of 'law' in *Leviathan* illustrates this conception. "[L]aw in general," Hobbes writes, "is not Counsel but Command; nor a Command of any man to any man; but only of him whose Command is addressed to one formerly obliged to obey him."[2] And Hobbes completes the conception by connecting the idea of a command with that of the will. Thus his definition of 'command' is "where a man says, *Do this*, or *Do not this*, without expecting other reason than the Will of him who says it."[3] God's laws, then, on this version of divine command theory, express his will, and therefore, following the theory's principal idea, his will determines universal standards of right and wrong.

Hobbes's definition of law includes a distinction between commands and counsels. A counsel, Hobbes writes, "is where a man says, *Do*, or *Do not this*, and deduces his reasons from the benefit that arrives by it to him to whom he says it."[4] The point of the distinction is to sharpen the understanding of law that Hobbes's definition conveys. For in defining laws as commands as distinct from counsels, Hobbes makes crystal clear that when a ruler issues a law to his subjects, he means for them to obey it because he has commanded them and not because they can deduce from his issuing the law that

---

[2] Hobbes, *Leviathan*, ch. 26, par. 2.   [3] Ibid., ch. 25, par. 2.   [4] Ibid., ch. 25, par. 3.

he thinks they will benefit from acting as he has commanded. Laws, in other words, are authoritative because they express the ruler's will and not because they represent wisdom the ruler has about actions that his subjects will benefit from doing. The point is evident in the case of bad laws. A bad law, a law, for example, that a corrupt ruler of an impoverished country enacts to enrich himself at the expense of his subjects is still authoritative in that country as long as the ruler legitimately holds power and has enacted the law in accordance with the protocols for legislation in that country's system of government.

That such laws are authoritative in that country does not mean of course that anyone who is subject to the authority of the country's ruler acts rightly in obeying those laws and wrongly if he disobeyed them. He acts legally in obeying them and would be acting illegally if he disobeyed them, but what it is legal to do in a country is not necessarily what it is right to do, and similarly, an action that it would be illegal to do in a country is not necessarily an action that it would be wrong to do. Huck Finn, for example, acted illegally in helping Jim in his attempt to escape slavery, but he did not act wrongly. A country's laws, therefore, though they are authoritative for all who are subject to the authority of the country's ruler or rulers, are not for those same subjects standards of right and wrong. The possibility of bad laws enacted by corrupt rulers makes this point clear.

But the same point, you might think, could not possibly apply to God's laws. In Christian thought, in particular, the authoritativeness of God's laws necessarily coincides with their being universal standards of right and wrong. To assume otherwise would be to assume that God could make bad laws, and because of God's attributes, specifically, his being a loving God who is all-knowing and all-powerful, that is not possible. God could not be corrupt; he could not misjudge what laws would best serve the interests of humankind; nothing could prevent him from imposing such laws on his subjects. Being a loving God, he has the good of all human beings as his end when he acts to impose laws on them, and being infinitely wise and all-knowing his judgment as to what is best for human beings is error-proof. Consequently, the laws he imposes are the best laws for establishing a moral order within human society. There can be no basis, therefore, to doubt that they are the standards of right and wrong for all human beings.

Nonetheless, the point does reveal a problem in divine command theory. The theory's principal idea is that what makes an act right is its being in compliance with God's will and what makes it wrong is its opposing his will. But if it is necessary to invoke God's being loving and all-knowing to show the impossibility of God's imposing bad laws on humankind, then the reason that actions that comply with God's will are right and actions that oppose his will are wrong is not that God has commanded the former and forbidden the latter. Rather it is that one can deduce from his having commanded the former and forbidden the latter that he judges that the former are actions human beings will benefit from doing and the latter are actions human beings will suffer harm as a result of doing, and that his judgment in either case could not possibly be wrong. In other words, if the theory must invoke God's being loving and all-knowing to certify the coincidence of the authoritativeness of his commands with their being universal standards of right and wrong, then God's telling human beings to do this and not to do that – e.g., to love their neighbors as they love themselves and not to kill – may as well be a matter of his giving counsels as commands. Compliance with God's will in that case is not what makes an act right; opposition to his will is not what makes it wrong. For the act would still be right even if God had only counseled men and women to do it, wrong even if he had only counseled against their doing it. Hence, to invoke God's being loving and all-knowing to show the impossibility of his imposing bad laws on humankind means that one has abandoned the principal idea of divine command theory.

Unfortunately, abandoning the theory's principal idea means giving up the thesis that God, by virtue of the commands he issues to humankind, is the author of universal standards of right and wrong. It is to give up the thesis that standards of right and wrong originate in God's will. The reason why is plain. To identify God's commands with universal standards of right and wrong because they are the commands of a loving and all-knowing ruler is to suppose that God, in issuing those commands, takes the good of humankind as his end and imposes laws according to a standard of effectiveness, through organized human action, in realizing that end. It is thus to suppose that God, in determining which acts to command and which to forbid, follows a standard of right action that exists independently of his will. But to acknowledge such a standard is to acknowledge a foundation of morality that is independent of God's will. All other standards of right and wrong would then derive from this foundational standard and likewise be independent of God's will. These standards, while they coincide with God's commands, do not originate in his will.

A divine command theorist must therefore maintain the theory's principal idea if he is to hold on to the thesis that morality springs from God's will. Yet maintaining this idea means holding that God's will precedes every standard of right and wrong. It means, that is, holding that no standard of right and wrong exists independently of God's will or serves to guide the judgments he makes in issuing commands. And because God is all-powerful, there are no limits on what he can command. These propositions constitute the doctrine of theological voluntarism to which divine command theory, in its most clear-eyed formulation, reduces. It follows then that no matter what act God commanded, it would be right to do that act and wrong not to do it. For no command of God could fail to be authoritative for human beings, and therefore no command of God could fail to be a universal standard of right action. Such is the import of theological voluntarism. Consequently, however horrific or bizarre the act, if God commanded it, then it would be right to do it and wrong not to do it. If God commanded, say, that blue-eyed infants be tortured to death, then it would be right to torture blue-eyed infants to death and wrong not to. But this result throws the theory into a real muddle. No one, after all, would allow that someone would be acting rightly in torturing infants to death, yet of course Christian belief in God requires taking God's commands as standards of right and wrong. The only way out of the muddle, therefore, is to give up theological voluntarism. It is to give up the thesis that the standards of right and wrong originate in God's will.

3. Rational intuitionism

Giving up theological voluntarism does not, to be sure, mean that Christian thought must give up its conception of God as the supreme ruler of the universe. What it means is that, to retain this conception, a Christian thinker must suppose that God imposes laws in accordance with standards of right and wrong that exist independently of his will. That is, a Christian thinker must suppose that such standards are evident to intelligent beings and therefore to God, whose intelligence is infinitely greater than human intelligence, and that God's rule over human beings accords with his knowledge and understanding of these standards. At the same, it is understood that their validity is independent of his will and that his actions can be judged by them. What is more, because God cannot err in determining his will, the standards necessarily inform it and therefore the commands that he issues to human beings. These are the laws he imposes on humans, and indeed he is often praised for the justice of his laws. Such praise, it is worth noting, entails judgment of his action and therefore presupposes standards of justice that exist independently of his will. For praising God's rule over human beings as just would be an empty encomium if there were no standards of justice independent of that rule by which to judge it. As Leibniz once observed, why praise God for acting in accordance with justice if calling his actions "just" says nothing more than that he acts?

The upshot, then, of this conception of God, the conception of him as the supreme ruler of the universe whose laws are just, is that ethics does not rest on premises about God's will. Indeed, it need not rest on any theological premisses. The point was controversially made by Hugo Grotius (1583–1645), when he declared that human beings would have the duties to one another that God's law imposes, "even if we should concede that which cannot be conceded without the utmost wickedness, that there is no God or that the affairs of men are of no concern to him."[5] Grotius, in this famous passage from his great work, *On the Law of War and Peace*, at once affirmed God's position as supreme ruler of the universe and abandoned theological voluntarism. The two points combined to yield a view of ethics as grounded in propositions or principles whose truth or validity, while present to God's intellect, is independent of his will.

It will be useful to compare the intellectualism to which Grotius' declaration leads with the view we considered earlier that identifies the standards of right and wrong with the laws that a loving God, who is all-knowing and all-powerful, imposes on human beings. This earlier view is most naturally formulated as a theological version of rule utilitarianism. As such, it includes theological premisses. In particular, it includes a premiss about God's love of humankind. It identifies the highest good with the well-being of the object of God's love and attributes to God the will to bring about the realization of this good to the greatest extent possible. Thus, one can obtain a version of rule utilitarianism once one uses the theological premiss about God's love to identify the well-being of humankind as the highest good, since from this identification and God's being sovereign over humanity one can infer that the laws God imposes on human beings are such that

---

[5] Hugo Grotius, *On the Law of War and Peace*, F. W. Kelsey, trans. (Oxford: Oxford University Press, 1925), p. 13.

general compliance with them best realizes that good. In imposing these laws on human beings, God acts in accordance with a principle of efficiency or optimality in the realization of the highest good. And as the view in question opposes theological voluntarism, the principle is understood to exist independently of God's will. In this regard, the view shares with the intellectualist view of ethics that Grotius advanced a commitment to principles of practical reason whose validity does not depend on God's existence or his being concerned with the affairs of human beings. At the same time, this version of rule utilitarianism departs from Grotian intellectualism in taking God's love to be what determines the good whose realization God brings about through the imposition of laws on human beings. For in doing so it represents God's existence and concern with human affairs as essential to there being universal standards of right and wrong.

Of course, a version of rule utilitarianism that is fully consistent with Grotian intellectualism is also possible. On this version, God imposes laws on human beings in accordance with the Principle of Utility, which is taken as the fundamental standard of morality and also as existing independently of God's will. That is, the Principle is understood to be evident to God as the fundamental standard of morality but not to depend for its validity on his existence or his concern with the affairs of human beings. Still, while this version of rule utilitarianism is possible, it is not the most credible theory within the intellectualist program that Grotius' view inspired. The reason is that our best gauge of whether a standard of right, when taken as a fundamental standard, is evident to God is that it is evident, on reflection, to us, and the Principle of Utility is decidedly less evident to us, on reflection, than other standards of right and wrong. The difficulties with it that we saw in the last chapter are ample proof of the uncertainty it brings. In this respect, the instability we noted in rule utilitarianism is particularly telling. The instability, recall, consists in a tension between the deontological character of the theory's secondary principles and the logic of utilitarianism, and this tension is due to our having greater confidence in the validity of the secondary principles than in that of the Principle of Utility. Consequently, because the main thrust of the intellectualist program that Grotius' view inspired is to fix, as the fundamental standards of morality, those that, on reflection, seem self-evident, the most credible theories that have developed within the program are those identifying as fundamental those standards that agree more with common sense than does the Principle of Utility.

In particular, it is a matter of common sense that acts are sometimes right in themselves regardless of their consequences. Nothing opposes utilitarianism more, for instance, than the common-sense maxim *fiat justitia, ruat coelum*. Similarly, common-sense morality condemns lying in the harshest of terms and seldom makes exceptions on account of its good effects. The most credible theories, then, within the Grotian program identify a plurality of standards as fundamental to morality, many of which correspond to features of an action that can make it right apart from its having good consequences. Such features include an action's being a piece of speech that expresses the truth, its being the timely returning of an object that one had borrowed, its being a showing of gratitude for advantages another has freely given one, and its being the performance of an action one had promised to do. The theories, then, identify as fundamental standards of right and wrong, not only standards of nonaggression and charity toward others and a standard of care for one's own well-being, but also standards of justice, honesty, fidelity, and gratitude. How different standards are identified and enumerated varies from theory to theory. Some theories identify a small number of very general standards each of which comprehends several more specific right-making features. Others identify a larger number and, accordingly, take each more specific feature as corresponding to a separate fundamental standard. These differences are unimportant, however. What is important is that all theories in this program identify a plurality of fundamental standards of right and wrong some of which qualify an action as right apart from its good consequences.

The program's main epistemological supposition is that these fundamental standards, being objects of God's intellect rather than deliverances of his will, can be grasped and affirmed through the exercise of one's rational powers. That is, one can see, from reflection on what rules people must observe in their relations to each other, the validity of certain standards, and seeing the validity of these standards, one is compelled to affirm them. What is more, on this supposition, one sees their validity immediately and does not infer it from considerations of the means necessary to achieving peaceful social relations. Accordingly, their validity is self-evident, and as such one grasps it by exercising the intuitive powers of reason rather than its inferential powers. The theories that developed from this supposition are thus themselves products of a general epistemological theory aptly called *rational intuitionism*. On this theory, the moral order that the fundamental standards of right and wrong constitute is an object of the intellect, and one's knowledge of it comes from directly perceiving its elements and structure through the exercise of the intuitive powers of reason.

The theory's debt to Plato's theory of forms is obvious. In either, the objects of the intellect are held to be distinct from the objects of sensory experience and known without recourse to the latter. Similarly, just as on Plato's theory one's knowledge of the forms consists in grasping ideas that are necessarily true, so on rational intuitionism one's knowledge of the moral order consists in recognizing standards of right and wrong that are necessarily valid. Such knowledge, in either case, is different from empirical knowledge, which concerns contingent facts. It is different, that is, from our knowledge that Mercury is the planet in the solar system whose orbit is closest to the sun. That fact is contingent on the events occurring eons ago that brought about the formation of the solar system. If those events had been different, there might now be a planet whose orbit is even closer to the sun than Mercury's. By contrast, knowledge of the forms, on Plato's theory, and knowledge of the moral order, according to rational intuitionists, is not knowledge of things that could have been different. The intuitionists' rejection of theological voluntarism makes this clear. Even if God had commanded the torture of all blue-eyed infants, such torture would still have been wrong. As the intuitionists might put it, its being wrong is not contingent on anything, not even God's will.

4. Ethics and mathematics

The force of rational intuitionism lies in the great confidence we have in the truth of such simple matters of right and wrong as that torturing infants is wrong. The same confidence is at work in our immediately seeing serious problems with act utilitarianism in its yielding prescriptions that conflict with basic standards of justice and honesty. Our verdicts in either case seem unshakeable. Of course, we are confident, too, in our belief that Mercury is the planet in the solar system whose orbit is closest to the sun. But that confidence would vanish if astronomers from the world's leading observatories and research universities were to announce the discovery of a planet whose orbit lies entirely within Mercury's. By contrast, no similar announcement about the newly discovered permissibility of torturing infants, even if it were made by leaders of the world's major religions and past winners of the Nobel peace prize, would shake our confidence in the truth of its being wrong to torture infants. Our confidence in this truth is not merely greater, then. It is, so it seems, of a different order.

Rational intuitionism explains this difference by sharply distinguishing between the objects of intellect and the objects of sensory experience and attributing necessity – one might say metaphysical necessity – to the truths about the former and contingency, metaphysical contingency, to the truths about the latter. Yet the problem with this explanation is that the attribution of necessity to truths about matters of right and wrong may be nothing more than a reiteration of our great confidence in their being true. And similarly for the intuitionists' companion thesis that we have knowledge of these matters through the exercise of intuitive powers that enable us to apprehend directly their truth, that their truth is self-evident to reason. Either thesis, in its own way, expresses a belief in the certainty of one's judgment on simple matters of right and wrong, but it offers nothing further to back up that certainty.

What is needed, then, is support for these theses that does not depend on our confidence in the truth of certain propositions of right and wrong and our recognizing that this confidence comes from something other than confidence in the methods of empirical science. To this end rational intuitionists have adduced mathematics as evidence of the type of truths and knowledge that they hold moral truths and moral knowledge to be. Surely, they argue, the necessity of such mathematical propositions as the simple truths of arithmetic, like $2 + 5 = 7$, will be granted. And surely it will be granted, too, that such truths are known without recourse to sensory experience. Further, in so describing them, we are not merely expressing belief in the certainty of our mathematical judgments or reiterating our confidence in their being true. Rather our description captures an understanding of mathematical objects that anyone familiar with the methods of the discipline, methods that are as old as Euclid, will have acquired. Anyone, that is, who is familiar with these methods will have come to understand mathematical objects as objects of pure intellect whose existence and nature could not be other than they are. Accordingly, mathematics furnishes us with the right model for understanding the necessary existence and character of moral standards and the certainty of moral knowledge. Or so rational intuitionists have often maintained.

The principal method that they have invoked is that of developing a branch of mathematics as an axiom system. Such a system consists of a set of propositions a small number of which are the axioms or postulates, the fundamental propositions of the system, and the rest of which are theorems, propositions that one can derive from the postulates and previously derived theorems. The paradigm of the method is Euclidean geometry, and for centuries thinkers followed Euclid in taking the postulates of geometry to be self-evident truths and the procedures by which one proved the theorems of geometry to be truth preserving. The self-evidence of the postulates and the truth-preservingness of the proof procedures meant that the theorems of Euclidean geometry were truths whose necessity was as certain as the necessity of the postulates. And one could be certain of the postulates because, being self-evident, one could directly apprehend their truth through exercising one's intuitive powers of reason. The match between this common understanding of geometrical truth and knowledge, on the one hand, and the understanding of moral truth and knowledge that rational intuitionism promotes, on the other, should be plain. For rational intuitionism takes the fundamental standards of right and wrong to be like the postulates of Euclidean geometry, treats other moral principles as analogous to theorems of geometry, and sees the moral order these standards constitute as an object of the intellect on a par with the geometrical space that the Euclidean postulates define.

Unfortunately for rational intuitionism, advances in mathematics beginning in the latter half of the nineteenth century overturned this understanding of axiomatic treatments of a branch of mathematics. In particular, mathematicians no longer regard the postulates of an axiomatic system as self-evident. They gave up this view once they began to construct and explore alternative systems within a single branch of the discipline. The most influential of these constructions are the axiomatic systems for geometry that are alternatives to Euclidean geometry. In each of these alternatives, the crucial difference between it and Euclidean geometry is found in its postulate about parallel lines. In Euclidean geometry the relevant postulate is Euclid's famous parallel postulate, that given a point p and a line l that does not contain p, there exists one and only one line that contains p and is parallel to l. In a non-Euclidean geometry this postulate is replaced by a postulate that contradicts it either by denying that there is any line parallel to l that contains p or by holding that there is more than one. Since a proposition and any proposition that contradicts it cannot both be true, they cannot both be self-evident. Hence, entertaining an axiomatic system that is an alternative to Euclidean geometry means giving up the idea that to be a postulate a proposition must be self-evident. Of course, one could still insist that Euclid's parallel postulate is self-evident and that the contradictory propositions that are postulates in non-Euclidean systems are mere logical possibilities, as are the systems themselves. But such insistence would amount to no more than a mere expression of one's belief in the certainty of Euclid's parallel postulate, a reiteration of one's confidence in its being true, and would not represent anything mathematics supports. The same points, moreover, hold true of axiomatic treatments of the discipline's other branches.

The consequence of these advances in mathematics is devastating for the appeal that rational intuitionists make to mathematics to support their theses about the necessity and self-evidence of fundamental standards of right and wrong. In view of these advances, as we've seen, these intuitionists cannot offer the postulates of an axiomatic system in mathematics as evidence of propositions whose truth one can, through exercising the intuitive powers of reason, directly apprehend. Nor can they adduce the axiomatic method as evidence of the necessity of mathematical truth. The reason is that the method upholds only the necessity of the theorems of an axiomatic system relative to the necessity of the postulates from which those theorems are derived. It does not uphold the necessity of the postulates themselves. To be sure, this point need not stop rational intuitionists from continuing to attribute necessity to these postulates if they like. But should they continue, it would be rather unclear what this attribution means in the case of postulates whose contradictories are logically possible. Calling it mathematical necessity would be vacuous. Calling it metaphysical necessity would be unilluminating.

There remains the sharp distinction rational intuitionists draw between objects of the intellect and objects of sensory experience. That distinction, to be sure, is unaffected by the construction of alternative axiomatic systems within a single branch of mathematics, since one can still distinguish the methods of mathematics from the methods of empirical science and take the subject of the former to be objects of pure intellect. At the same time, we can now see that an important assumption about these objects that is implicit in the rational intuitionists' appeal to mathematics is unwarranted. Because the intuitionists explicitly assume that the postulates of a branch of mathematics are necessary truths, they must further assume, albeit implicitly, that the objects defined by those postulates are the only objects with which that branch deals. Obviously, the construction of alternative axiomatic systems within a single branch makes this implicit assumption untenable. No one nowadays would even suggest that geometry, for instance, deals exclusively with geometric objects in Euclidean space and that the distinctive postulates and theorems of non-Euclidean geometries are simply false propositions about the properties of those objects. The point by itself merely reinforces our earlier criticism of rational intuitionism's appeal to mathematics. But it should also remind us that rational intuitionists must be making an analogous assumption about the objects of ethics and that this assumption, too, is unwarranted. Its being unwarranted, moreover, spells even deeper trouble for the theory.

Specifically, rational intuitionists must be assuming that the objects of intellect that the fundamental standards of right and wrong define – particularly, the moral order that those standards constitute – are the only objects with which ethics deals. Yet nothing warrants this assumption. This point may at first seem odd. If the fundamental standards of right and wrong are universal, if every human society, regardless of its laws and customs, instantiates the moral order they constitute, then that order and its related objects must be the subject of ethics. So how could this assumption be unwarranted? But the question rests on a confusion of two kinds of study, a confusion that revisiting the analogy with geometry should clear up. If we understand geometry as a study of certain objects of pure intellect, then it is a study of geometric objects and the different forms of space, Euclidean and non-Euclidean, that contain them. These different forms of space correspond to alternative axiomatic systems. Apart from this study, there is also the study of physical space, for the universe exists in space and one can ask what the form of the space in which the universe exists is. Specifically, one can ask, "Which of the different spaces, Euclidean and non-Euclidean, does the universe instantiate?" The study that this question initiates is not a study of objects of pure intellect. It is rather a study that requires recourse to our sensory experience of the position and motion of material objects. By analogy, then, rational intuitionists must distinguish within ethics the study of objects of pure intellect, specifically, the different forms of moral order that could be instantiated in human society, and the study of the form that is so instantiated. The latter study, given that the fundamental standards of right and wrong are universal, must be a study of the one moral order that every human society instantiates. But nothing warrants the assumption that the former study deals with only one set of universal standards and thus with only one form of moral order. And it is this assumption, which rational intuitionists, by virtue of their taking the objects of ethics to be objects of pure intellect, make, that is unwarranted.

They need the assumption, however. They need, that is, to avoid the possibility of there being alternative sets of fundamental moral standards and thus different forms of moral order. For this possibility would open the door to asking what determined which of these forms was the moral order that every human society instantiates, which of these alternative sets of standards was the set of fundamental standards of right and wrong that we recognize and follow. In the context of Christian thought, it would open the door to asking what explains God's choice of the set of standards in accordance with which he issues laws to human beings. Clearly, the answer cannot be that God chooses to issue laws in accordance with the set of standards of right and wrong whose validity is self-evident, for as objects of pure intellect no set stands apart from the others as self-evident, no more than the postulates of one axiomatic system within a branch of mathematics stand apart from the postulates of the alternative systems as self-evident. It appears, then, that the distinction between objects of intellect and objects of sensory experience provides no support for the rational intuitionists' theses about the necessity and self-evidence of the fundamental standards of right and wrong. Without some support for these theses, however, or warrant for the assumption that there is only one form of moral order with which ethics deals, rational intuitionism is in danger of collapse. And in the context of Christian thought such a collapse would amount to a reversion to theological voluntarism.

5. Kant's way

Immanuel Kant (1724–1804) shared the rational intuitionists' belief that knowledge of right and wrong was knowledge of the requirements of moral law and that such knowledge was a matter of common sense. On Kant's and the intuitionists' view, moral knowledge does not require a deep

understanding of human nature or complicated calculations of the consequences of the various actions open to one in the situations one faces. Of
course, Kant and the intuitionists granted that sometimes we face situations
in which it is hard to know what the right thing to do is. But for the most
part, they held, we have no trouble determining in the situations we face
what the moral law requires. Our ordinary powers of reason, they maintained, are sufficient for this purpose.

Kant broke with rational intuitionism, however, on the question of how
we know, through the exercise of reason, what the moral law requires.
According to rational intuitionism, the moral law corresponds to fundamental standards of right and wrong, and these standards are self-evident.
We directly see their validity through use of our intuitive powers of reason.
That is, we know directly and by intuition that we ought not to kill human
beings, that we ought to tell the truth, that we ought to keep our promises,
and so forth, and we then apply these precepts to the situations we face.
Kant, by contrast, did not appeal to the intuitive powers of reason to explain
our knowledge of the moral law. He did not think we directly saw the
validity of fundamental standards of right and wrong that corresponded
to that law. Rather he thought that each of us knows whether an act is
required by the moral law, whether we have a duty to do it, by a process of
reasoning about it. The process is one of practical thought as distinct from
speculative thought, a distinction that is of the utmost importance in Kant's
philosophy and of no importance to the rational intuitionists'. Kant understood the process of reasoning by which we determine whether an act is
required by moral law as embedded within other processes of practical
thought. Accordingly, he drew his account of our knowledge of right and
wrong from a general account of the operations of practical reason. And it
will therefore be necessary to set out this general account of practical
reason before examining Kant's account of our knowledge of right and
wrong.

In Kant's view, the workings of practical reason in human action are
what set the actions of human beings apart from all other actions and
events in nature. Human beings, Kant held, are rational agents. Reason,
that is, has a practical as well as theoretical function. Its powers include the
power to direct action. Thus, according to Kant, when a man acts rationally,
he acts in accordance with a rule or principle that, through the exercise of
practical reason, he sees as applying to his situation and suited to his ends.

"Everything in nature," Kant wrote, "works in accordance with laws. Only a rational being has the power to act in accordance with his idea of laws – that is, in accordance with principles – and only so has he a will. Since reason is required in order to derive actions from laws, the will is nothing but practical reason."[6] This passage from Kant's *Groundwork of the Metaphysics of Morals* begins his celebrated argument for understanding the moral law as the promulgation of reason.

What does Kant mean by acting in accordance with principles? In the first instance and as a first approximation, he means acting according to a generalization that connects an action in a given situation with a result that the agent intends. The result is therefore the agent's end, and the generalization captures the agent's understanding of the action as, in the situation he is in, a good means to this end. A man, for example, who turns on a faucet with the intention of washing his hands acts on the generalization that turning the handle of a working faucet releases water from the supply to which it is attached. His end is to get water for washing hands, and his means is turning a handle on a faucet attached to a supply of water large enough for that purpose. Getting water, needless to say, is only his immediate end. He also has the end of washing his hands, preventing infection or perhaps the ingestion of disease-producing microbes, and ultimately being happy. All of these ends are objects of human desire, and while different people have different desires, that is, different tastes and interests, hopes and ambitions, each person desires his or her own happiness as an ultimate end. It is, in that individual's life, the ultimate end consisting in the satisfaction of his or her individual tastes and interests, hopes and ambitions. Practical reason, then, in the first instance, guides human beings in the pursuit of happiness by providing, in the form of principles, intelligence about the best means to achieving their ends.

Kant introduces the term 'imperative' to denote certain principles of practical reason. It is a technical term in his philosophy. It applies to those principles with which reason dictates compliance. The dictatorial character of imperatives is essential to Kant's understanding of them. Because human beings have appetites and passions, because many of our desires and

---

[6] Immanuel Kant, *Groundwork of the Metaphysics of Morals*, H. J. Paton, trans. (New York: Harper & Row, 1964), p. 412. References are to page numbers in the Preussische Akademie edition.

emotions originate in animal instinct, we often act on those desires and emotions without giving enough thought to the consequences and implications of our actions. Such is particularly likely when a person is subject to strong desires or in the grip of a powerful emotion. In these cases, the person acts on poor judgment but not necessarily against reason. Sometimes, though, a person does not act merely on poor judgment but irrationally. That is, the person knows that reason requires his taking a certain course of action, yet he fails to take it. You know, for instance, that to get to your chemistry class on time, you will have to leave your apartment by 9:45, and there is no question of your wanting to be in class on time more than your wanting to remain in your apartment reading your favorite blog. Yet 9:45 comes and goes, and you continue to read the blog. In this case, your leaving at 9:45 is a requirement of reason. As Kant would see it, reason does not merely propose a 9:45 departure as the best course of action, but demands it as the only course, given that your end is to be in class on time. Departing at that time is necessary for achieving this end. Such necessity is what qualifies the principle you would be acting on, if you acted rationally in this situation, as an imperative.

Kant distinguishes different types of imperative according to the kind of necessity they imply. The type in our example is what Kant calls a hypothetical imperative. It is hypothetical because the necessity of taking the action is conditional on the agent's having the end relative to which the action is a means. In the example above, given that you want to be in class on time, it is necessary that you leave your apartment by 9:45. But it wouldn't be necessary if you had a different end whose achievement did not also require a 9:45 departure. The imperative, in other words, that you leave your apartment by 9:45 is valid only if the end relative to which your leaving by that time is a means is an end that you in fact have. Let us call such an end a validating end. Accordingly, Kant distinguishes, within the class of hypothetical imperatives, between two further types of imperative, technical and pragmatic, according as the validating end is the end of an activity or enterprise that human beings engage in at their discretion or is an end of an activity or enterprise that all human beings, just in virtue of their having natural desires, are engaged in. An example of the former would be the imperative, with regard to cooking a hard-boiled egg, that one cook the egg in boiling water for more than three minutes. An example of the latter would be any hypothetical imperative whose validating end was the agent's happiness, for in Kant's view all human beings pursue happiness, not because they choose to but because it is part of their nature as human beings. Consequently, the necessity with which pragmatic imperatives dictate action is a higher grade than the necessity with which technical imperatives dictate action.

Neither, however, dictates action with the highest grade of necessity. The highest grade would be the necessity of an imperative whose validity was not conditional on any of the agent's ends. The highest grade, that is, would be an imperative whose validity was unconditional. Kant calls such an imperative a categorical imperative. It is distinct from every type of hypothetical imperative. His bold thesis is that moral laws are categorical imperatives.

This would not be such a bold thesis, of course, if all that Kant meant in identifying moral laws with categorical imperatives was that moral laws were the commands of God, for there would be nothing bold in characterizing God's commands as unconditionally valid. Hobbes's distinction between commands and counsels, to which we referred earlier, makes this clear. While the validity of a counsel depends on the ends of those to whom counsel is given, the validity of a command does not. It depends instead on the commander's having authority over those to whom the command is given, and God, being the supreme ruler of the universe, has unconditional authority over human beings. Accordingly, his commands are unconditionally valid. But Kant meant something else. Given his special use of the term 'imperative' to mean principle of practical reason that dictates action, he meant that the moral laws were principles of practical reason and valid as such rather than as expressions of an authority's will. Hence, being categorical imperatives, they are unconditionally valid as principles of practical reason rather than as expressions of a supreme ruler's will. Consequently, any rational agent, regardless of his or her ends, would be acting contrary to reason if he or she violated a moral law. And this is a bold claim.

How could one substantiate such a claim? Or as Kant put the question in the *Groundwork*, how is it even possible that there are categorical imperatives?[7] It is evident, Kant pointed out, how there can be hypothetical imperatives. Someone who decides to pursue a certain end thereby sets himself to

[7] Ibid., p. 419.

take whatever means are necessary to achieving that end. This person may later, to be sure, on realizing the lengths to which he would have to go to achieve this end, decide that achieving it isn't worth the trouble, but at that point he will have also abandoned his decision to pursue it. In other words, as long as it is his will to pursue this end, it must be his will to take whatever means are necessary to achieving it. There would be an incoherence in his will if this were not so. Hence, an imperative that directed him to take this means makes sense as a requirement of reason. But how could there be any incoherence in his thinking or his will if he decided to act dishonestly or cruelly in the pursuit of some end? By what process of reasoning could a person be led to see the necessity, as a matter of coherent thinking or willing, of acting honestly or forbearing from acting cruelly? Kant answers these questions by taking such actions to be lawless and arguing that only by keeping one's actions lawful can one avoid incoherence either in one's thinking or in one's will. Categorical imperatives are possible, then, according to Kant, because lawfulness itself can be a condition of rational action.

Kant's idea, in proposing lawfulness as a condition of rational action, is that the agent, in acting on principles, act only on those principles that could be made into laws for all human beings. That is, we are to test the principles on which we act to see whether they could be adopted as universal laws, and if they can, then our acting on them is lawful action. Moreover, Kant understands this test as purely formal. A principle of action does not fail the test just because it is predicated on the pursuit of a certain, substantive end. Rather, failure occurs only when there is something incoherent either in the conception of the principle as a universal law or in the act of will required to make it a universal law. To Kant's way of thinking, as long as you are able to form the idea of everyone's acting on the principle of your action when they find themselves in situations similar to yours and as long as you can will consistently with your decision to act on this principle that you live in a world in which everyone acts on the principle in situations like yours, then your acting on the principle is lawful. When you cannot form the idea because of some incoherence in it or, though you can form it, you cannot will its realization consistently with your decision to act on the principle, then acting on the principle is unlawful. In either case, the incoherence or inconsistency makes it necessary that you forbear from acting on the principle. The imperative, then, that you not act on it is categorical. Or rather it would be categorical if acting lawfully in Kant's sense, that is, acting on principles that could be made into laws for all human beings, were a condition of acting rationally.

Kant, as I said, proposed that it was. He put his proposal in the form of a second-order principle. It is second order in that it is a principle regulating the first-order principles on which rational agents act. The first-order principles are the generalizations that connect an action in a given situation with an intended result and that an agent follows in pursuing an end to whose advancement the intended result contributes. Kant calls these first-order principles maxims.[8] Accordingly, the second-order principle he formulates is this: *Act only on that maxim through which you can at the same time will that it should become a universal law*.[9] This principle, given that it represents a requirement of practical reason, is itself, then, an imperative that dictates with unconditional necessity. Indeed, Kant in recognition of its being the source of all particular categorical imperatives or imperatives of duty refers to it singularly as the Categorical Imperative. It is thus, in his system, the fundamental principle of morality. Fidelity to it in our deliberations about what acts it would be right to do, he believes, leads us to make moral judgments coincident with common sense. Faithful application of the Categorical Imperative in one's deliberations, that is, not only shows what the moral law requires but also reinforces the judgments of ordinary men and women about right and wrong.

Kant's identification of moral laws with categorical imperatives turns, then, on whether lawfulness is a condition of rational action. Kant did not think it would be easy to show that it is or that if he did, he would have established as a matter of general psychological fact that human beings, when they act honestly, honorably, kindly, and the like, act on categorical imperatives rather than on other motives. He did maintain that anyone who firmly believed in the validity of universal standards of right and wrong and did not think they were, as he put it, "chimerical" must accept his conception of them. But firm belief falls short of knowledge, and it is knowledge that Kant sought. Still, we can at this point see whether his conception of universal standards of morality as categorical imperatives is cogent and leave for later, if it is, examining the complex case he made for his proposal that lawfulness is a condition of rational action.

---

[8] Ibid., p. 421n.   [9] Ibid., p. 421.

6. Formalism in ethics

The main objection to Kant's conception is that it is too formal to be a useful guide to telling right action from wrong action. "Empty formalism" is the standard charge that its critics have raised against it. The Categorical Imperative directs rational agents to determine whether they can will that the maxims of their actions become universal laws, and the procedure for determining this is purely formal. It involves no substantive criterion of right and wrong. On this procedure, the agent first identifies the maxim of his action, whether it be an action he has already done or one that he is contemplating doing. The agent then determines whether he can form a coherent idea of a world in which everyone whose circumstances are like his does the same action. That is, he determines whether he can form a coherent idea of a world in which his maxim has become a universal law regulating the conduct of human beings in such circumstances. And finally, supposing he can form this idea, he determines whether he can will that such a world be created consistently with his willing the action. The criteria the agent uses to test the maxim's suitability for being willed as a universal law are coherence and consistency. These are formal criteria, and such criteria, Kant's critics have maintained, cannot alone yield definite conclusions about whether an action is right or wrong. While Kant, to be sure, meant the procedure to be one that yielded definite conclusions about the rightness or wrongness of a course of action one had taken or was contemplating taking, one can in fact, so the criticism continues, always rig things at the procedure's first step so that the maxim one identifies at this step passes the tests that one applies at the following steps. Hence, Kant's critics conclude, the procedure for applying the Categorical Imperative – let us call it *the CI procedure* – is ultimately arbitrary.

Let us take up this charge of arbitrariness first. It will be useful, in seeing how serious the charge is, to work with a concrete example. Our example of your finding a lost purse containing a huge wad of cash will do nicely. Recall that you find the purse, notice the cash, and recognize that you ought to return both to its owner. It would be wrong, you conclude, to keep the cash for yourself. But how can the CI procedure explain your coming to this conclusion?

Its first step requires that you identify the maxim you would be acting on if you kept the cash. Let us assume that if you did keep the cash, your reason would be to make yourself richer. Accordingly, the maxim of your action would be something like the following:

(M1) Given circumstances in which I can appropriate for myself something valuable that belongs to another without fear of punishment or retaliation, I will take the valuable thing in order to enrich myself.

At the next step, you form the idea of a world in which everyone who finds himself in a situation in which he can, without fear of punishment or retaliation, enrich himself by appropriating something valuable that belongs to another does so. This idea, you should then immediately realize, is incoherent. It is incoherent because a world in which no one respects the property of others would be a world in which, in effect, there would be no property and none of the rights of ownership that go with it, and in such a world people cannot appropriate for themselves things that belong to others. The incoherence of the idea therefore tells you that you cannot act on this maxim. It tells you, in other words, that it would be wrong to keep the cash in order to enrich yourself.

Admittedly, what conclusion the procedure yields depends on the directive you identify as the maxim of your action. Suppose, for example, you identified the following as your maxim:

(M2) Given circumstances in which I can appropriate for myself cash contained in a lost purse that I find in a public park, without fear of punishment or retaliation, I will keep the cash in order to enrich myself.

Taking this as your maxim, you would then, at step two of the procedure, form the idea of a world in which everyone who finds a lost purse in a public park keeps whatever cash the purse contains whenever they can do so without fear of punishment or retaliation. You would thus form the idea of a world in which universal disrespect of the property of others was limited to cash contained in lost purses found in public parks. Since universal disrespect that was so limited would not amount to the wholesale dissolution of property rights, you would not see anything incoherent in this idea. Nor need you discover any opposition in your will to the creation of such a world that would be inconsistent with your deciding to keep the cash so as to make yourself richer. M2 therefore passes both the test of ideational coherence at step two and the test of volitional consistency at step three. In other words, if it were the maxim of your action, the CI procedure would tell you that it would not be wrong to keep the cash.

Obviously, if M1 and M2 were equally plausible candidates for being the maxim of your action, then the CI procedure would be open to manipulation.

In that case, you could, by deciding to identify one directive rather than the other as your maxim, rig the procedure so that it yielded the conclusion you wanted. For this reason critics have long charged Kant's procedure with being arbitrary. But the charge is overblown. Using the procedure to determine whether an act is right or wrong is not a game. It presupposes a genuine interest in knowing the moral status of your act, whether it is right or wrong, and therefore presupposes sincerity in identifying the maxim you would be acting on in doing it. Given that you are sincere in identifying this maxim, there should be few if any cases in which you are genuinely torn between two formulations of it on each of which the CI procedure yields a conclusion opposed to the conclusion it yields on the other.

Further, you can tell whether you have properly identified your maxim by determining whether you have included in its formulation only those features of the action and its circumstances that would make a difference to your decision about whether to do it. Thus, with regard to M2, it should be clear on several counts that this would not be the maxim on which you would be acting if you kept the cash. First, that you found the purse in a public park makes no difference to your decision whether to keep the cash it contains. Had you found the purse in an alley instead, the decision would still be the same. Second, that the cash is contained in a purse is likewise irrelevant. Your decision would not be affected by its being contained in a wallet, a briefcase, or even a gym bag. Third, and what is most important, your decision is not about keeping or returning someone else's cash as such. It is about keeping or returning something valuable that belongs to another and that you have come to possess. Leaving aside questions of safety from punishment or retaliation, your decision would be the same even if what the purse contained were not cash but rare stamps, an endorsed cashier's check, or a winning lottery ticket. M1, then, because it does not, as it were, descend to the level of irrelevant specificity about the action and its circumstances that M2 does, is far more plausible as a candidate for being the maxim of your action.

The question of whether there could be an equally plausible candidate that was even less specific than M1 is trickier. Thus consider the following:

(M3) Given circumstances in which I can gain possession of something valuable without fear of punishment or retaliation, I will take the valuable thing in order to add to the stock of valuable things that I possess.

If this were the maxim of your action, then again you could form a coherent idea of a world in which everyone took possession of valuable things whenever they could do so without fear of punishment or retaliation. In such a world there would be no property or rights of ownership, to be sure, but M3, unlike M1, does not presuppose the existence of property or ownership rights and therefore your forming the idea of a world in which it became a universal law would not be similarly incoherent. Indeed, the idea you would form would correspond to Hobbes's account of the natural condition of humankind, and no one has ever thought there was something incoherent in Hobbes's account. At the same time, whether you could also will that such a world be created consistently with a decision to keep the cash is questionable at best, since in such a world you are likely to possess a smaller stock of valuable things and a decision to take the cash manifests a will to possess a larger one. But even before considering whether M3 passes the tests of ideational coherence and volitional consistency at steps two and three of the procedure, there is the question of whether M3 could even be your maxim.

It could be, if you were either completely innocent of notions of private property and knew nothing about the rights that owners of property have or had rejected these notions and denied that anyone could privately own anything or have the rights that private ownership entails. Either possibility is extremely unlikely, of course, but neither can be ruled out without ruling out other instances of ignorance or rejection of an aspect of the moral culture in which an agent finds himself that are not so unlikely. People, after all, are sometimes ignorant of the moral culture that partly defines the circumstances of their actions, or they are sometimes sufficiently opposed to it as to have rejected it wholly or in part. Recent immigrants from faraway lands are often ignorant of much of their new country's moral culture. Committed anarchists reject government and the laws that governments enact. The maxims of their actions, in either case, may therefore be directives that exclude references to cultural or legal aspects of their circumstances that people who are at home in the culture and accept the authority of government and the laws it enacts would include in the directives that are the maxims of their actions. In general, then, an agent's maxim of action includes reference to all and only those features of his circumstances that are relevant to his decision to act, and for agents who are familiar with the moral culture that partly defines their circumstances and have not rejected any aspect of it that is relevant to their decisions, their maxims must include reference to those aspects of it. M1, therefore, is the maxim on which you would be acting if you kept the cash in order to enrich yourself, except in the extremely unlikely event that you are innocent of the ideas of property and ownership rights or have rejected them. In that event, M3 could be your maxim.

7. The problem with Kant's formalism

The CI procedure can thus survive the charge of arbitrariness that its critics commonly make against it. Sincere identification of your maxim gives you no leeway to rig the procedure. There remains, then, the more general charge that the procedure is excessively formal. While this charge is vaguer than the charge of arbitrariness, we can nonetheless understand it as at least criticizing the CI procedure for lacking a substantive criterion of right action. And there does appear to be something to this charge, for the CI procedure is not, as turns out, completely reliable. Sometimes it yields false negatives. That is, sometimes it yields a conclusion about its being wrong to act on a maxim of action that, as a matter of common sense, it is not wrong to act on. Moreover, that it yields such conclusions is due to the purely formal notion of law that Kant assumed. This deficiency is most readily seen in examples concerning the application of the second of the procedure's two tests, the test of volitional consistency. How Kant meant this test to apply to an agent's maxim is itself somewhat obscure, however. So let us first, to clarify it, work through one of his primary examples.

Kant, in this example, imagines a prosperous man coming upon others who are in great distress and whom he could easily help. This man, Kant writes, "[then] thinks, 'What does it matter to me? Let every one be as happy as Heaven wills or as he can make himself. I won't deprive him of anything; I won't even envy him; only I have no wish to contribute anything to his well-being or to his support in distress!'"[10] Implicitly, then, the man's maxim is:

> (N1) Given circumstances in which I can easily help others who are in distress, I will withhold assistance to them in order to avoid the inconvenience to my own pursuits that it would entail.

Kant observes that such a maxim would pass the first test of the CI procedure, for one can form a coherent idea of a world in which no one freely inconveniences himself to help others who are in distress. But he

[10] Ibid., pp. 423.

maintains that the maxim would fail the second. The reason, he argues, is that occasions may arise in this man's life in which he will need the help and support of others, and he would be depriving himself of that help if he were, through his will, to bring about a world in which no one ever helps others who are in distress and whom they can easily help. Hence, there would be an inconsistency in his will if he were to act on N1. And from this result it follows that he has duty to help the people in distress he has encountered.

Though the argument as it stands has gaps, filling them is not a problem. To begin with, let us observe that N1, when it is one's maxim, manifests a will to advance one's happiness. Kant's argument, then, must show that, given N1 as the agent's maxim, the agent would be thwarting his will if he brought about, through it, a world in which no one helps others in distress when he or she can easily do so. Showing that the agent's will would be so thwarted shows the requisite inconsistency in the will, an inconsistency that consists in the agent's deciding to act so as to advance his happiness and at the same time willing the creation of a world in which his prospects for happiness are significantly diminished. And to show this inconsistency requires the supposition that a person, no matter how prosperous he may be, at least tacitly knows that there may be occasions in his life when he will need the freely given help of others and that without such help his life would become significantly worse. In effect, then, Kant must be supposing that people, however prosperous, at least tacitly know that they may eventually be the victims of accidents, mishaps, or crimes, that they may find themselves lost in unfamiliar places or stranded far from home, that they may become targets of unprovoked vengeance, that they may lose their homes to floods, fires, tornadoes, or other natural disasters, and so forth and that in any of these circumstances they would look to others for help and hope to receive it. For knowing this, the person will recognize that his prospects for happiness are better in a world in which people have goodwill toward each other than in a world in which they are indifferent to each other's well-being and accordingly, given a will to advance his happiness, he would will the creation of the former and oppose the creation of the latter. To will the creation of the latter, in other words, would be inconsistent with his will to advance his happiness. Once we add this supposition and its implications to the argument, Kant's conclusion that N1 fails the CI procedure's test of volitional consistency follows directly.

It is sometimes said, in criticism of Kant's argument, that it is an essentially prudential argument for a duty of to help others. Yet this criticism misses the point of the second test. The point of the test is to see whether one's will, if fixed by a given maxim, would be thwarted were that maxim to become, through one's will, a universal law. When the given maxim is prudential, as N1 is, then the reasoning by which the agent determines whether his will would be thwarted were his maxim to become, through it, a universal law is *perforce* prudential. But the test itself is not restricted to prudential maxims, and if the given maxim were, for instance, the maxim of an agent seeking to promote world peace, then the agent's reasoning in applying the test would be oriented toward the achievement of world peace rather than prudentially oriented. Kant's argument therefore appears to consist of prudential considerations in favor of a duty to help others only because the maxim that fixes the will, N1, is prudential. What the agent actually determines, when he sees that his will would be thwarted if N1 were to become, through it, a universal law, is that he would not be acting lawfully if he acted on N1. This consideration is what establishes that he has a duty to help others in the situation he faces. He discovers an inconsistency in his will, and realizes that the only way to resolve it, if he is to act in accordance with law, is to abandon N1.

It is now possible to see how the CI procedure overreaches in determining whether courses of action are right or wrong. Specifically, the condition that one's maxim be suitable for being willed as a universal law of nature places too great a constraint on the courses of action a person can pursue without acting wrongly. The trouble arises because many courses of action will not, in fact, be pursued by everyone, and to let considerations of what the world would be like if everyone pursued a course of action determine the rightness of that course is, in some cases in which relatively few people would in fact pursue it, to exclude as wrong courses of action that are in fact permissible.

Here is an example. Suppose you live in an area where the incidence of violent crime has risen high enough to cause you some concern about going out at night. To protect yourself you decide to carry a handgun concealed on your person. Doing so, let us further suppose, is permitted by the state and the smaller units of government that are responsible for public safety. The maxim of your action would then be something like:

(N2) Given circumstances in which I am in some danger of being the victim of violent crime, I will carry a concealed handgun in order to protect myself from this danger.

Following the CI procedure, you test this maxim by first seeing whether you can form the idea of a world in which everyone who is in some danger of being the victim of violent crime carries a concealed handgun. It is certainly a coherent idea. Next you determine whether you can will that such a world be created consistently with your decision to carry a concealed handgun for protection. At this point you should see that you cannot will that such a world be created consistently with your will's having been fixed by N2, for in bringing about such a world, through your will, you would be creating even more dangerous circumstances for yourself, ones in which you are in fact at greater risk of being the victim of violence, criminal and otherwise. This is because a world in which everyone who is concerned about being the victim of violent crime carries a concealed handgun is a world awash in handguns, and such a world is a much more dangerous place than a world in which only a relatively small number of people carry handguns. Consequently, you see that you would be thwarting your will if you brought about, through it, such a world and must therefore conclude that it would be wrong to carry a handgun to protect yourself. Yet surely it is not wrong for someone to carry a handgun for protection, as long as the state and other units of government responsible for public safety permit it.

The reason the CI procedure runs into trouble when applied to examples like this one is that the notion of law implicit in the procedure's tests is entirely formal. It is the notion of a supremely authoritative rule by which every rational agent is governed, and it is entirely formal in that it does not contain the idea of the rule's having an end or purpose beyond that of prescribing lawful conduct. In particular, it does not contain the idea of the rule's having the purpose of helping to sustain human society by either restraining people from doing things that, if done too often, would threaten the society's stability or requiring people to do things that, if not done often enough, would also threaten the society's stability. Rather the application of either test appears to express an interest on the agent's part in acting lawfully for the sake of acting lawfully and not for the sake of participating in a scheme for bringing about social good through general obedience to law. In this respect, the notion of law implicit in the procedure's tests is more like Hobbes's notion than a notion that implies a social purpose to law as such. It is more like Hobbes's notion in that the agent is not supposed to look for reason to obey beyond the fact that he is subject to the law, subject, that is, to the authority of the ruler who imposes it. As a result, the CI procedure invites criticism similar to the one that proved fatal to theological voluntarism. It invites the criticism that the unlawfulness of an action is not itself a reason against doing the action if the relevant notion of law is entirely formal, for such a notion does not preclude innocuous or sensible actions from being unlawful.

Trouble arises, in particular, then in the application of the second test, because whether one can, consistently with a decision to act on a certain maxim, will the creation of a world in which that maxim is a universal law will sometimes appear to be an idle consideration if one thinks the lawfulness of an action matters to its being reasonable to do only if the social good would not be jeopardized by letting people do it. It is not an idle consideration, of course, if one can expect people generally to be similarly motivated in similar circumstances and to forbear from acting on the maxim from a shared understanding that the action must be forborne for the sake of social good. But it does appear to be idle if one knows that few others would be similarly motivated in similar circumstances, too few at any rate, for one to regret the collective effect of their acting on that maxim. For in that case letting people do the action will not jeopardize the social good.[11]

The charge of excessive formalism against Kant's CI procedure has significant merit, then, when it is understood as an objection to the formal notion of law implicit in the procedure. The notion is implicated in the false negatives that the procedure yields. It is also, on account of the notion's being divorced from any end or purpose that law has as an instrument of maintaining order and stability in human society, hard to see what interest

[11] One might, in light of this observation, think that the trouble arises only because N2 does not accurately express your maxim, since it omits from the description of your circumstances that few people carry handguns. But obviously if your maxim included this feature of your circumstances – that is, if your maxim were: (N3) Given circumstances in which I am in some danger of being the victim of violent crime and only a few people are carrying handguns, I will carry a concealed handgun in order to protect myself from this danger, then you would again find that it would be unlawful to act on this maxim. The reason is that the conception of the maxim as a universal law of nature is incoherent; you cannot coherently conceive of a world in which everyone carries a handgun in circumstances in which few people do.

a rational agent could have in acting lawfully except that of doing so for the sake of acting lawfully. Such an interest, however, seems no more reasonable than the interest of a political subordinate in blind obedience to his political superiors. It borders on idolatry toward law. In any case, the notion is markedly different from the notion that originally inspired the deontologists' answer to the question of how human beings could know the requirements of moral law through reason and without consulting a text in which those requirements are laid down. That notion corresponded to an understanding of morality as based on substantive criteria of right and wrong that arise from a need to impose order on human society. Kant's notion, by contrast, corresponds to a different understanding of morality, one that springs from his idea that lawfulness is a condition of rational action. The idea, as we noted at the close of section 5, is not easy to show, and our subsequent criticism of the CI procedure has only added to the difficulty. Kant thus carries the heavy burden of having to vindicate this idea. Unless he does, the charge of excessive formalism commonly made against his ethics will stick.

6   The ethics of self-determination

1. Kant's step into metaphysics

What interest could rational agents have in acting lawfully if not the order, stability, and other collective goods that law brings to society? Why should it otherwise matter to them that their actions are lawful? It would matter to them, of course, if acting unlawfully made them liable to punishment. But in that case their interest in acting lawfully would not come from seeing it as a good thing. It would come, rather, from seeing it as the surest way to avoid a bad thing, something they have an interest in escaping. Yet the challenge to an ethics like Kant's that represents lawfulness as the essence of moral action is to explain what could interest rational agents in acting lawfully regardless of how the law is enforced, regardless, that is, of whether it is enforced by threats of punishment or incentives to obey. The question then that confronts a defender of Kant's ethics is why a rational agent should regard an action's being lawful as a condition of its being reasonable to do. If he cannot give an answer to this question, the charge of excessive formalism will stick.

Kant himself was fully aware of the importance of this question. He understood that a person must realize some value through acting lawfully, else making lawfulness a condition of the reasonability of an action would be pointless. It would have no rational basis. This value, moreover, had to be recognized by all who possessed reason by virtue of their possessing reason. It could not be due to a desire, sentiment, feeling, or other contingent affection, not even one common to all human beings. For if it were, then the point of insuring that one's action was lawful would be due to something in the agent's psychology that, being contingent, he could lack, and therefore there could be circumstances, if only hypothetically, in which the agent's forbearing from an act because it was unlawful would be pointless. That is, when he forbore from it in those circumstances he would not realize

157

the value of acting lawfully that normally gives such forbearance a point. Consequently, only if the point of insuring that one's action is lawful is due to a value of which one could be cognizant regardless of the desires, sentiments, feelings, and other contingent affections to which one is liable, could the lawfulness of an action be, for any agent, a necessary condition of its being reasonable to do. Hence, Kant observed, for categorical imperatives to be possible there must be a value that rational agents realize through obedience to them, and it must be a value that these agents could recognize regardless of the desires, sentiments, feelings, and other contingent affections to which they are liable.

With this observation, Kant begins to build a deeper theory of morality. Or as he puts it, he takes his first step into metaphysics.[1] Before taking this step, he had, as we saw, divided imperatives into hypothetical and categorical, used this division to distinguish different degrees of necessity with which an imperative dictates action, and then identified the Categorical Imperative – the second-order principle whose application to first-order principles yields imperatives of the highest degree of necessity – as the fundamental principle of morality. Kant's aim, in expounding these ideas, was to fix the type of experience in which moral law appears to rational agents and to describe the character of the thinking by which they typically determine what the moral law requires. Our experience of moral law, according to Kant, is thus the experience of being directed by unconditional dictates of reason, dictates we determine by seeing whether in taking a certain course of action we would be allowing ourselves more liberty in the pursuit of our ends than we would permit others to have in the pursuit of theirs. It is, in short, the experience of being bound by a universal rule that has the backing of reason, and Kant's step into metaphysics initiates a theory of what in the nature of human existence must lie behind and make possible such an experience if the experience is not illusory.

The first step in the construction of this theory, then, is Kant's introduction of a value that a rational agent realizes through acting lawfully. Some such value is needed to guarantee that acting lawfully always has a rational basis. And for there to be such a basis, Kant holds, the value realized through

---

[1] Kant, *Groundwork of the Metaphysics of Morals*, p. 426.

acting lawfully must have its source outside of the agent's ends. Hence, Kant is led to the idea of two radically different kinds of value in human life. On the one hand, human beings find value in the satisfaction of their natural desires and personal interests, the determinants of their ends as sensuous beings. Accordingly, such value is relative to these desires and interests and varies among human beings to the degree that the corresponding desires and interests likewise vary. On the other hand, because human beings are rational agents and thus capable of acting lawfully, they are all cognizant of the value that lawful action realizes. This value provides them with a rational basis for such action, and because it is a value that rational agents recognize by virtue of their being rational, Kant characterizes it as absolute. Unlike values that are relative to natural desires and personal interests, it does not vary among human beings. It is constant for all rational beings and necessarily so by virtue of there being no variation in reason across rational agents.

Kant's idea of there being two radically different kinds of value in human life corresponds to his view of human beings as having a dual nature. It corresponds to a view of human beings as both sensuous beings, beings in whom sensory experience composes, at least partly, their mental lives, and rational beings, beings in whom the processes of reason compose, at least partly, their mental lives. Humans, in Kant's view, are unlike beasts who, if sentient, are wholly sensuous beings. At the same time, humans do share a sensuous nature with such beasts. But possessing reason, they also have a nature that beasts lack. This duality in human nature is reflected, then, in two kinds of activity in human life, the pursuit of happiness and the exercise of reason for its own sake, and through each of these kinds of activity human beings realize one or the other of the two kinds of value that Kant's deeper theory of morality assumes.

Thus Kant regards the pursuit of happiness as the pursuit of things that satisfy one's natural desires and personal interests, and these things have value for one as constituents of that happiness. Their value corresponds to the contribution they make to one's happiness, and the greater the contribution the more they are worth to one. Accordingly, Kant characterizes their value as a kind of price, for having measured the value of each by its contribution to one's happiness, one would be willing to forgo it – that is, pay the price of not having it – in return for attaining something that would contribute even more to one's happiness. By contrast, Kant regards the exercise of reason for its own sake as a self-sufficient activity. One needs no external reward to engage in it. The value of engaging in it inheres in the activity itself. There is value, Kant holds, to being a rational agent, and this value has no price. For its value does not consist in its contribution to one's happiness, and hence there is no common measure by which to compare it with those things that do. The value realized through rational activity is independent of, and indeed, incommensurable with, the value of the things that contribute to one's happiness.

The absolute value of rational activity or of being a rational agent therefore provides the rational basis of acting lawfully. Kant arrives at this crucial tenet of his theory by reasoning hypothetically. Let x, he supposes, be that which has absolute value and whose absolute value provides the rational basis for acting lawfully. There must be such an x if there is a point to acting lawfully. And, further, x must ground the same set of imperatives as the CI procedure yields, else it would not explain the experience of being bound by a universal rule backed by reason. It would not, in other words, explain our experience of moral law. To explain this experience, then, the value of x must be such that one realizes it through obedience to moral law as popularly understood, for moral law, as popularly understood, is what the CI procedure is meant to capture. And only if this value inheres in rational activity itself or in rational agency itself could it explain this experience. Thus Kant comes to identify our rational nature as a possible ground of all categorical imperatives. x, he declares, is humanity or, more generally, rational agency. It is that which, as an end in itself, grounds the moral law.[2]

2. The formula of humanity

But what does Kant mean by describing human beings, and rational agents generally, as existing as ends in themselves? And does he mean something more than that the value of rational agency is absolute? These questions arise because the phrase 'end in itself' is rather odd. Indeed, it is peculiar to Kant's ethics. No other philosopher before Kant used it. Rather his predecessors, in referring to an action's end, meant either a goal of the action, or

---

[2] Or as Kant puts it, having supposed that there is something whose existence has absolute value, "Now I say that man, and in general every rational being, *exists* as an end in himself, and *not merely as a means* for arbitrary use by this or that will." Ibid., p. 428.

an effect that its agent intended to bring about, or an objective that the agent hoped to accomplish. Kant, by contrast, does not mean any of these things in describing human beings as existing as ends in themselves. He does not mean that human beings are goals to be pursued or effects one can intend to bring about, or objectives one can hope to accomplish. Indeed, he could not mean any of these things since, procreation aside, none is a coherent idea.

What is even more important, though, Kant could not mean any of these things, because he understands the function of humanity's being an end in itself (or what for Kant comes to the same thing, our rational nature's being an end in itself) as the same as the function of the Categorical Imperative. Like the latter, it applies to one's maxims and not to one's actions directly. It is not, therefore, an end that one sets for oneself and chooses means to achieve. It is rather a value that, being inherent in reason, regulates the rational activity of setting ends and choosing means to them. Specifically, it is a value inherent in reason that, if upheld, keeps one from setting ends the pursuit of which would denigrate one's own humanity or the humanity of others. And likewise it is a value inherent in reason that, if upheld, keeps one from choosing means the use of which would denigrate one's own humanity or that of others. In short, it regulates the activity of practical reason by guiding rational agents toward setting ends and choosing means that comport with the agent's value as an end in himself and the like value of those whose lives are touched by his actions.

Accordingly, Kant draws from his notion of humanity as an end in itself an alternative formulation of the Categorical Imperative: *Act in such a way that you always treat humanity, whether in your own person or the person of any other, never simply as a means but always at the same time as an end.*[3] Following a common practice in recent Kant scholarship, let us refer to this formulation as the formula of humanity and to the earlier formulation as the formula of universal law.[4] Kant means these to be different formulations of one and the same principle. He does not regard them as different principles. They are, in his view, alternative formulations of the fundamental principle of morality, the Categorical Imperative. It follows, then, that on his view, each formulation yields in every case the same result as the other. Thus, on his view, if you apply the formula of humanity to the situation in which you find a lost purse

---

[3] Ibid., p. 429.   [4] See above, p. 146.

containing a huge wad of cash in the bushes of a neighborhood park, you will come to the same conclusion as to what you ought to do as you would reach in applying the formula of universal law. And similarly if you apply the formula of humanity to the situation in which you happen upon a person in immediate need of help whom you can, thanks to your own prosperity, easily help, you will come to the same conclusion about what you ought to do as you would reach in applying the formula of universal law.

Kant's view may seem surprising, even untenable. How could a principle predicated on the idea of universal law be identical to a principle predicated on the idea of humanity or rational nature as an end in itself? Neither idea implies the other. They are wholly independent of each other. So why aren't the two formulations similarly independent? And if they are, then in what sense can they be formulations of one and the same principle? In the strictest sense, of course, they cannot be, for two principles cannot be identical if the concepts that constitute each are different from those that constitute the other. Presumably, Kant would agree, for he clearly does not mean that the two formulations are synonymous. That is, he does not mean that they are formulations of the same principle in the sense that to for-mulate Euclid's parallel postulate as a postulate about there being, with respect to a line l in a plane p and a point r also in p but not lying in l, one and only one line in p that both contains r and is parallel to l and to formulate it as a postulate about there being with respect to l and r only one line in p that contains r and contains no point intersecting l is to give two formulations of the same postulate. So it must be in some looser sense that he means that they are the same. The most likely possibility is that he conceives of the two formulations as equivalent in that each yields the same conclusion as the other when applied to the same practical situation. Each then serves equally well as the fundamental principle of morality. Or in other words, taking morality to be founded on a single principle, one can take either to be that principle without it affecting one's judgments about where one's duties lie.

Some recent defenders of Kant's ethics reject even this weaker thesis about the relation between the two formulations of the Categorical Imperative. They deny that the two are equivalent. They hold, instead, that the formula of humanity, despite Kant's own view of the matter, is superior to the formula of universal law and in some situations yields results differing from the results one gets from applying the latter.

Because the CI procedure is not, as we saw, foolproof, because it produces false negatives, one attraction of this view is that it offers a reconstruction of Kant's ethics that avoids the problem of excessive formalism that these false negatives represent. For instance, one could very plausibly argue that if you apply the formula of humanity to the situation in which you are in danger of being the victim of a violent crime, you will not reach the conclusion that it is impermissible to carry a concealed handgun for the purpose of self-protection, since neither will you be using anyone as a means when you take such action nor will you be failing to treat anyone as an end. By contrast, when you apply the formula to the situation in which you find a lost purse containing a huge wad of cash, you will conclude that you may not keep the cash since to do so would be to ignore that the cash belongs to another and to treat its owner as merely a supplier of funds for your use. It would be to treat her, in other words, simply as a means. Similarly, when you apply the formula to the situation in which you happen upon someone in immediate need of help and are prosperous enough to be able to help, you will conclude that you ought to help since to deny someone in such distress help when you can easily provide it would be to fail to treat him as an end.

3. Is the formula of humanity an independent principle?

This modern view of Kant's ethics conceives of the formula of humanity as an independent principle for assessing maxims of action. In other words, on this view, it is understood to provide separate and distinct criteria for assessing maxims of action from those that the formula of universal law provides. This understanding plainly departs from Kant's own understanding of the relation between the two formulae. For it is clearly Kant's intention, in introducing the formula of humanity, to be developing a theoretical substructure to the formula of universal law. It is clear, that is, that he believes that there is a structure to moral thought in which the formula of humanity is at a deeper level than the formula of universal law and which his step into metaphysics is meant to uncover. So to conceive of the formula of humanity as an independent principle is to abandon Kant's own conception of it as a formula that undergirds the formula of universal law. One immediate worry, then, to which this departure from Kant's thought gives rise is that the criteria for assessing maxims of action that the formula provides are, when detached from those of the formula of universal law, too vague to yield definite conclusions in more than a few stock situations.

Their vagueness is due, on the one hand, to the obscurity of Kant's notion of an end in itself and, on the other, to its being largely indeterminate whether in one's actions one is treating someone simply as a means. What, for example, explains why you treat a news vendor as an end and not simply as a means when you buy a newspaper from him? How does this purchase differ from your buying the same paper from a machine, since in that case you are not treating the machine as an end and since in both cases the transaction may consist in little more than your giving up three quarters to the vendor or the machine and picking up a paper?

Suppose, as some would argue, that the reason why you treat the vendor as an end but not the machine is that your transaction with him involves mutual consent. The vendor's consent implies that your exchange with him satisfies some end of his, and your understanding that it does so is sufficient for denying that you treat him simply as a means. But now we must wonder about examples, like those of the gigolo and the gold digger, in which someone takes advantage of another's love without reciprocation. Because of the one-sidedness of the relationships in these examples, we describe them as ones in which one party simply uses the other. Thus a man who has no feelings for a woman but nonetheless takes advantage of her love by allowing her to pay the rent on his apartment, put him through dental school, buy him expensive gifts, and so forth is simply using her, we would say, and we would not withdraw this description even if we knew that she was not blind to his lack of feelings for her. Her consent to the arrangement, though it implies that it satisfies some end of hers and though he understands this, would still not alter our perception of him as simply using her as a means to his living a more comfortable life. But how, then, does the vendor's consent differ?

Nor is this conundrum the only problem with determining what counts as using another simply as a means. When a photojournalist takes photographs of people involved in events that are making news, war refugees, say, or protesters at a public demonstration, is he using his subjects simply as a means to reporting the news? It might seem so, especially since photojournalists seldom ask their subjects for consent and since some of the latter undoubtedly do not wish to be photographed. Yet Kant surely did not mean to condemn such actions (or their eighteenth-century counterparts) as contrary to moral law. Similar uncertainties arise with consideration of such actions as those of someone who is writing an unauthorized biography of a famous person for the purpose of making money from sales of the work or people who bet on sporting events like tennis matches for the sheer fun of it. Perhaps these are not examples of using people as a means in the sense that Kant meant, because in none of them is someone being manipulated by another into doing something he would not otherwise do. But if one cannot use someone as a means in Kant's sense unless one manipulates that person, then the typical actions of peeping Toms and malicious gossips will not be contrary to law according to the formula of humanity. And who would deny that a man who spies on his neighbor for the excitement of watching a stranger undress was using that neighbor simply as a means to gratifying his prurient interests?

There is, moreover, a further worry about the view of Kant's ethics on which the formula of humanity is conceived of as an independent principle. This worry is that such a view erases the difference between Kant's ethics and the ethics of the rational intuitionists. For unlike the formula of universal law, which one applies *through* the CI procedure, the formula of humanity taken by itself does not appear to be similarly embedded in a process of practical reason. There is no distinctive form of practical reason that it structures. Rather one applies it to the maxims of one's actions as one would apply any substantive principle, such as a principle that prescribes honesty and forbids deception or one that prescribes loyalty and forbids betrayal. In other words, the use of the formula to determine whether one may act on a given maxim entails no form of reasoning other than that of applying a general principle to a particular object or fact, and this form of reasoning is not peculiar to practical thought.

Perhaps those who have offered reconstructions of Kant's ethics on which the formula of humanity is independent of and superior to the formula of universal law would object to this point on the grounds that to determine whether someone is being treated as an end and not simply as a means, because it requires thinking about ends and means, must make use of the form of practical thought that means-to-ends reasoning entails. But applying the formula does not in fact require such reasoning, for Kant's notion of someone's being an end, his notion of humanity as an end in itself, does not, as we noted earlier, imply the ordinary notion of an end, and determining whether you are using someone simply as a means is not a matter of determining a means to an end but rather of determining whether there is anything more to your using someone as a means to an end than that you so use him. The upshot, then, of these recent attempts to reconstruct Kant's ethics appears to be not so much an improvement on Kant's ethics as a reversion to rational intuitionism.

How then shall we understand Kant's conception of the formula of humanity as depending on the formula of universal law? The answer to this question lies in how the formula of universal law enters into the way you determine whether you would be, in acting on a certain maxim, treating humanity in yourself or another as an end. For to treat humanity, either in yourself or another, as an end requires honoring the dictates of reason. This requirement follows from Kant's distinction between humanity and animality, a distinction reflected in his view of human beings as having a dual nature. Thus Kant identifies humanity with our rational nature and animality with our sensuous nature. So to treat humanity as an end is to treat the rational nature of human beings as such, and one treats man's rational nature as an end by honoring the dictates of reason. Plainly, then, one treats humanity in your own person as an end by acting only on those maxims that pass the two tests the CI procedure comprises, for to act on a maxim that failed one of these tests would be to disregard a dictate of reason in order to satisfy some natural desire or personal interest, and in doing so one would be subordinating one's humanity to one's animality, which is to say, failing to treat the former as an end. Similarly, one treats humanity in the person of another as an end by acting with respect to this person only on maxims that he would regard, if he were reasonable, as acceptable maxims to act on. And what determines whether a reasonable person would regard a maxim as acceptable is the CI procedure, for it represents the deliverances of reason on the permissibility of acting on the maxims to which it is applied, and a reasonable person is one whose judgments correspond to these deliverances.

Kant, it is worth noting, expressly makes it a condition of your not treating another simply as a means that the latter agree with your maxim.[5] At the same time, Kant clearly does not mean by agreement with a maxim consent to it. Criminals, he observes, do not as a rule consent to their punishment, yet it does not follow that a judge who imposes

---

[5] Kant, *Groundwork of the Metaphysics of Morals*, pp. 429–30.

punishment on a criminal who does not wish to be punished treats him simply as a means. The criminal does not consent, but having a rational nature, he is able to understand when punishment is just and lawful. He knows what justice and the law demand of those who commit crimes even if he does not exercise that knowledge at the time of his sentencing. He thus agrees with the maxim on which the judge acts in imposing punishment even if he refuses to acknowledge the judgment that demonstrates the agreement. Or as I put this point in the paragraph above, he would regard the maxim on which the judge acted as an acceptable maxim to act on, if he judged it reasonably. Hence, one can say that the judge treats him as an end and not simply as a means.

Generally speaking, then, you treat others as ends and not simply as means when you act on maxims that they, too, if they are reasonable in their judgments, would judge to be maxims on which it is permissible to act. Their possessing reason guarantees agreement with the maxim on which you act if it is a maxim on which it is permissible to act, for no matter who applies the CI procedure to the maxim the result will be the same. To treat others as ends and not simply as means requires therefore acting on maxims that fulfill the conditions of the formula of universal law. In this way you honor the humanity, the rational nature, of all with whom you deal.

4. The formula of autonomy and the kingdom of ends

During the course of his account of the formula of humanity, Kant notes that every person attributes absolute value to his or her own existence as a rational being. Everyone, that is, realizes that his or her powers of reason are to be honored as having value that nothing else matches. This recognition of the absolute value inherent in one's rational nature is subjective, Kant says, by which he means that one cannot appeal to it as proof of rational nature's absolute value. At the same time, Kant maintains that one's recognition of this value does not come through experience. In this respect it differs from the relative value one finds in objects of natural desire. One finds relative value in such objects upon experiencing them and thus seeing in the enjoyment this experience brings how these objects can contribute to one's happiness. Or alternatively, on the basis of a desire for some object, one projects onto the future such an experience and then infers from the resulting prospective enjoyment of the object how it can contribute to one's happiness. In either case the value is discovered through experience of the world and its impact on one's well-being. By contrast, Kant denies that the value of rational nature is discovered in any such experience of the world. Rather one sees it as the result of reflection on the limits that categorical imperatives place on the pursuit of the ends on which one has staked one's happiness. The limits reveal the authority of these imperatives. Hence, they reveal the authority of the principle, the formula of universal law, and the procedure that it defines and that yields them. The procedure being a form of practical reason, it follows that in the revelation of its authority the inherent value of one's rational nature is revealed as well. From these observations Kant draws the idea of reason's being the sole, authoritative source of categorical imperatives, which is to say, the maker of universal law. This idea is the most fundamental idea of his theory.

Kant, then, identifies it with a third formulation of the Categorical Imperative. This formulation, he declares, is a synthesis of the other two. It resembles the first more than the second, but unlike the first, it represents the universal law that one constructs out of one's maxim and accepts when the construction passes the two tests of the CI procedure as a law that one issues to oneself through an exercise of one's reason. And given Kant's identification of the will with reason,[6] the third formulation becomes: *Act only from a will that makes universal law through its maxims*.[7] The formulation expresses an ideal of self-government. It is the ideal of one's actions being governed exclusively by laws that one has given to oneself. It is, in other words, the ideal of being autonomous, of being an agent who is subject to no laws but those he himself has authored. Accordingly, Kant introduces the phrase 'autonomy of the will' to express the idea with which he identifies this formulation.[8] And the formulation itself is commonly known as the formula of autonomy.

In reaching this formula, Kant believes he has found the explanation of the motive to act lawfully, the motive of duty, as he sometimes calls it, from which lawful actions must spring if every such action has a rational basis. Lawful actions that lack a rational basis are possible when the laws are externally imposed on their subjects. Examples of externally imposed laws are laws that kings impose on their subjects and laws that colonial rulers

---

[6] Ibid., p. 412.   [7] Ibid., pp. 431–32.   [8] Ibid., p. 433.

impose on theirs. In these examples, the subjects require incentives to obey the law, particularly, in circumstances in which, without the incentives, they could advance their interests by disobeying but not by obeying. Or in other words, without these incentives, there is nothing to insure that someone subject to externally imposed laws will have in such circumstances a rational basis for obeying them. Specifically, without the incentives, the subject's being rational is no guarantee that his obeying the laws in such circumstances is not baseless. Matters are different, however, if the laws are self-imposed as the formula of autonomy requires. If they are self-imposed in this way, if they are laws that a person gives to himself by making his maxim a universal law, Kant argues, then there are no circumstances in which incentives are necessary for providing a rational basis to obey them. For such laws express a will formed by reason alone, and it is therefore unnecessary to suppose of a person whose will is so formed that he needs an incentive to act as the law requires. That it is his will is alone sufficient. It means that when he acts lawfully, he acts without regard to external influences and consequently, unlike actions that obey laws another has imposed on him, he acts on initiative that does not originate in the will of another. He acts, that is, from a motive that originates in his own will.

To help illuminate his idea of the autonomy of the will, Kant introduces the idea of a kingdom of ends. The former is the idea of the will of a rational agent as making, through its maxims, universal law. And the idea of a universal law made through such a maxim is the idea of a law to which every rational agent, insofar as he or she might disobey it, is subject.[9] Since the idea of the will of a rational agent making universal laws through its maxims applies to every rational agent, it is possible, then, to think of all rational agents as being joined together under laws made through the maxims of any one of them. And since the identity of the agent makes no difference to what laws would be made through his or her maxims, this thought is essentially the thought of all rational agents as members of a legislature that makes laws to which each is subject insofar as he or she might disobey them. It is the thought, in other words, of a community of all rational agents governed by laws that they give to themselves collectively.

---

[9] The qualification is necessary because Kant includes God in the category of rational agents along with human beings. God, unlike human beings, is not subject to law because he can never will to act contrary to law. Hence, while both God and man are makers of moral law, only human beings are subject to it.

Such a community is what Kant has in mind in speaking of a kingdom of ends. It is a kingdom, he says, in being "a systematic union of different rational beings under common laws."[10] And it is a kingdom of ends, because the laws join together different rational agents simply as ends in themselves and therefore without regard to their different identities or to the sort of personal ends they pursue in their lives. In short, it is a community whose laws are enacted by the members collectively and are such that the members through compliance with them treat each other as ends and never simply as means. When one acts from a will that regards itself as making universal law through its maxim, one acts as if one were a lawmaking member of such a community.

The idea of being a lawmaking member of a kingdom of ends appears to be Kant's version of the deontologists' ideal of living in fellowship with others as one's equals under the rule of law. For it, too, is an ideal of belonging to a community in which all men and women are equally subject to law and equally protected by it. Yet Kant, in constructing this ideal of egalitarian fellowship, goes further than his deontological predecessors in the natural-law tradition. For them equality within the fellowship meant that all were equally subjects of the law that governs and protects them. Kant, by contrast, made the fellowship explicitly democratic. In his version, all men and women are equally and collectively the makers of the laws that govern and protect them. Moreover, his ideal has an importantly different place in his theory than the corresponding ideal had in those earlier deontological theories.

The difference follows from the difference we noted earlier between Kant's conception of law and that of those earlier theories. On the earlier theories, recall, laws are instruments for maintaining peaceful and stable social relations. They are needed because human beings cannot live together peacefully without the imposition of a moral order on their society, and such an order is established when they command sufficient obedience from the society's members. More generally, they serve to promote the common good, and obedience to them, when not due to self-interested motives, such as fear of the punishment inflicted for disobedience, is due to motives of public spirit. Plainly, this conception of moral laws goes against Kant's conception of them as commanding obedience independently of any

---

[10] Kant, *Groundwork of the Metaphysics of Morals*, p. 433.

social benefits that obedience might bring. For Kant moral laws command obedience because reason requires unconditionally that one act as they command. By so acting one fully realizes one's nature as a rational being. One acts as an autonomous agent and not as an agent whose behavior is subject to the arbitrary influences of natural desire and animal emotion. It is the full realization of one's rational nature, then, and not social peace or other benefits accruing to one's society, that for Kant explains the place of morality in human existence. And being a lawmaking member of a kingdom of ends is thus, in Kant's theory, only incidentally an ideal of living harmoniously with others as one's equals. Its principal place in the theory is to enrich our understanding of what it means fully to realize our rational nature.

5. Answering the charge of excessive formalism

The deeper theory of morality Kant expounds, beginning with his preliminary reflections on the value realized through acting lawfully, has the burden of answering the charge of excessive formalism that is commonly made against Kant's ethics. The answer the theory gives should now be evident. The value one realizes through acting lawfully is that of autonomy or the full realization of one's rational nature. Lawful action, in other words, is the same as autonomous action. Consequently, lawful action as such has a rational basis. For the laws obedience to which qualifies one's actions as lawful are laws that one gives to oneself, and such laws are in every case the enactments of practical reason. The charge of excessive formalism, then, according to this answer, represents an incomplete understanding of lawful action. When the charge is made, it is made against Kant's ethics as defined by the formula of universal law. Kant's deeper theory of morality is not considered. Hence, that the agent is the maker of the laws obedience to which qualifies his actions as lawful goes unrecognized. But once lawful action is understood to be the same as autonomous action, action through which one fully realizes one's rational nature, the seeming pointlessness of acting lawfully in the examples on which the charge is based disappears. So too does the charge. Or at least that is the answer Kant's theory gives.

What this answer implies is that we should not expect to find in Kant's deeper theory of morality a way to correct the application of the CI procedure in the cases that yield false negatives so that the procedure yields more acceptable conclusions. Rather, we should expect to get from the theory a defense of the conclusions the procedure delivers in those cases. That is, we should expect to get from it a defense of the conclusions that up to now we have described as false negatives. These are, in each case, a conclusion that to act on the maxim in question would be to act unlawfully. Specifically, each is the result of one's having determined, by applying the CI procedure, that the maxim is unfit to be made, through one's will, a universal law. Formally, its unfitness is seen in the contradiction one finds either in one's conception of the maxim as a universal law or in one's will when one regards it as becoming a universal law through one's will. But these formal criteria shed no light on why one should regard acting on it as wrong. They indicate only that reason is confounded when one considers whether the maxim can become through one's will a universal law. Hence, Kant's ethics appears excessively formalistic when one looks only to these criteria for explanation of why acting on this maxim is wrong. One must therefore look to the other formulations of the Categorical Imperative and the criteria by which they determine that the maxim is unfit for being made through one's will a universal law to see why acting on it is wrong. And in this regard, looking to the third formulation, the formula of autonomy, is particularly illuminating when its core idea of a will that regards itself as making law through its maxim is interpreted as that of being a lawmaking member of a kingdom of ends.

When the formula is so interpreted, its test for whether your maxim is fit to be made a universal law becomes whether you could, as a lawmaking member of a kingdom of ends, enact it as a law. All such enactments necessarily proceed without regard to anyone's identity or special interests, for lawmaking in a kingdom of ends must be impartial. If it were not, then there would be laws designed to work to the benefit of some and at the expense of others, and the existence of such laws is contrary to the ideal of a kingdom in which all, being ends in themselves, are always treated as such. After all, a law designed to benefit some at the expense of others could not be the product of the will of any of the latter, since whatever maxim was the basis of its enactment could not be one that any of them found reasonable. It would not satisfy the CI procedure. It follows that a maxim action on which would achieve its end only if the agent is alone or among a small number in so acting is unfit for enactment as a law in a kingdom ends. The reason is that the benefits of acting on this maxim cannot be shared by all who act on it should everyone choose to do so. Hence, because the benefits are available to those who act on it only if a limited number do so, it makes sense to act on the maxim only if one can be confident that enough people will refrain from so acting as to enable one to gain the benefit. In other words, it makes sense to act on the maxim only when one can take advantage of their refraining from acting on it. In taking this advantage, however, one would be treating oneself as different from others, and to do so would be inconsistent with the impartiality toward all that acting only on maxims that can be made laws in a kingdom of ends entails. The wrongfulness of the action, then, consists in the favoritism toward oneself implied in one's acting on a maxim that one could not will that everyone act on.

To illustrate the point, consider again the example of your carrying a handgun for protection in circumstances in which an increase in the incidence of violent crime in your neighborhood has made you concerned about going out at night. This action, as we noted before, makes sense as long as only relatively few people carry handguns, for if everyone carried one, the risk of your being harmed by violence would increase rather than decrease, notwithstanding the protection your carrying one provides. You would therefore be acting on a maxim whose end is achievable only if the number of people who act on it is limited, which is to say that the greater personal safety you would gain by acting on this maxim is not available to all who act on it should everyone do so.[11] By acting on this maxim, then, you would be advancing your interest in personal safety in a way that you could not will that everyone take advantage of. Consequently, you would be displaying an attitude of favoritism toward yourself since the action would express your willingness to seek a benefit for yourself that you would not will that everyone seek for him- or herself in the same way. Such an attitude is inconsistent with the impartiality toward all required of every lawmaking member of a kingdom of ends. It expresses, in Kant's view, a lack of respect for others as ends in themselves. Thus one can explain why the action is wrong in a way that is intuitively more satisfying than citing the failure of its maxim to satisfy the formal criteria necessary for it to become a universal law through the agent's will.

---

[11] For the statement of the maxim (N2) on which you would be acting, see above, p. 154.

6. Rationalism revisited

Of course, this explanation, though intuitively more satisfying, may still leave doubters. It will not convince everyone that it would be wrong for someone concerned about the rise of violent crime in his neighborhood to carry a handgun for protection. If you are among the unconvinced, then you might still think that Kant's ethics is unsound. And one reason why is that you think his account of morality is too austere. Morality, you might think, does not prohibit people from carrying handguns for protection in circumstances in which there is a heightened risk of their being victims of violent crime. And more generally, it does not require us to forgo advantages that come from actions that we know many people will not do and that are advantageous so long as this is true. Kant then, on this view, simply errs in holding the contrary. Nonetheless, you might still wonder whether this view is really sufficient to prove Kant's ethics unsound. If Kant's ideal of a kingdom of ends in which all rational beings are legislative members uncovers something about morality of which you were previously unaware, perhaps there is room to weigh the certitude with which you hold these moral convictions that contradict the conclusions of the CI procedure against the attractiveness of this ideal and its support for those conclusions. This possibility should seem especially strong if you have no competing ideal to which you could appeal to support and unify your convictions.

Be this as it may, there is a second reason why you might still think Kant's ethics is unsound. For not only are some of the conclusions the CI procedure yields contrary to common-sense judgments about what we are free to do and what we have a duty to do, they also imply that to act contrary to them is to act against reason, and the idea that a person acts unreasonably by, for example, carrying a handgun to protect himself from violent crime in circumstances in which such crime in his neighborhood is on the rise is, if anything, much harder to fathom than the idea that he violates a duty by so acting. What, after all, could be more rational than one's taking suitable means to achieving a reasonable personal end, an end on the achievement of which one has staked one's happiness? Accordingly, you may find, in questioning the credibility of Kant's bold thesis that obedience to moral law is essential to rational action, an even more powerful reason to think his ethics unsound. Indeed, this challenge to Kant's rationalism will prove to be the greater threat. Ultimately, as we will see, it reveals a serious gap in his system.

At the core of Kant's rationalism is the thesis that moral laws are categorical imperatives. What Kant understands by this is that obedience to moral law is obedience to an unconditional dictate of reason. The chief corollary of this is that one cannot disobey a moral law without going against reason. And this corollary is especially striking given Kant's austere conception of morality. For on that conception, as we've seen, a person who seeks advantages for himself by acting on a maxim that he cannot will that everyone act on is not only in breach of a moral duty but also acting unreasonably, and this latter proposition defies belief. To be sure, the person acts on a maxim that he can neither conceive of as a universal law nor will that it become one, but this observation only moves our skepticism about Kant's rationalism back one step. Why, after all, is it unreasonable to act on such a maxim? The problem is this. Whether or not the CI procedure correctly tracks the reasoning that yields conclusions about what our duties are, the question remains why rational deliberation requires that these conclusions supersede conclusions about how best to achieve our personal ends. They would, of course, if they were categorical imperatives, for reason requires that one follow a categorical imperative whenever its directive conflicts with the directive of some hypothetical imperative.[12] But one cannot credit the conclusions of the CI procedure with being categorical imperatives just in virtue of their being the conclusions of this procedure. For a categorical imperative is a dictate of reason, and as we've seen, neither the procedure nor the formula of universal law that the procedure implements alone provides a rational basis for following its conclusions. So to resolve the problem we need to look to Kant's deeper theory of morality. It is there

---

[12] Reason requires this because categorical imperatives are unconditional dictates of reason and hypothetical imperatives are conditional dictates of reason, the condition on which each dictates being the agent's having willed a certain end. Thus if the agent, in deliberating, sees that he cannot follow a hypothetical imperative without ignoring a categorical one, reason requires that he follow the latter. He must follow the latter, for in doing so he avoids violating either dictate of reason, which is to say he avoids acting against reason. Specifically, he does not violate the hypothetical imperative when he follows the categorical one but rather invalidates it by ceasing to will its validating end (i.e., the end the necessary means to which the imperative directs him to take). In effect, then, when he follows the categorical imperative, he removes the condition on which the hypothetical imperative is valid and so avoids violating it. Were he to follow the hypothetical imperative instead, he would violate the categorical imperative, which is to say, he would go against reason. Hence, reason prohibits him from following a hypothetical imperative when doing so means ignoring a categorical one.

that we find Kant's answer to the question of why rational deliberation requires that the conclusions of the CI procedure supersede conclusions about how best to achieve one's personal ends.

The answer would appear to fall directly out of a comparison of the rational bases for following the two types of imperative. Recall that the rational basis for following a categorical imperative is the value one realizes through acting lawfully. This is the value of acting autonomously, and being inherent in rational nature and therefore a value for every rational being, it is absolute and constant across different rational beings. In both respects it differs from the value that explains the rational basis for following a hypothetical imperative. This is the value of achieving the personal end the necessary means to which the imperative directs one to take. Achieving this end has value by virtue of its contribution to one's happiness, and therefore different actions and conditions have value for different people depending on the natural desires and personal interests whose satisfaction constitutes their happiness. Accordingly, the value of achieving a personal end is relative, and moreover its magnitude varies according to how great a contribution the achievement makes to one's happiness. Yet however great the achievement's contribution, its value, according to Kant, cannot be compared to the value of acting autonomously. To the contrary, the latter, being absolute, limits what one can do in pursuit of ends whose achievement has the former. There is, then, no basis for trade-offs between autonomy and the means for achieving one's personal ends. Rather one must choose the latter within the constraints set by the respect due the former. Conformity to categorical imperatives, in other words, constrains what hypothetical imperatives one can follow. And this constraint means that one cannot ignore a categorical imperative in order to follow a hypothetical one.

Plainly, Kant in this answer rests his conclusion on his distinction between the absolute value of autonomous action and the relative value of achieving a personal end. Yet the distinction cannot by itself support the conclusion. For the distinction does not imply that one type of value is superior to the other. It does not imply that an absolute value is superior to a relative one. Rather, to say that something has absolute value is to say that its having that value does not depend on the existence of anything contingently related to it, whereas to say that something has relative value is to say that its having that value depends on the existence of something that is contingently related to it. In the case at hand, autonomy has value and there are no conditions under which it could fail to have it. By contrast, achieving a personal end has value only so long as it satisfies some desire or interest the object of which is that end. For only then does it contribute to one's happiness. Hence, since the end's being the object of some desire or interest is a contingent relation, since it is possible, that is, for one to will an end without that end's being the object of any desire or interest, there are conditions under which the action could fail to have value. Specifically, if the desire or interest whose object is the end one has achieved did not exist and the end was not the object of some other desire or interest, then achieving the end would not have value. This possibility, however, though it explains why the value of autonomy is absolute and the value of achieving a personal end is relative, does not support regarding either value as superior to the other.[13] After all, while the achievement's having value depends on the existence of a desire or interest whose object is the end one has achieved, there is nothing in this dependence to imply that the value it has is inferior to the value of autonomy.

   Kant believes otherwise. The soaring language by which he characterizes the difference between the value of autonomy and that of achieving a personal end implies as much. Thus, having identified the idea of relative value with that of a price, he writes, "[T]hat which constitutes the sole condition under which anything can be an end in itself has not merely a relative value – that is, a price – but has an intrinsic value – that is, *dignity*."[14] And he further characterizes the dignity that ends in themselves have as "exalted above all price."[15] Similarly, he attributes to the mental attitude distinctive of autonomous action "an intrinsic worth … [that] puts it infinitely above all price, with which it cannot be brought into reckoning or comparison without, as it were, a profanation of its sanctity."[16] Finally, distinguishing human beings as free when the laws that govern their action are laws that they give to themselves and unfree when the laws that govern their action are the laws of nature that regulate the stimulation of their

---

[13] At one point Kant writes, "[I]f all value were conditioned – that is, contingent – then no supreme principle could be found for reason at all" (*Groundwork of the Metaphysics of Morals*, p. 429), from which one may be tempted to infer that the existence of absolute value implies that there is a supreme principle. But the inference in that case would be faulty, an instance of the fallacy known as denying the antecedent.

[14] Ibid., p. 435.   [15] Ibid., p. 434.   [16] Ibid., p. 435.

appetites and passions, he characterizes the lawmaking essential to this ideal of human freedom as having "a dignity – that is, an unconditioned and incomparable worth – for the appreciation of which, as necessarily given by a rational being, the word '*reverence*' is the only becoming expression. *Autonomy*," Kant concludes, "is therefore the ground of the dignity of human nature and of every rational being."[17]

But the distinction between dignity and price to which Kant appeals in these passages to capture the distinction between the value of autonomy and the value of achieving a personal end is a different one from the distinction between an absolute value and a relative one to which he first appealed in distinguishing the value of autonomy from the value of achieving a personal end. For the distinction between dignity and price includes a ranking of one value over the other, and as we already noted, nothing in the distinction between absolute and relative value supports taking one type as superior to the other. Consequently, the distinction between absolute and relative value does not support the thesis Kant intends when he attributes dignity to autonomous action and price to achieving a personal end. This is the thesis that the value of the former is incomparably superior to the value of the latter. And unfortunately for Kant, without it he cannot maintain that the conclusions of the CI procedure are categorical imperatives and so cannot maintain that ignoring any of them in order to follow a hypothetical imperative is never reasonable. His shift to the language of dignity, reverence, and infinite value helps, then, to obscure the gap in his argument for this conclusion. It does not close it.

What leads Kant to shift to this language? Why does he think he has shown that the value of autonomy is incomparably superior to the value of achieving personal ends? The answer must lie in his view of human beings as having a dual nature. At the same time, it should be evident that the duality of human nature alone is insufficient to explain why the value of autonomy is the superior value. At most it could explain why the two values are incommensurable. Their being incommensurable, however, merely means that comparing the worth of acting autonomously with the worth of achieving a personal end is like comparing the worth of a well-performed ballet with that of well-played violin concerto. While individuals will differ about which performance they prefer – ballet enthusiasts will prefer the

---

[17] Ibid., p. 436.

former, devotees of classical music the latter, there is no grounds for taking one performance to be superior to the other absolutely. So if the answer lies in Kant's view of human beings as having a dual nature, that view must involve more than the mere duality of our nature.

What more it involves is the chief doctrines of rationalism: that the sensuous aspect of human nature gives rise to motives of desire and emotion that conflict with motives originating in reason and that the values implied by the latter must be supreme in a human life else that life will be given to unreasonable pursuits of pleasure and unreasonable abandonments of morally worthy ends. For Kant, therefore, any conflict between a conclusion of the CI procedure and a hypothetical imperative that directs one to take necessary means to the achievement of a personal end can be understood as a conflict between reason and some desire or emotion that arises from the sensuous aspect of one's nature. At the same time, this understanding of such conflicts requires recourse to his deeper theory of morality to ground the CI procedure's conclusions in reason. But this grounding, as we have seen, is insufficient to support regarding them as superseding in deliberation any conclusion about how best to achieve a personal end and so superseding any hypothetical imperative that directs one to take the necessary means to such an end. So ultimately Kant must fall back on the very doctrines of rationalism his theory is meant to uphold to maintain that the conclusions of the CI procedure supersede in deliberation conclusions about how best to achieve one's personal ends. The doubts about the soundness of Kant's ethics that arise from resistance to the thesis that there is some defect in your reason if you choose to carry a handgun for protection despite its being contrary to the CI procedure reflect doubts about these rationalist doctrines. Kant's ethics, one could say, is a profoundly modern elaboration of the doctrines. But it falls short of vindicating them.

7. Personal autonomy

Part of the profundity of Kant's ethics is its use of the theme of self-government to explain morality's authority. To propose that men and women are the authors of the moral laws that govern their lives is to break completely from traditional conceptions of morality as externally imposed on human beings or as implanted in their frame by nature or some other external force. Seventeenth- and eighteenth-century political thought had produced various ideals of republican freedom according to which, on the one hand, no adult human being of sound mind and intact reason was subject by nature to the rule of any other man or woman and, on the other, political rulers, to whose authority men and women were subject, ruled by their consent. The most progressive strains in this thought not only founded the authority of governments on such consent but also made governments subject to democratic control. An ideal of popular sovereignty, then, came to represent the most forward-looking programs in the political philosophy of the late eighteenth century. And Kant's genius as a moral philosopher lay in his seizing on this ideal and extending it to morality. The kingdom of ends is nothing less than an ideal of popular sovereignty in which the people are all rational beings and the society over which they are sovereign is a fictional union of them. Thus Kant extended the spirit of emancipation from feudal and hierarchical social institutions that animated modern political thought to the fixed moral order that, on traditional conceptions of morality, structured the lives of human beings. Morality, on Kant's view, ceased to comprise standards whose authority one was subject to as a servant is subject to the authority of the master's rules or a trainee is subject to the authority of a trainer's regimen. Rather being the author of these standards, one obeyed them as one obeys one's own freely made decisions about how to act. Obedience to them, on this view, is a form of self-determination.

This idea that each person is the author of the moral standards that govern his or her life has had a powerful hold on philosophical thought even among Kant's sharpest critics. For one can reject his rationalism and the austere conception of morality that goes with it and still retain this idea. It is consistent, for instance, with the view that, faced with a choice between following a conclusion of the CI procedure that directs one to forgo advantages one could gain as long as few others did so as well and pursuing a personal end by taking those advantages, one does nothing wrong in choosing the latter. To choose the latter may require that one abandon the ideal of being a lawmaking member of a kingdom of ends, but one need not uphold this ideal to conceive of oneself as the author of the standards one follows. It is sufficient if one has freely, reflectively, and sincerely decided to live according to certain standards and not others. The point is that Kant's notion of the autonomy of the will is not the only notion of individual self-determination available to moral philosophers once they entertain the idea that the moral standards a person lives by are themselves determined by that person's own choices. And a number of such philosophers in the two centuries since Kant published his great works have realized this point and advanced alternative notions and a corresponding ethics of self-determination based on them. The term 'existentialism' is often used to refer to the movement of thought they represent, though Jean-Paul Sartre (1905–80) may well be the only major philosopher among them to have embraced the term. Nonetheless, I will follow this usage.

The starting point of existentialism is human thought. Unlike Kant, however, existentialists do not focus on the powers of reason in characterizing what is distinctive about human thought. Rather they focus on the powers of decision and choice. What makes these powers distinctive of human thought is that their exercise typically resolves matters presented to the mind. Someone, for instance, finds himself in a situation in which he hears screaming of an uncertain kind that is coming from a house nearby, and he must decide whether the screams he is hearing are those of a child in need of help or those of a child engaged in exuberant play. Similarly, someone finds himself in a situation in which, at a time when he is rather busy, he is asked by a stranger for assistance and offered payment in return, and he must decide whether the payment would be worth the time and effort that assisting the stranger requires. In these examples, the decision is about some matter in the world external to the thinker's mind that is presented to him, screaming in the first example, an offer from a stranger in the second, and he must decide how to resolve it because what is presented to him is ambiguous or uncertain. Resolution, in other words, depends on his judging on the basis of the evidence or considerations before him rather than on his merely responding to the force of the different images and sensations that the world impresses on his mind. While the latter may characterize how such ambiguity or uncertainty is resolved in the thought of nonhuman animals, the former is, arguably, distinctive of human thought. The famous plight of Buridan's ass, immobilized by being situated at equal distance from two equally large and equally appetizing piles of hay, illustrates the point.

This contrast highlights the difference between an active mind and a passive one. It is a major theme of existentialist thought that human beliefs are, far more often than is typically acknowledged, the product of the mind's being active in their formation, which is to say that human beliefs result, far more often than is typically acknowledged, from decisions like the ones in these examples. Recognizing that a belief one holds resulted from such a decision means also recognizing a certain degree of personal responsibility that one has for holding the belief. A second major theme of existentialist thought, then, is that men and women are far more responsible for many of the beliefs they hold and the states of mind that flow from them than is typically acknowledged. And because accepting responsibility implies assuming a kind of burden, which many people would prefer to avoid, a third major theme of existentialism is the flight from accepting this responsibility that is common to human life. The reason therefore why people seldom acknowledge the role of their own decisions in the formation of their beliefs is that they wish to be free of responsibility for those beliefs. This wish, in turn, gives rise to a strong tendency to regard their beliefs as formed in direct response to the sensations and images that impress their minds and other external forces with respect to which they are also passive. And some of the most celebrated existentialist writing consists of portrayals of the different ways people deny and hide from themselves their own complicity in the forming of beliefs central to their outlook on life.

In addition to decisions about matters in the world external to the thinker's mind, a person also makes decisions about matters internal to his mind. Someone, for instance, finds himself in a situation in which he feels threatened or anxious, and he must decide whether the object that is the source of his apprehensiveness is properly to be feared and shrunk from or faced with confidence and challenged. Similarly, someone finds himself in a situation in which he is invited to do something illicit, and troubled by his conscience, he must decide whether to listen to it and heed its warnings and reproaches or ignore it and act on whatever desires the illicit action appeals to. Or again someone faces a situation in which remaining loyal to a friend means jeopardizing a mission of national importance, and he must decide what matters to him more, friendship or the public good. In these examples, the decision is about some matter interior to the thinker's mind, what emotion to feel, what motive to act on, what most to care about, and he must decide how to resolve it because in each case it is a question of what sort of person to be, a question that, according to existentialism, is always and necessarily open. It is always and necessarily open, for human beings would not otherwise be capable of the kind individual self-determination that existentialism attributes to them. In short, they would not be capable of what I'll call *personal autonomy*.

The decisions in these examples represent exercises of personal autonomy. As such, they presuppose capacities for self-reflection and self-assessment. They are, therefore, if anything, even more indicative of distinctively human thought than the decisions in the earlier examples. The minds of nonhuman animals respond to the images and sensations presented to them, and these responses – the whetting of appetite, the stirring of emotion – define the significance of those images and sensations in animal life. What is distinctive of human minds are the capacities to take such responses and other mental states as objects of reflection and evaluation. For self-assessment consists in large part in the evaluation of the ends that define one's life pursuits and the motives predominant in how one lives one's life, and the evaluation of ends and motives is the evaluation of states of mind that contain one's purposes and move one to act. While a good watchdog responds with anger and prepares to attack when it sees a stranger trespass on the property it guards, the dog never reflects on this anger or wonders whether it is proper to feel it at the sight of a stranger. No watchdog has ever been known to decide to be more gentle in its disposition towards strangers, to greet them with a wag of its tail rather than a growl or a bark. Nor has any been known to have brought about such changes in its demeanor on its own. Human beings, by contrast, are capable of questioning their emotions and motives, assessing their importance, and deciding whether or not to maintain and act on them. This is the essence of their personal autonomy. And however reluctant people may be to exercise it, this capacity implies a far greater degree of responsibility for who they are than is typically acknowledged. This attribution of responsibility to human beings is at the core of existentialist ethics. And the three major themes of existentialist thought mentioned above extend to these decisions as well.

8. Existentialist ethics

When someone hears a child screaming and decides that the screaming is a cry for help, his decision can, at least in principle, be checked against the facts. And if, as a matter of fact, the screams he hears express the excitement of children at play and are not cries for help, then his decision is mistaken.

Similarly, when someone is asked for assistance and promised payment in return, his decision as to whether such assistance is worth the time and effort it entails can, at least in principle, be judged with respect to how well it fits in with the more general plans and values around which he has organized his life. And if, as a matter of fact, his assisting the stranger and receiving payment in return does more to thwart those plans and to betray those values than to forward and promote them, then his decision is a mistake.

By contrast, when someone finds himself in a situation in which remaining loyal to a friend will jeopardize a mission of national importance and he must decide whether friendship or the public good should ultimately matter more to him, there are no facts against which the decision can be checked. Some people in this situation would, no doubt, put patriotism ahead of friendship and choose to betray a friend in order to protect the mission. But there are, with equal certainty, others whose choice would correspond to E. M. Forster's memorable statement, "If I had to choose between betraying my country and betraying my friend, I hope I should have the guts to betray my country."[18] And one cannot say of those in either group that their decision is the correct one and that the decision of those in the other group is not. If the facts are the same in either case, then they do not resolve the question of which should matter more, loyalty to a friend or loyalty to country. It is up to the individual to decide.

Nor is there a standard that all who deliberate soundly must apply to the situation and that resolves this question. One's deliberation can, of course, be more or less sound, but the standards one applies in deliberating are not among the factors that make it sound. Rather what make it sound are the clarity and cogency of the thinking, the correctness of the understanding of the situation, and the sincerity with which some considerations are given more weight than others. Decisions like this one, then, decisions about what sort of person to be and by what values and principles one should lead one's life, while they may be more or less soundly made, are not of a kind that can still be wrong if soundly made. They are decisions in which the discretion to choose one way or the other is unbounded. They represent radical choices, choices for which there are no criteria of correctness beyond their resulting from sound deliberation. And the existentialist

---

[18] E. M. Forster, *Two Cheers for Democracy* (New York: Harcourt Brace, 1951), p. 68.

doctrine of radical choice is that occasions for making such choices are essential to human life, however much people may try to avoid acknowledging them. In making these choices one exercises one's capacity for personal autonomy, and in avoiding acknowledgment of an occasion for making a radical choice, one hides from oneself the fact of one's having this capacity. This doctrine challenges directly the very idea of an ethical theory. Indeed, it suggests that the enterprise of ethical theorizing is yet another stratagem for avoiding acknowledging one's capacity for autonomous choice.

Sartre, in a famous public lecture on existentialism, pressed this challenge to ethical theory with a detailed example of a student of his who, during World War II, while the Germans occupied France, came to him for advice.[19] The student yearned to join the Free French Forces in England. His older brother had been killed fighting the enemy during the 1940 invasion, and wanting to avenge his brother's death, the student felt the need to join in the struggle to rid his country of her Nazi overlords. At the same time, he was living alone with his mother, who had separated from his father because of the latter's inclination to collaborate with the enemy, and she was wholly dependent on him. His departure, he knew, would cause her enormous hardship, aggravating her grief over the loss of her eldest son and leading to crippling despair. What is more, realizing his aim of joining the Free French and advancing the cause of liberating France was only a remote possibility, given all that could interfere with his plans, whereas he was certain to be of help to his mother on a daily basis if he remained at home with her. This student's quandary, Sartre argued, demonstrates the futility of relying on ethical theories for help in deciding what one should do. The standard of neighbor love in Christian ethics, for example, is unhelpful; for it does not say whether neighbor love is shown more in acts of patriotism or in acts of filial duty. And Kant's formula of humanity is equally unhelpful and for similar reasons. Indeed, any theory, Sartre maintained, is bound to fall short of providing a satisfactory answer. It is merely a set of abstractions, and concrete situations like his student's necessarily outrun them. Ultimately, then, it is up to the student to decide which course of action is

---

[19] Jean-Paul Sartre, "L'existentialisme est un humanisme"; reprinted as "Existentialism Is a Humanism," Philip Mairet, trans., in *Existentialism from Dostoevsky to Sartre*, Walter Kaufmann, ed. (Cleveland: The World Publishing Co., 1956), pp. 287–311, esp. pp. 295–96.

the right one, and there is no way for him to determine this independently of his making that decision. As Sartre put it, the student does not find the right answer to the question of what he should do; he invents it.

This last point highlights the existentialist view of human beings as creators of the values by which they lead their lives. It captures their understanding of the capacity for personal autonomy, just as Kant's idea of one's being the maker of the moral laws that govern one's life captures his understanding of the autonomy of the will. And just as the latter yielded the idea of one's being a lawmaking member of a democratic republic whose citizenry was all rational beings, so the former yields the idea of a solitary artist who creates value through the artistic endeavors in which he or she engages. Sartre, in particular, finds the similarity between the artist's decisions and those of moral life ethically instructive. The point, however, is not to compare moral value to aesthetic value. Rather it is to compare the creative acts of artists, for which there is no question of their being responsible, to actions in human life that imply decisions concerning the sort of person to be or the things that should ultimately matter to one. By implication, then, a person who relies on doctrines and theories in ethics in deciding how to live is like someone who paints by the numbers or follows the instructions in a manual for would-be painters. In either case, the person avoids exercising his or her own distinctively creative powers and substitutes instead something mechanical or automatic. He does not want to acknowledge that what is done or what is put on the canvas is something of which he is the author and for which he is thereby responsible. He wants instead to shift responsibility to some external authority. He wants, that is, not to have the freedom he in fact has to decide how to live his life or what to display on the canvas before him.

Existentialist ethics takes this freedom, the capacity for personal autonomy, as the sole condition with respect to which actions are morally evaluated. The standard it applies, however, is not a universal standard of right action. Indeed, on existentialist ethics there are no such standards. The standard it applies, rather, concerns the self-understanding with which a person exercises this freedom in acting. It is the self-understanding of someone who wholly identifies with his actions. Such a person recognizes and accepts his actions as the products of his own decisions, which he understands in turn as resulting from his exercising his freedom. He understands, then, that he is the author of these actions and as such is responsible for them. In a word, it is a standard of integrity. One who meets it does not try to put distance between himself and his actions by regarding them, say, as caused by alien forces or compelled by external authorities. And he does not try to avoid responsibility for them by regarding his doing them as necessitated by his nature, his upbringing, or his place in society. Someone who does regard his actions in any of these ways, notwithstanding their having resulted from his deciding to do them or from his being passive in situations in which he could have so decided and acted accordingly, denies that he has the capacity for personal autonomy. He acts under a false view of himself as unfree, as having no choice in the matter. The self-understanding with which he acts is that of someone who deceives himself about his actions and his responsibility for them and therefore falls short of the standard of integrity by which the defenders of existentialist ethics evaluate the morality of actions. In Sartre's well-known expression, he acts in *bad faith*. In existentialist ethics, then, someone acts well when his or her actions display integrity. He or she acts badly when they are done in bad faith. And any other judgments about the morality of one's actions are a matter of personal decision.

Of what use is this ethics in answering questions about how one ought to live and what actions ought one to do in the conduct of one's life? How, for instance, does it help you to determine what to do in the situation in which you have found a lost purse containing a huge wad of cash? Plainly, you will not find in existentialist ethics an answer to the question of what to do in this situation. None of its doctrines generates for you a reason for returning the purse and the cash to its owner, nor does any of them generate for you a reason for doing something else. Instead, they bid you to see this situation as one of radical choice. It is a situation in which you must decide what sort of person to be and in which there are no facts determining what the correct decision is and no standard that you are required to apply in deliberating about what you should do. The only standard to be applied is that of integrity, and that standard does not enter your deliberations as a standard of right action. Rather it enters by calling on you to be conscious of the freedom you have to decide whether to be the sort of person who respects property and seeks to restore lost valuables you happen to find to their rightful owner or who disregards property and takes advantage of other people's losses.

Hence, a decision to keep the cash is a decision to be someone of the latter sort. If in making it, however, you try to justify keeping the cash on grounds that implicitly deny the freedom you have to be a different sort of person, then you fail to meet the existentialist standard of integrity. If you think, for instance, that your needs of the moment justify your keeping the cash or that you were destined to find it and to use it as you see fit or that it is a windfall and thus fairly kept by you, etc., you act in bad faith. If, by contrast, you recognize the decision to keep the cash as an exercise of your freedom, an exercise in which you freely choose to be someone who does not respect property and takes advantage of other people's losses and do not try to explain your choice as permitted or justified by extenuating circumstances or some special dispensation, then nothing in existentialist ethics speaks against your keeping it. It would be an unusual thief, to be sure, who had such integrity, but if what defines human beings as moral agents is a capacity for personal autonomy, then the possibility cannot be gainsaid.

9. The excesses of existentialism

Does attributing the capacity for personal autonomy to human beings have the striking implications for ethics that existentialism draws from it? Does the attribution imply, for instance, that there are no universal standards of right action? Does it imply that there are no values inherent in human life by which to evaluate the ends people pursue? These implications, if sound, would represent a powerful objection to ethical theory. But are they sound? A review of Sartre's arguments shows that he at least, in drawing these implications, overstates the existentialist case. Consider, first, his argument in criticism of ethical theory that he bases on the example of the student who was torn between joining the Free French Forces and looking after his mother. Sartre maintains that no ethical theory can resolve the student's quandary because the complexity of a concrete situation, such as the student's, exceeds what the abstract principles a theory consists of can comprehend. But the premiss of this argument is mistaken. Utilitarianism certainly has no difficulty comprehending the situation. Nor does Kant's ethics, despite Sartre's remarks to the contrary.

Utilitarianism has no difficulty because by design the principle it identifies as at the foundation of ethics, the Principle of Utility, comprehends all practical situations. This point should be obvious, since in any situation in which a person must decide what to do, no matter how complex it is, at least one of the actions open to him will satisfy the utilitarian standard of right action. At least one of them, that is, will bring about as much or more happiness overall than any of the other actions open to him. To be sure, complex situations like the student's present practical difficulties in carrying out the calculation necessary for determining which action satisfies the utilitarian standard. But these difficulties are no different in kind from the difficulties of making such a calculation in less complex circumstances. After all, one can never be certain of all the consequences of an action one contemplates doing, and these difficulties simply contribute to the uncertainty that is present in a situation. Sartre, then, though he has described a situation in which there is a great deal of uncertainty about the outcome of one of the courses of action a person is contemplating, has not described a situation to which the utilitarian standard is inapplicable. His student could still have applied it in trying to resolve his quandary, and while his assessment of the consequences of his following each course of action and their likelihood would be crude, his making a decision on the basis of that assessment, in accordance with the Principle of Utility, would give it theoretical support.

So too Kant's ethics has no difficulty comprehending the student's situation. This is because the complexity of the situation does not prevent the student from identifying either the maxim on which he would act if he opted for joining the Free French Forces or the maxim on which he would act if he opted for staying with his mother. Therefore it does not prevent him from determining whether either maxim satisfies the two tests that the CI procedure comprises. To be sure, applying the CI procedure to these maxims might still leave him undecided about which course of action to take, since both maxims may satisfy the two tests. But this is not a defect in Kant's ethics, for his theory is not designed to yield an answer to every question about what one ought to do. Rather the principle it identifies as at the foundation of ethics, the Categorical Imperative, determines whether acting on a certain maxim in a given situation is lawful, and in any situation there may be more than one maxim on which one could act lawfully, in which case the theory is silent on which maxim to act on. Thus Sartre is simply mistaken in thinking that Kant's ethics must be useless if it cannot resolve his student's quandary.

Of course, Sartre may think the student's situation is a crucial test of the adequacy of an ethical theory because the situation entails a conflict of obligations and he thinks the adequacy of an ethical theory depends on its ability to resolve such conflicts. But this thought, too, would be mistaken. We should not think that every conflict of obligation puts an ethical theory to the test. It does so only if the person faced with the conflict could act wrongly by fulfilling one of the conflicting obligations rather than the other, and not every conflict is like this. Sometimes the conflict is between two obligations that are specific forms of a more general obligation, and as long as you fulfill the more general obligation by fulfilling one of these specific forms, you do nothing wrong by disregarding the other. Those of us who are prosperous and healthy, for instance, have obligations to help the needy and to help the sick, yet we shouldn't expect a theory like Kant's to resolve any conflict we have between donating to a food bank and donating to a hospital. Donating to either would presumably be found lawful if the CI procedure were applied to the maxim on which we would act, for in so acting we would be fulfilling our obligation to contribute to the good of the less fortunate. Consequently, there would be nothing further for a theory like Kant's to say. And if the situation Sartre's student faced is similarly one of conflicting obligations either of which the student could fulfill without acting wrongly, then the situation does not provide a test of the theory's adequacy.

Sartre's argument fails, then, to show that ethical theories are incapable of providing guidance in complex situations. There is, however, a different criticism of them he could have made. He could have criticized them as falsely offering us safe havens from having to make radical choices. This is the signature criticism of ethical theories that is implicit in existentialist ethics. And indeed, Sartre, in considering the possibility that his student could resolve his quandary by consulting a priest, makes just this criticism of moral expertise. Thus he observes that the student, were he to seek guidance from a priest, would first have to choose his advisor, and this decision is both as much up to him and as determinate of what he will do as his deciding the matter directly. He cannot, in other words, avoid having to exercise his freedom by turning the decision over to someone else. For as Sartre points out, different priests would give different advice, and inasmuch as the student would choose an advisor in view of that person's faith, principles, temperament, and sensibilities, he would decide what kind of advice he would get. Choosing someone to be one's advisor on such a weighty personal matter is itself a reflection of one's values and principles and is therefore no less radical a choice than the choice of what action to take.

The same points, existentialists should argue, apply *mutatis mutandis* to using an ethical theory to determine what one should do. For different theories give you different answers to this question, depending on the circumstances you face, and inasmuch as in deciding to consult one theory rather than another you choose a system of thought in view of the values and principles it elaborates, you decide what kind of answer you will get. Because each theory, as we have already noted in the several we have examined, implies a different moral ideal, a decision to consult one theory rather than another is a choice of an ideal of human life by which to live. Choosing this ideal implies an aspiration to be a person of a certain sort. So it, too, represents a radical choice. And to think otherwise, to think that your decision to use a particular theory is correct because it squares with the facts of your situation or brings to bear on the matter at hand standards that no sound deliberation on that matter can ignore, is to deny your freedom by supposing that the matter is to be decided by inescapable facts and standards. From the viewpoint of existentialism, it is to choose in bad faith. This is the criticism of ethical theories that is proper to existentialist ethics. Sartre's criticism, by treating the example of the student as showing that ethical theories are necessarily too weak to provide useful guidance in complex concrete situations, goes too far. In making it, he misreads the import of his own example.

What of his further point that a radical choice does not follow from the chooser's seeing the values that he should pursue but rather acting on a radical choice creates the values that define his pursuit? Here, too, Sartre appears to have misread the import of his example. This is evident from the very fact of the student's being in an ethical quandary. He is torn between fighting for the Free French Forces and looking after his mother. Yet he would not be torn in this way if he didn't see value in both options. His quandary consists in his being unable to decide between two courses of action of whose values he has no doubt, patriotism and filial devotion. It does not consist in his being unable to decide on a course of action that will, as a result of his choosing it, have value. That condition would be better captured in an example of someone in despair about life, someone who sees no value in anything he might do in life. Such a person might well be advised to choose an activity in which he can immerse himself, even if he sees no value in it, as a way of eventually coming to see value in things. But such advice would be offered as therapy for someone who had fallen into a funk and needs a means to escape it. It is not the sort of direction one gives to someone who, like Sartre's student, faces a situation in which he sees value in each of two or more actions open to him and is conflicted about which to pursue. The latter situation is a typical occasion for exercising personal autonomy. Yet Sartre, it would seem, thinks that one's integrity is compromised if one chooses a course of action in view of the value one sees in it, and this is surely a mistake. For a person who sees value in a course of action is not compelled to pursue it. He is still free to turn away. In choosing to pursue it, he affirms or embraces the value. He does not create it.

Some existentialist writers, notably Albert Camus (1913–60), have in effect proposed that acting with integrity requires taking up the perspective of despair about life and choosing from it the values and principles by which one will live. Only by first regarding the world as valueless and absurd and then committing oneself to action from such a perspective does one take full responsibility for one's choices and actions, so these writers maintain, and anything less than taking full responsibility for one's choices and actions is a loss of integrity. But this thought, too, is a philosophical extravagance, similar, I suspect, to Descartes's conceit that to attain knowledge he had to start from a position in which he had no beliefs and find a cornerstone from which to build a solid body of them. Even the person in despair about life, although he cannot see value in anything, still has beliefs about values. He knows, for instance, the difference between a boxing match and a barroom brawl, or between the performance of a symphony and the clamoring of taxi horns on a crowded New York City street. He can recognize the event in the former of each of these pairs as a human activity organized to exhibit something of value when it is done well, athleticism in the one case, music in the other. And thus, he understands, if only tacitly, how cultures, traditions, customs, and the like are the substrata of different values in human life. So if Camus is proposing that integrity requires our making radical choices from the perspective of despair about life, he is not proposing that we suspend all belief about value in making these choices. But in that case it is a mystery as to why he thinks choosing from such a perspective is necessary for choosing with integrity.

Alternatively, he is proposing that integrity requires our making radical choices from a perspective in which, not only does nothing appear to us to have value, but all of our beliefs about value are suspended. That is, we must suppose that in making these choices not only do we not see any value in the different things we could do or make but we also do not believe there is a difference between human action and production that can be done well and the movements and products of random or purposeless human behavior. Not only do we not see any value in music that we might produce, say, or gymnastics that we might engage in, but we do not believe there is a difference between music and mere noise or gymnastics and the movements of an epileptic during a seizure. On this proposal, it is by virtue of a radical choice to do something or make something that what one does or makes has value. One invests it with value, so to speak, by the sheer act of one's will in choosing to do or make it. Thus, if a person chooses to devote his life to driving a car down busy New York City streets and repeatedly honking its horn, he gives value to the activity and to the noise he thereby creates. In this case, then, there is no mystery as to why Camus thinks choosing from such a perspective is necessary for choosing with integrity. For he must think that choosing and acting with integrity means taking responsibility not only for the action one chooses but also for its having value, and one could not be responsible for its having value unless the value were a product of one's will. But if this is Camus's proposal, then it is false if not incoherent.

Someone who chooses to play the violin, for example, can decide either to play it well, if he knows how, and produce music, or to play it badly and produce mere noise. But if he does the latter, he cannot make it the case, no matter his intentions, that he is playing the violin well. He cannot make it the case that the mere noise he makes has value. Though what he produces, music or noise, is up to him, whether or not it has value is not. Similarly, while he can choose to drive a car down a busy New York City street and repeatedly honk its horn, his doing so does not give the sounds he creates value. Honking a car horn for the purpose of warning pedestrians or other drivers is something one can do well or badly according as it is done in a way that augurs success or failure. The sounds one makes in that case can have value as a means of warning others. But honking the horn for its own sake is not something that can be done well or badly, and correspondingly the sound one makes in this case cannot have value in and of itself. To think otherwise, to think that one can give such horn honking value simply by choosing to do it, is somewhat like Humpty Dumpty's belief, in *Through the Looking Glass*, that the words he speaks can have whatever meaning he chooses to give them simply by virtue of his so choosing.[20] The impossibility of this belief is transparent. While one can choose what words one speaks, one cannot choose what they mean. Camus's proposal, on this second construction of it, is similarly impossible.

10. Existentialist ethics pruned of excess

What, then, is left of existentialist ethics once one removes its excesses? At its core there is the doctrine of radical choice. This doctrine, when understood apart from the faulty lessons about ethical theories and the origin of values that existentialists tend to draw from it, is the view that certain decisions, decisions about what sort of person to be and by what values and principles to lead one's life, cannot be wrong if the thinking from which they follow is clear and cogent, if they are based on a correct understanding of the facts of one's situation, and if one is sincere in the way one weighs the different considerations that bear on them. This is a not an implausible view. Nor is it trivial. For it contradicts the belief that some ends in life and some principles of right conduct are not optional if one is a rational agent. To decline to pursue the former or comply with the latter, according to the philosophers who hold this belief, goes against reason. One thing that remains, then, is a powerful thesis about the limited scope of practical reason. On this thesis, to exercise practical reason is to determine means to some end and not to determine an end whose achievement is not also a means to some further end. Or as Aristotle put it, deliberation is of means only.[21]

At the same time, existentialist ethics assumes that one's ultimate ends are themselves an object of choice. It thus rejects the conception of human action Aristotle assumed in asserting his thesis. For in asserting it, Aristotle meant to be observing that people do not choose the ultimate ends of their actions. To the contrary, he held that every human action has the agent's well-being as its ultimate end.[22] Hence, choice must always be choice of a means to this end. This view plainly contradicts the doctrine of radical choice. Existentialist ethics, in attributing personal autonomy to human beings, takes determination of the ultimate ends of one's actions to be a

---

[20] Lewis Carroll, *Through the Looking Glass (and What Alice Found There)*, ch. 6.
[21] Aristotle, *Nicomachean Ethics*, 1112b11–12.   [22] Ibid. 1095a13–20.

matter for the agent to decide. The ultimate ends of one's actions are thus optional in the sense of its being open to a rational agent, consistent with his being rational, to choose what his final ends are. In other words, there are no ends he must pursue as a condition of his being rational.

Existentialist ethics, then, once one removes its excesses, consists of two theses. One is a thesis about personal autonomy: that there is no end (such as one's own well-being) whose pursuit as an ultimate end in one's life is a condition of one's being rational. The other is the thesis about practical reason's limited scope: exercises of practical reason are limited to determinations of means to one's ends. This pair of theses, even though lacking the audacity of the views from which it descends, constitutes nonetheless a significant view within contemporary ethics. Other views, corresponding to the teleological and deontological theories of ethics that moral philosophers have expounded, take human rationality or practical reason as fixing the ultimate ends men and women ought to pursue in life or determining the principles they ought to follow in pursuit of the ends around which they have organized their lives. Each of these theories yields a moral ideal whose realization gives meaning to their pursuing those ends and complying with those principles. Existentialist ethics, by contrast, treats all such moral ideals as objects of choice similar in this respect to other ideals of human existence that a person might choose as a model of how to live. Neither human rationality nor practical reason fixes or dictates which is to be chosen. The choice rather is a radical one. Ethical theories then become guides to realizing a moral ideal, and one comes to accept an ethical theory as a result of having embraced the moral ideal it yields rather than having decided that it represents the soundest account of morality. Existentialist ethics can thus acknowledge a role for ethical theory in an autonomous life, though it is not the traditional role of systematizing morality and supplying the grounds on which its standards are rationally justified. The challenge it represents to traditional ethics is a challenge to the very idea of morality as the subject of a philosophical study whose aim is to formulate its basic standards and to determine the rational grounds of their authority to govern our lives.

7   Practical reason

1. Meta-ethics

Our study of different ethical theories began with reflection on a hypothetical question about whether you would have good reason to do the
honest thing if you found a lost purse containing a huge wad of cash. The
question generated an inquiry into the rational basis of the standards of
honesty and justice. These standards, and standards of morality generally,
appear to have an authority in our lives superior to that of the conventional
standards embedded in local social practice. For one thing, they appear to
have such authority because we measure our local social practices and the
conventional standards embedded in them against standards of justice and
morality. For another, we commonly praise and honor those who resist
conforming to conventional standards when those standards create privileges for some and hardships for others that are unjustly enjoyed and borne.
This is especially true where such resistance carries personal costs like
ridicule, ostracism, or worse. Huck Finn's actions in helping Jim in his
attempt to escape slavery are exemplary. The assumption of our inquiry,
then, has been that the authority of the standards that morality comprises is
founded on reason and truth and not on mere custom or prejudice.
Otherwise it would be hard to explain its superiority. Accordingly, we
have treated the different ethical theories we surveyed, up to existentialist
ethics, as systems of thought constructed to confirm this assumption. As
such, they represent competing accounts of morality as comprising standards of conduct and character whose authority has rational foundations.

Existentialist ethics is different, however. It does not offer such an
account. To the contrary, its doctrine of radical choice opposes the assumption of the inquiry in which we have been engaged and which has produced
such accounts. It is not hard to see why. The doctrine derives from a conception of individual self-determination according to which each of us, as

individuals, is the final authority on questions about what sort of person to be and by what values and principles to guide our lives. On this conception there are no criteria by which to assess someone's answers to these questions as right or wrong independent of the sincerity of those answers and the soundness of the deliberations that yield them. Each person alone determines the actions it is imperative for him to do. Were he to look instead to external standards in deciding what to do, standards he regarded as authoritative independently of his own decision to follow them, he would be denying the very freedom he has to decide how to live. He would be denying his own autonomy. Implicitly, then, existentialist ethics denies that morality comprises standards of conduct and character whose authority is founded on reason and truth. Rather it holds that such standards have authority in a person's life only by virtue of the person's sincerely deciding to live his life by them. Consequently, according to existentialism, inquiries in ethics into the rational basis of the authority these standards have, inquiries of the kind with which our study began, are essentially mistaken.

The opposition of the doctrine of radical choice to the assumption on which traditional inquiries in ethics proceed presents us with questions of a new kind. Does our capacity for personal autonomy imply that no answer to a question about what it is right to do or what one ought to do is ever true independently of our attitudes towards the different actions we can do? Are disagreements about whether an action is right or ought to be done resolvable, at least in principle, through consideration of the relevant facts and what they imply? And is universal knowledge of right and wrong possible? What makes questions like these different from questions of right and wrong that arise in the course of everyday life and that lead, when we reflect on them, into ethical inquiry is that they turn the very project of ethical inquiry into an object of study. Accordingly, they introduce a higher level of inquiry. Each asks something about the very nature of the everyday questions of right and wrong – what I will refer to as *the ground-level questions of ethics* – with which traditional ethics is concerned. Thus the first asks, in effect, whether these ground-level questions of ethics admit of objectively true answers given human freedom. The second asks whether there is a rational procedure or method by which disputes over such questions can, given enough time and factual knowledge, be resolved. And the third asks whether answers to them could ever qualify as human knowledge. Other higher-level questions one might ask are whether ground-level questions of ethics are essentially different from questions of natural science and whether one's answers to them, if sincere, entail some disposition of one's will. These and similar higher-level questions define the field of meta-ethics.

Ground-level questions of ethics include not only questions about right and wrong but also questions about values. We want to know not only whether one ought always to do the honest thing in circumstances in which dishonesty would be more profitable but also whether anything has value in itself besides pleasure and freedom from pain, whether, for instance, human life would still be of infinite value, as we say, if it excluded experiences of pleasure and pain. Such questions about values are also the objects of meta-ethical inquiry. Typically those engaged in such inquiry do not distinguish between these two kinds of ground-level question. Typically, that is, they ask the same higher-level questions about both kinds. Nonetheless, it is useful to distinguish between them, for the considerations that bear on how the higher-level questions are answered may differ according to whether one asks them about ground-level questions concerning right and wrong or ground-level questions concerning values. In particular, while the doctrine of radical choice bears on how one answers higher-level questions about the former, it has no bearing on how one answers the same questions when asked about the latter. It has no bearing because the freedom the doctrine affirms, while it entails the freedom to decide whether to pursue some values and ignore others, does not entail freedom to decide what has value and what does not. While it calls the authority of moral standards into question, it yields no such consequence for the reality of values. Failure to appreciate this, as we saw, led existentialist thinkers like Camus grossly to overstate the implications of their ideas about human freedom.

Accordingly, we need to limit our examination of the challenge to traditional ethical inquiry that the doctrine presents to meta-ethical questions as they concern ground-level questions about right and wrong. Let us call the answers to these ground-level questions *normative statements* or *directives*. They are to be distinguished, then, from the answers to ground-level questions about values, which I'll call *evaluative statements* or *valuations*. It will also be useful to expand the class of normative statements to include directives that are not answers to questions about right and wrong, that is, what morality requires and prohibits, but rather are answers to questions about personal and practical matters. Accordingly, the class of normative statements includes all hypothetical imperatives, in Kant's sense, as well as any that are categorical. It includes as well ordinary pieces of advice such as "You should buy the tickets now; the show will be sold out soon" and "You ought to keep a flashlight in the car in case of emergencies."

The advantage of expanding the class of normative statements to include all hypothetical imperatives and other pieces of practical advice that do not concern moral matters is that the conditions under which such directives are valid imperatives or sound bits of advice are evident. They therefore represent either a good model for understanding the conditions under which directives that concern moral matters are true or a good contrast class – as Kant saw – for the same purpose. In general, normative statements are meant to guide the choices and actions of the people to whom they are addressed. If the statements are true, then they offer those to whom they are addressed reason to choose to act as they direct. In other words, their being true implies that one could come to this choice on the basis of sound deliberation. Hence, we can formulate the challenge that the doctrine of radical choice presents to traditional ethical inquiry as a challenge to the thesis that some choices and actions are the outcome of deliberations that would be sound no matter who the deliberator was or what his or her personal feelings or attitudes were. In short, it is a challenge to the idea of universal truths of practical reason, true normative statements that apply to every rational agent.

2. Meta-ethical disputes: an illustration

One answer to this challenge is to deny that human beings have freedom of the kind that the doctrine of radical choice implies. If you accept psychological egoism as Hobbes did, and hold that all voluntary actions are self-interested, that the aim of every voluntary action a person takes is to advance his interests,[1] then you deny that people have this freedom. For in agreeing with Hobbes, you are agreeing that no one can voluntarily act contrary to his or her own interests, and if people have the kind of freedom the doctrine of radical choice implies, then they can deliberately choose to do something that hurts their interests and to act on that choice.

---

[1] Hobbes, *Leviathan*, ch. 14, par. 8.

This implication of accepting psychological egoism carries over, then, to the opposition between Hobbes's thesis that the laws of nature are true directives applying to all rational agents and the existentialists' skepticism about there being such directives. For if you accept psychological egoism, then you believe with Hobbes, at least implicitly, that there are such directives. The reason is clear, as Hobbes explained. People have as their primary interests the necessities of life: food, shelter, clothing, mobility, safety, and the like, and in some situations, some actions will be more conducive to securing those interests than others. Accordingly, directives to do the former rather than the latter in those situations will be true and apply to all rational agents. The brilliance of Hobbes's ethics lies, then, in the arguments he made to show that the basic standards of right and wrong, such as those of honesty, gratitude, and fairness, qualify as directives of this sort. Their brilliance notwithstanding, however, the arguments have no force if one accepts the doctrine of radical choice. Since, according to this doctrine, a rational agent need not take his own interests as an end to be pursued, the basic standards of right and wrong need not apply to every rational agent.

The lesson in this clash of meta-ethical views is twofold. First, Hobbes's program of deriving basic standards of right and wrong from the fundamental principle of egoism is a good example of a program in ethics that takes sound pieces of personal advice as a model for understanding the conditions under which directives that concern matters of right and wrong are true. On this model, if you know a person's aims and do not think they are contrary to his interests, then sound advice consists in a directive to do what is necessary or most conducive to his realizing those aims. If a friend, say, who wants to visit a foreign country and knows nothing about traveling abroad comes to you for advice, one piece of sound advice you could give him is that he ought to get a passport. This would be sound advice, a true directive, since his aim is to visit a foreign country and having a passport is necessary for achieving that aim safely.[2] Hobbes's program, in effect, generalizes on this model. It starts with very general aims that Hobbes attributes to all human beings – those of securing for oneself the necessities of life – and then offers arguments to show that following fundamental standards of right

[2] On Kant's account of hypothetical imperatives, "You ought to get a passport" is a valid hypothetical imperative for someone whose end is to visit legally a foreign country, for having a passport is a necessary means to legal travel to another country.

and wrong is necessary for achieving these aims. Fittingly, then, in Hobbes's terms, these standards are to be taken as counsels rather than commands.[3]

Second, the opposition between Hobbes's program and the existentialists' skepticism about true directives applying to all rational agents is an instance of a general opposition between such skepticism and teleological theories of ethics that are premised on doctrines, like psychological egoism, that restrict the motives on which humans act to those of a certain kind or restrict the ends that humans pursue to those of a certain character. All teleological theories of this kind explain the truth of directives about matters of right and wrong on the model of sound advice. All take such directives as hypothetical imperatives whose validity rests on the attribution of certain motives or ends to every man or woman and in the correlative thesis that these at bottom are the only motives or ends in the agent's psychology. Each then answers the challenge that the doctrine of radical choice presents to traditional ethical inquiry by denying that human beings have freedom of the kind that the doctrine implies. The most influential of these teleological theories is Aristotle's eudaimonism. Among such theories, it offers, perhaps, the strongest opposition to the doctrine, and for this reason its answer to the doctrine merits careful study.

3. Aristotle's answer and an existentialist response

Aristotle held that the final end of every action is the actor's well-being. No one, on his view, can aim to make his own life worse or to bring harm overall upon himself. Hence, it is not, on this view, open to people to choose a life of misery or to seek their own ruin. It is no more open to them to choose such a life or to seek such an outcome than it is open to them to choose immortality or to seek to live the life of a blue jay. Of course, the limits to what humans can choose or seek in these latter cases are due to our nature as physical and biological beings, and no adherent to the doctrine of radical choice disputes the existence of such limits. In the former cases, by contrast, the limits, if they exist, are due to our nature as rational beings, and adherents to the doctrine dispute any view that takes human rationality to be the source of such limits. Aristotle's view, in other words, yields limits on human freedom that are contrary to what the doctrine implies.

---

[3] See p. 128 above and Hobbes, *Leviathan*, ch. 15, par. 41.

Few contemporary philosophers, however, accept Aristotle's view. Most allow, as at least tenable in an ethical theory, that it represents morality as requiring people in some circumstances to sacrifice their own well-being for the greater good or for the cause of justice, and such a theory would be untenable if it were impossible for people intentionally to act against their own good.[4] In addition, studies in literature, psychiatry, and clinical psychology of men and women driven by self-destructive or self-belittling motives have persuaded most contemporary philosophers to abandon the view of human beings as always and necessarily striving to better their lives and promote their own good. Indeed, one such study, Fyodor Dostoyevsky's novella *Notes from Underground*, is among the most important sources of existentialist thought. Its protagonist, a former lowly official in the Russian civil service, recounts, as if writing in a diary, the many times he deliberately acted contrary to his best interests. He relishes, it seems, telling of how he often acted out of spite to get revenge on those who had annoyed him and of his tendency to court humiliation and suffering. "Sometimes," he declares, "a man is intensely, even passionately attached to suffering – this is a fact. About this there is no need to consult universal history: ask yourself if you are a man and have ever lived even in some degree. As for my own personal opinion, I find it somehow unseemly to love only well-being. Whether it's a good thing or a bad thing, smashing things is also sometimes very pleasant."[5] This compelling portrait of a small-minded and mean-spirited contrarian, a

---

[4] You might think Aristotle's ethics, being a version of Platonic eudaimonism, is not open to this objection. After all, on any version of Platonic eudaimonism, doing what morality requires and acting to advance one's well-being cannot come apart. But because Aristotle, unlike the Stoics, say, held that virtue does not guarantee that one will achieve the highest good, because he allows that a virtuous person is still vulnerable to tragic or grievous loss in life, there is still a question of whether, on his ethics, the two can come apart. Hence, to maintain, as he does, that all actions aim at the agent's well-being and so to keep them from coming apart, he must hold that to act shamefully always damages one's well-being more than suffering a great personal loss. And to maintain this thesis, it would seem, is too high a price to pay for keeping them from coming apart. Surely not every shameful act does worse damage to one's well-being than the most grievous and tragic of losses. If Agamemnon is required by morality to sacrifice his daughter to the gods, the loss he suffers from killing his own daughter may surely be a greater blow to his well-being than the disgrace he would have suffered if he had declined to make the sacrifice.

[5] Fyodor Dostoyevsky, *Notes from Underground/The Double*, J. Coulson, trans. (Harmondsworth, England: Penguin Books, 1972), p. 41.

not uncommon product, Dostoyevsky (1821–81) assures us, of nineteenth-century urban European life, confounds any view of human beings, Aristotle's included, as constant seekers of their own good and vigilant guardians of their well-being.

While Aristotle's view of human action as in every case having the agent's well-being as its final end now has few adherents, there is a weaker view that he also holds and that could serve, too, as a basis for denying that men and women have the kind of freedom the doctrine of radical choice implies. This weaker view enjoys much greater support among philosophers. Some may even see it as a piece of common sense. This, at any rate, is how Aristotle saw it. Thus book I of his *Nicomachean Ethics* opens with the statement that every action and every pursuit aims at some good.[6] Aristotle immediately and problematically infers from this statement that there is some good at which all actions and pursuits aim, and this inference is what leads him to the stronger view that the aim of every human action and pursuit is the actor's own well-being. But one need not follow Aristotle in making this inference in order to find in his account of human action ammunition with which one can attack the doctrine of radical choice. The statement with which book I of the *Nicomachean Ethics* opens alone provides it. For it entails that a person cannot choose as a final end of action a condition or activity that he regards as either without value or positively bad. It places, in other words, limits on human freedom of a kind that is contrary to what the doctrine of radical choice implies.

Nor should there be any doubt that those who advance this doctrine would see the opening statement of book I of the *Nicomachean Ethics* as antithetical to their understanding of our capacity for personal autonomy. They would see it, that is, as expressing a view someone might hold unreflectively because the idea of a person's choosing to be an enemy of what is good is beyond the grasp of conventional thought. Or perhaps they would see it as expressing a view someone might hold defensively as a way to hide from himself possibilities too unsettling to be faced. In any case, they would maintain that the question of whether to be a friend or an enemy of what is good or merely a neutral party is one that a person can and should decide for himself or herself. The capacity for personal autonomy, though it does not, as I argued in the last chapter, include the

---

[6] Aristotle, *Nicomachean Ethics*, 1094a1–3.

capacity to determine what is good, includes at least this much. And the person who thinks he is bound to pursue only that which he sees as good is not yet, they would argue, fully exercising this capacity. He is not yet a self-determining agent.

Camus, for instance, sees the capacity in this way. Recall that the Archimedean point of his philosophy is the perspective from which the world appears absurd. It is the perspective of existential despair. Why, Camus wonders, once one has taken up this perspective, should one continue with one's life? This question, he thinks, the question of whether to commit suicide, is the first question of practical philosophy. When nothing in the world appears to matter, one must first find an answer to the question why go on.[7] And Camus treats the question as truly open. That is, he takes suicide to be an option a man who sees the world as absurd might actually choose, not because the man thinks he could achieve some good by ending his life, but because all of the other options available to him appear equally pointless. Hence, if the man were to choose to commit suicide, his ending his life would be an action whose end he did not see as good. It would therefore confound Aristotle's thesis that the end of every action or pursuit is something the agent sees as good. For Camus, then, the first question of practical philosophy defines, at least for those who confront it, a radical choice, a choice that Aristotle's ethics cannot comprehend.

Of course, the idea that suicide is something a person could deliberately commit on account of his seeing nothing worth doing in life may just be an existentialist conceit. It may represent nothing more than an abstract possibility. After all, it is one thing to have the idea of doing a certain action, and quite another to be able to bring oneself to do it. For one's being able to do an action in circumstances of the kind that call forth sufficient motive for doing it does not mean that one can do it in any circumstance in which there is nothing physically stopping one from doing it. Think, for instance, of deeply religious people who martyr themselves in protest like the Buddhist monks in Vietnam during the Diem regime who immolated themselves to protest the regime's persecution of Buddhists. That they could set fire to themselves in such circumstances does not mean that any of them could have brought himself to do the same thing in peaceful circumstances

---

[7] Albert Camus, "The Myth of Sisyphus," in *The Myth of Sisyphus and Other Essays*, J. O'Brien, trans. (New York: Vintage Books, 1955), p. 3.

when Buddhists had no complaints against their government. Nor, needless to say, does it mean that anyone who gets the idea of self-immolation from their martyrdom could walk out onto a public plaza, douse himself with gasoline, and set himself on fire. So too that there are circumstances that drive people to commit suicide privately does not mean that existential despair is one of them. Camus treats suicide as if it were a real choice that someone who came to an understanding and view of the world as a hopeless arena of meaningless phenomena might make, but his doing so may just reflect his overestimating the agential power of human beings to realize the ideas of actions they can contemplate doing. We should not therefore take Camus's treatment of suicide as a refutation of Aristotle's thesis that all actions aim at some good. What it does show is that rejection of the thesis is basic to his philosophy and that of like-minded existentialists.

4. Can there be motives that aim at doing evil for its own sake?

How then shall we resolve the opposition between the thesis with which the *Nicomachean Ethics* begins and the existentialists' doctrine of radical choice? Fortunately, its resolution may not require our deciding the question about human agential power that Camus's treatment of suicide raises. For that question is equivalent to the question of whether human action can ever be motiveless, and the thesis with which the *Nicomachean Ethics* begins, the thesis that every human action aims at some good, is stronger than the thesis that every human action springs from some motive. Hence, we can examine the soundness of the thesis by considering the possibility of a motive to act that does not imply that the actor is aiming at some good. If such a motive is possible, then the thesis is unsound, and we will therefore have removed the objection to the doctrine of radical choice that it yields without having to take up the question about human agential power that Camus's treatment of suicide raises.

For this purpose, let us consider a version of the thesis due to Thomas Aquinas (1224/5–74): whatever is desired is desired *sub ratione boni*, that is, under an aspect of goodness.[8] This version nicely reveals a source of equivocation in Aristotle's view. On the one hand, one may desire an object

---

[8] Aquinas, *Summa Theologica* I–II, q. 8, a. 1.

because one sees something good in it. That is, it is the object of one's desire because there is something good in it that one sees and one's seeing it excites the desire. On the other hand, one may see something good in an object because one desires it. That is, when one desires something, one finds the thought of one's having it in whatever way would satisfy that desire agreeable or pleasant, and if the thought of having something is agreeable or pleasant, then one is disposed to see that thing as good. Thus, in this case, too, the object is desired under an aspect of goodness. Since the end of an action is the attainment of the object of whatever desire is the motive of that action, Aristotle's thesis is equally equivocal. It may be true, on the one hand, because we act only from desires whose objects we desire because we see something good in them, or it may be true, on the other, because the desires from which we act provide the ends of our actions and we see something good in those ends because we desire the objects that constitute them.

The opposition between Aristotle's thesis and the doctrine of radical choice depends on which of these ways, if either, the thesis is true. The thesis stands in substantial opposition to the doctrine if it is true in virtue of our seeing something good in the objects of our desires independently of our desiring those objects. For in that case, because we are limited in what we can desire to what we can see to be good independently of our desiring it, we are limited, in what we can choose to do, to actions whose ends we see, independently of that choice, to be good in some way. And while we might pursue ends that are in fact bad, we can do so only under the misperception of them as good and thus only in error. This, then, is a substantive limit on our freedom of the sort whose existence the doctrine of radical choice denies.

If, on the other hand, one takes Aristotle's thesis to be true on the grounds that we regard anything we desire as good in virtue of our desiring it, then the thesis does not stand in any real opposition to the doctrine. The thesis, when taken in this way, places no limits on what we can desire, so it does not limit us, in what we can choose to do, to actions whose ends we must perceive independently to have some choice-worthy property. In being free to choose whatever we desire and to desire whatever appeals to us regardless of the properties it has independently of that appeal is as much freedom as the doctrine of radical choice need imply. To be sure, as we've seen, the doctrine may also imply freedom to choose to act independently of one's desires, which is to say, independently of all motives. But the possibility of such choice is a highly contentious metaphysical thesis, and for that reason, the opposition between the doctrine and Aristotle's thesis that it creates may be treated separately. Leaving it aside, then, we may conclude that Aristotle's thesis opposes the doctrine only if it is true by virtue of our seeing something good in the objects of our desires independently of our desiring those objects.

Aristotle's thesis, however, if it is taken to be true in this way, is open to the same kind of objection that throws his stronger view that all actions aim at promoting the agent's well-being into doubt. Men who have soured on life, like Dostoyevsky's underground man, not only exemplify people inclined to actions that do not aim at promoting their own well-being but exemplify as well people inclined to actions whose final end is to spoil or damage something they see as good. And because the very point of these actions is to spoil or damage something good, they go against Aristotle's thesis that every action or pursuit aims at some good. When, for instance, a person's youthful aspirations and ambitions for himself go bad, when things don't turn out for him as he once expected, which is to say dreamed, the disappointments can come hard and embitter. Such bitterness about one's reduced prospects in life typically leads to petty and nasty conduct toward others and to conduct that is self-abusive and self-injurious. The underground man is a case in point. Recall his earlier remark in which he enthusiastically comments on how he likes smashing things even when this is a bad thing to do. He has lost interest in his life and esteem for himself, and his self-contempt manifests itself in degrading and destructive actions. These are not actions whose ends the underground man sees as good.

Dostoyevsky asks us to look beneath our social selves, the personae, as it were, that we inhabit and to some extent shape in engaging publicly with others. Our actions in such engagements are generally construed as either competitive and self-advancing or cooperative and constructive. In either case, they easily fit Aristotle's thesis. We readily understand socially structured actions as having as ends the purposes embedded in those structures, and those purposes are beneficial either to the individual agents or to society generally. Buying a pack of gum or a candy bar at a local convenience store is a mundane example of the former. Discarding gum or candy wrappers in public trash cans is an example of the latter. Our lives are filled with such actions, and even when we are alone, in the privacy of our homes, the conventions of housekeeping and of the preparations we make to present ourselves to others define much of what we do. But not everything we do contributes to our public engagements with others. Privacy is not only something we require to prepare for public engagements but is also a cloak for actions that make no contribution to our self-presentations. These are both actions that take place in private spaces and are done for their own sake – actions such as making faces at oneself in the mirror or sharpening all the pencils in a desk drawer, even though one has no need of sharp pencils – and actions done in public space whose ultimate ends are disguised and whose true motives are kept hidden – actions such as a malicious prank one secretly plays on a co-worker who has rebuffed one's advances or an accident one who cannot cope with success provokes to insure failure. If we think of our public lives as conducted openly and above ground, then these are actions that we must unearth and bring to light to observe. They are actions that generally need a cover of darkness to be done; if done publicly, they would be a source of embarrassment or shame. It is surely with this point in mind that Dostoyevsky characterizes the protagonist of his strange novella as an underground man.

Aristotle, who conceived of men and women as social animals, likely came to his views of human action from this conception. While he does not require a social context for the intelligibility of actions, it is plausible to read him as regarding actions as always fitting within some social structure. One bit of evidence for this reading is his assuming without argument that justice and honesty are moral virtues, which is to say, excellences of rational functioning. That Aristotle seems untroubled by the core problem of Plato's *Republic*, the problem Glaucon and Adeimantus set for Socrates, strongly suggests a view of rational action that cannot accommodate the anti-social strain in Dostoyevsky's underground man. It suggests a view of deviations from the norms of human social life, like those the underground man at once exhibits and applauds, as symptomatic of deficiencies in practical reason rather than the heterogeneity of human motivation. Perhaps, then, Aristotle's thesis that all actions and pursuits have some good as their end reflects preconceptions that preclude Aristotle from seeing those motives and actions that do not fit his view. Perhaps, they blind him to certain kinds of motives and actions in human life that are typically hidden from public view. Alternatively, though, his thesis may simply reflect the fact that he never knew any Russians.

5. The obsolescence of Aristotle's answer

Counterexamples have only so much force in philosophical argument. Dostoyevsky's underground man is no exception. Confronted with his actions and similar examples, diehard Aristotelians will respond by interpreting the motives of those actions consistently with Aristotle's thesis. The underground man, by his own admission, takes pleasure in his suffering and humiliation, so, they will argue, he makes himself suffer or seeks humiliation for the sake of this pleasure. His actions thus aim at some good. Or again, the man who plays a malicious prank on a co-worker who has rebuffed his advances does so, they will argue, for the sake of exercising power over his co-worker, and having and exercising power over another is typically seen as a good. These interpretations are plainly necessary to maintain Aristotle's view, and some such interpretation will always be available if only because it is reasonable to suppose, as we noted, that one generally takes pleasure in attaining the objects of one's desires. Hence, any action on a desire is interpretable as an action in which one seeks pleasure through attainment of the object of that desire.

Nonetheless, we have good reason to resist these Aristotelian interpretations. To have merit, they must be more than reflexive applications of a dogmatic belief that every human action aims at some good. Specifically, they must rest on some deeper account of why every human action essentially has such an end. Yet there is no such account that is consistent with understanding human actions as caused by the motives from which they spring. Motives such as love and compassion are, of course, naturally understood as prompting actions that aim at some good, for each implies a desire to benefit its object. Love implies a desire to make one's beloved happy. Compassion implies a desire to relieve the suffering of the individual with whom one commiserates. But motives such as hatred, spite, envy, and malice are not readily understood as prompting actions that aim at some good. To the contrary, because each implies a desire to hurt its object, we naturally understand them as prompting actions that aim at what is bad. Nor is it necessary for so understanding them that one suppose that the person who acts under their influence sees something good in hurting others or in making their lives worse. When we understand actions as caused by the motives from which they spring, we understand that the desires the motives imply explain, either by themselves or in concert with certain beliefs, those actions. For to have a desire to do something is to be disposed to do it in circumstances that appear to one propitious for doing it, and consequently what explains one's doing it is this disposition together with beliefs that the circumstances favor one's doing it. One's seeing it as good or as accomplishing some good has no role in this explanation. The desire and these beliefs alone suffice.

There is the temptation, as we have seen, especially when malicious desires are cited as counterexamples to Aristotle's thesis, to defend it by identifying such desires as at bottom desires for the pleasure one obtains from doing the action, from hurting others or making their lives worse. But to defend the view in this way is to confuse two distinct desires. Recall Butler's criticism of psychological hedonism from chapter 2. Because the pleasure one gets from hurting others presupposes the desire to hurt them, a desire for that pleasure must be a different desire. And the same point will apply wherever one tries to deflect counterexamples to the thesis by redefining desires to do certain actions or obtain certain external objects as desires for the pleasure that doing the action or obtaining the objects will bring. It may be true that whenever an action aims at pleasure it aims at some good, but given that not every desire is a desire for pleasure and some are desires for making another suffer, the assertion that every action aims at pleasure has nothing to recommend it.

Indeed, the general strategy of defending Aristotle's thesis by redefining any desire offered as a counterexample to it as a desire for some apparent good misconstrues the problem Aristotelian interpretations of these counterexamples face when we understand human actions as caused by the motives from which they spring. For the problem is that when human actions are so understood, one does not need to suppose that their agents regard their ends as good to explain them. Citing the desire implicit in the motive along with relevant beliefs about the circumstances of action is sufficient. Knowing, for instance, that someone desires a certain object and believes that he can attain it in these circumstances by taking certain actions is all one needs to explain why the agent takes those actions. Consequently, redefining the person's desire so that it is understood as a desire for some good adds nothing to the explanation. It becomes a strictly ad hoc maneuver, undertaken solely for the purpose of saving Aristotle's thesis. To defend Aristotle's thesis, then, requires opposing, as inadequate, explanations of human actions that consist in citing the motives from which the actions spring. Or what comes to the same thing, it requires opposing, as problematic, the conception of human action behind such explanations. The explanations are causal in the sense that events and conditions preceding an action are cited to explain it, so the allegedly problematic conception behind them is that of an event the cause of which consists in prior events and conditions. To oppose this conception one must believe that human actions are events whose nature does not lend itself to causal explanations. One must believe, in other words, that explanations of actions must take a different form.

Unsurprisingly, the most common defense along these lines appeals to explanations whose form is characteristic of Aristotelian naturalism. These are teleological explanations. Such explanations presuppose that the action being explained is done intentionally. The relevant conception of human action, then, is that of an intentional action. One explains an intentional action by citing its point, what the agent means to do or achieve in so acting. The point of an action is not a prior event or condition. It is, rather, what gives the behavior its meaning or intelligibility as a human action. Hence, the form of explanation is different from that of causal explanation. In giving such an explanation, one assumes that the agent saw something desirable or worthwhile in acting as he did, and the feature that makes the action seem desirable or worthwhile to the agent defines the action's point. For instance, when we explain a man's opening a window by saying, "He is letting in some fresh air," we give the point of his opening the window, and we recognize it as such because we understand that removing a barrier to fresh air's entering the room will make the room more comfortable. Specifying what is or seems to the agent to be desirable or worthwhile about the action makes sense of it as something one would intentionally do. Teleological explanations therefore uphold Aristotle's view. The action necessarily aims at some good in the sense that its end is necessarily something that appears to the agent to be desirable or worth achieving.

In teleological explanations the idea of an action's having a motive that is its cause is replaced by the idea that to act intentionally is to act under the guidance of practical reason, and to be a rational agent, that is an agent guided by practical reason, is to be a seeker or pursuer of what is good. People's appetites and emotions, which on a causal explanation of human action are or are the source of an action's motives, are on a teleological explanation states in which rational agents perceive or sense something good or bad. And while these perceptions are liable to error owing to the primitive, violent, or erratic character of the states of appetite and emotion behind them, neither they nor those states can change one's nature as a rational agent. They cannot turn one away from seeking or pursuing what is good. Thus, hatred, spite, envy, and the other emotions that, on a causal explanation of human action, can prompt actions aimed at doing something bad, are on a teleological explanation states that affect what a rational agent perceives as good or bad but do not change the agent's orientation toward bringing about what is good. In short, a rational agent, on the conception of rational agency on which teleological explanations are based, essentially functions as a seeker or pursuer of what is good. Accordingly, one explains an intentional action by pointing out how the action fulfills this function.

Any teleological conception of nature is now obsolete. Consequently, either teleological explanations of natural phenomena are replaceable by causal explanations and used solely as proxies for the latter, or they are anachronisms. A defense of Aristotle's thesis that rejects causal explanations of human action in favor of teleological ones therefore bears the burden of justifying its rejection of causal explanations. It has the burden of showing that the view is not anachronistic. Hence, the justification cannot consist in wholesale rejection of causal explanations of natural phenomena in favor of teleological ones, since that would be tantamount to affirming a teleological conception of nature. It must therefore consist in first distinguishing intentional action from mere behavior, whose status as natural phenomena is indisputable and is thus explicable by the prior events and conditions that are its causes, and then showing that what distinguishes intentional action from mere behavior also makes intentional action resistant to causal explanation. The distinction between the two that defenders of Aristotle's thesis would draw is plain. Intentional action has a point, they would say, whereas mere behavior does not. So the burden they bear is to show why intentional actions' having a point makes them resistant to causal explanations.

The argument by which the defenders of Aristotle's thesis discharge this burden is roughly that one can account for an intentional action's having a point only by taking the action as fulfilling a certain function. That is, the action has a point because the agent, being a rational agent, is conceived of as a seeker or pursuer of what is good and not just an organism whose behavior is due to the forces acting on it. Its point, then, is given in how the action serves the function of his rational agency, which is to say, how it contributes to his seeking or pursuing what is good. The forces acting on a person at the time of action, the events and conditions immediately preceding it, cannot by themselves account for this contribution. For accounting for it presupposes the existence of a function that the action is fitted to serve, and to explain the action as intentional by citing this function and how the action is fitted to serve it is to explain the action teleologically and not causally.

This defense of Aristotle's thesis rests on the supposition that the point of an intentional action is defined by a feature of the action that makes it seem desirable or worthwhile to the agent. In the example of opening a window, the feature that made it seem desirable to the agent was its making the room more comfortable by removing a barrier to fresh air's coming into it. This feature defines the point of the action because it shows how the action fulfills the function of rational agency, to seek or pursue what is good. The question, then, that this defense raises is whether one can understand the point of an intentional action without supposing that it is defined by a feature of the action that makes it seem desirable or worthwhile to the agent. If one can, then one need not suppose rational agency has this function to explain intentional action. The defense would then fail. And if the alternative way to understand an intentional action's having a point were consistent with causal explanations of action, then continued support for Aristotle's view would be nothing but exercises in anachronism.

6. The eliminability of teleological explanations

How, then, can we understand an intentional action's having a point without supposing that the function of rational agency is to seek or pursue what is good? To answer, let us begin with a truism. The point of an intentional action is to achieve its end. When one acts intentionally, one acts with foresight of the events and states that are more or less likely to come about as a result of one's acting as one does, and one of these or some combination of them is what one intends to bring about. This is the action's end. Consequently, the feature of the action that defines its point is its being more or less likely to result in this event, state, or combination of events and states. The action, to be sure, may therefore appear desirable or worthwhile to the agent in the sense that it gets him what he wants. But it does not follow that it appears desirable or worthwhile to him in the sense that it helps him attain what is good, where what is good is something independent of what he desires. Hence, if we can understand how a person's actions can come to have ends without supposing that the person regards those ends as good, then we can understand the point of an intentional action without supposing that its agent, as a rational agent, is a seeker or pursuer of what is good.

What we need to determine is how a person's actions originally acquire their ends. Let us start with the earliest of human desires, those that develop in infancy from the appetites and emotions that are already manifest in the first few weeks after birth. These would be desires for satiation, sleep, affection, relief of distress, among other states. Their satisfaction is a source of pleasure, their frustration a source of discomfort or pain. These experiences of pleasure and pain, when the desires are satisfied and frustrated, come to be associated with the things whose consumption or use brings satisfaction or whose opposition brings frustration. Accordingly, a child takes pleasure in or is upset by having these things or by their presence. It then acquires new desires and aversions, namely, desires for the things whose consumption or use brings satisfaction and aversions to the things whose opposition brings frustration. The new desires are for possession of the objects for their own sake and not merely for their usefulness in getting other things that one desires. Similarly, the new aversions are aversions to the objects in themselves and not to the frustrations that those objects cause. A child may come to be attached to a blanket or a stuffed animal, for instance, in virtue of its being an aid to sleeping. Initially, the blanket or stuffed animal may not have interested the child, but it later comes to be something the child desires to possess because it comforts the child when the latter is left alone to sleep. The pleasure of being so comforted is then associated with the blanket or stuffed animal, and as a result, its possession comes to be an end of the child's actions not only at bedtime but at other times as well. It becomes, that is, even at times when the child is not disposed or expected to sleep, the object of the child's searches, requests, and demands. The child seeks to have it for its own sake.

Mill, in the chapter of *Utilitarianism* in which he offers his famous proof of the Principle of Utility, appeals to essentially the same process to explain how people come to desire money, power, fame, and virtue for their own sake. Focusing on the love of money, he writes:

There is nothing originally more desirable about money than about any heap of glittering pebbles. Its worth is solely that of the things which it will buy; the desires for other things than itself, which it is a means of gratifying. Yet the love of money is not only one of the strongest moving forces of human life, but money is, in many cases, desired in and for itself; the desire to possess it is often stronger than the desire to use it, and goes on increasing when all the desires which point to ends beyond it, to be compassed by it, are falling off. It may, then, be said truly, that money is desired not for the sake of an end, but as part of the end.[9]

So too with other "great objects of human life" like power and fame. He concludes:

Life would be a poor thing, very ill provided with sources of happiness, if there were not this provision of nature by which things originally indifferent, but conducive to, or otherwise associated with, the satisfaction of our primitive desires, become in themselves sources of pleasure more valuable than the primitive pleasures both in permanency, in the space of human existence that they are capable of covering, and even in intensity.[10]

Clearly, a process by which something comes to be desired for its own sake as a result of repeated pleasurable experiences of it does not require one's regarding it as good in order for one's possessing it to become an end of one's actions. It would be natural of course to regard it as good, but doing so is inessential to this process. And similar things can be said of the process of becoming averse to something as a result of repeated unpleasant experiences of it. Further, it is worth noting that in Mill's example of the love of money, money originally serves as an instrument of obtaining other things. As such, the lover of money will naturally see it as good, for being useful is a form of being good. But to see money as useful is not to see it as an end. Hence, his seeing it as good is independent of its being an end for him. That is, he sees it as useful but also desires to acquire it for its own sake. What the lover of money develops is an emotional attachment to money just as the child in my example develops an emotional attachment to the blanket or stuffed animal. The development marks the difference between desiring something for its own sake and seeing it as useful to one's attaining something else that one desires. Such attachments are the source of motives for

---

[9] Mill, *Utilitarianism*, ch. 4, par. 6.   [10] Ibid.

action, for they are, in effect, emotional dispositions. That is, they are dispositions to have a range of different emotions with respect to the object or person to whom one is attached. The different emotions in this range then correspond to different motives: fear, anger, hope, jealousy, yearning, and so forth. This account of how something becomes the end of one's actions is therefore consistent with causal explanations of those actions.

Finally, nothing about the process precludes something's becoming the end of a person's actions, though he regards it as bad or evil. If a person repeatedly gets pleasure from damaging or spoiling things, then he may come to desire damaging or spoiling things for its own sake. Perhaps Dostoyevsky's underground man acquired his predilection for smashing things in this way. Be this as it may, the point is that the ends of action that result from this process may be such that one who desired them for their own sake could also regard them as bad. We can thus see how the underground man represents such an effective counterexample to the Aristotelian model.

7. Modern skepticism about practical reason

Modern philosophers abandoned teleological explanations of natural phenomena. They concentrated instead on causal explanations. Treating human actions as natural phenomena, they looked for causal explanations of them. That is, they sought to explain human actions as the effects of the events and conditions that precede them. This way of explaining human actions puts pressure on the traditional understanding of them as the work of reason operating in the practical sphere. Indeed, some modern philosophers, notably David Hume (1711–76), having replaced teleological explanations of human actions with such causal ones, went on to deny that actions were ever the work of reason. Because actions are not related to their causes as conclusions of an argument are related to the premises from which they follow, actions do not, strictly speaking, result from the operations of reason. The causes of human action, according to Hume, are appetites and passions, desires and emotions, along with the perceptions of the world that excite them, and the relation of an appetite or passion to the action it causes – the relation of fear, say, to fleeing – is not that of inference. Fear moves its subject to flee; it does not argue in favor of fleeing. While one can reconstruct a teleological explanation so that the good at which the action aims argues in favor of doing the action, one cannot similarly reconstruct a causal explanation so that an action's causes argue in favor of doing it. Consequently, Hume denied that the processes of reason ever directly yielded action.

Hume reinforced this view by characterizing reason as being limited in its reach. On Hume's characterization, reason works entirely in the service of its possessor's efforts to understand the world around him. It is the power by which one determines whether one's ideas of the world are true. Hume, in so characterizing reason, followed Hobbes. In *Leviathan*, Hobbes had declared, "Reason is but reckoning (that is, the adding and subtracting) of the consequences of general names agreed upon for the marking and signifying of our thoughts."[11] In the same vein, Hume restricted the powers of reason to demonstrative and probabilistic reason, or as we now commonly say, deductive and inductive reasoning. In either case, the conclusions of reason – the conclusions one draws in reasoning – are thoughts one can express in complete sentences. Actions, appetites, and passions are therefore never the conclusions of reason. Such a limited conception of reason marks Hume as breaking from the traditional understanding of reason as the power by which men and women ruled their appetites and passions. Indeed, Hume brashly asserted the opposite. "Reason," he wrote in a passage often quoted by his admirers, "is and ought only to be the slave of the passions."[12] His skepticism about the possibility of practical reason was unremitting.

Of course, in characterizing Hume as an unremitting skeptic about the possibility of practical reason I do not mean that he denied the possibility of reasoning about practical matters. This much should be clear from the foregoing discussion of practical reason. It should be clear, in other words, that the notion of practical reason I am using in my characterization of Hume is a peculiarly philosophical notion and not the notion you would use in everyday conversation. Thus, if, unfamiliar with the peculiarly philosophical notion of practical reason, you were asked what the difference was between practical and speculative thought, you would likely say something like, "Practical thought concerns practical matters like how late the local grocery store stays open or whether the dark spot on the garage floor

---

[11] Hobbes, *Leviathan*, ch. 5, par. 2.
[12] David Hume, *A Treatise of Human Nature*, bk. II, pt. 3, sec. iii.

means your car is leaking oil; whereas speculative thought concerns matters of intellectual curiosity like how human beings came to be bipedal or what explains the appearance of rainbows after storms." Ordinarily, that is, we think of the difference between the two as a difference in their subject matter. Practical thought is about practical matters. Speculative thought is about matters of intellectual curiosity. There is no basis for skepticism, obviously, on this way of identifying different areas of thought. It is a rough-and-ready division, serviceable perhaps for some purposes. At the same time, it is no more illuminating of the nature of thought than similar divisions between secular and religious thinking or scientific and humanistic thinking. The same goes for the distinction between practical and speculative reason. On their ordinary notions, skepticism about either of them does not arise. But there is also nothing illuminating in the distinction.

It is the peculiarly philosophical distinction that gives rise to skepticism. This is a distinction between modes of reasoning and not of subject matter. Being a distinction between modes of reasoning, it is a distinction within human psychology. Moreover, it is sharp. There are no gray areas between the two modes. Practical and speculative reason, on the philosophical distinction, are different inferential processes. The inferences that characterize speculative reason typically lead to beliefs as their conclusions. The inferences that characterize practical reason typically lead to actions as their conclusions. Take as an example of an exercise of speculative reason, your inferring, from your observing wet streets and sidewalks in the morning, as you leave your home for work or school, that it rained during the night. Your observations are judgments about the wet conditions of the streets and sidewalks near your home, and from these judgments you conclude that it rained the night before. The conclusion is a belief that you form by inference from these judgments. Consider, in contrast, as an example of practical reason, your taking an umbrella with you, as you leave your home, because upon looking outdoors you see dark clouds overhead and have a presentiment of rain. Your observations of dark clouds and the imminence of rain result in your taking an umbrella, provided of course that you wish to keep dry and understand that without an umbrella for protection you won't. Your taking an umbrella is the conclusion of this bit of means-to-ends thinking. It is the means to keeping dry you take following observations of your circumstances made under the influence of a wish to keep dry. Decisions too, in the sense of a resolve to do something, when made prior to their being carried out, are conclusions of practical thinking. In either case, actions or decisions, the inferential process that results in them is distinct from that of speculative reason.

Aristotle, in his account of the role of reason in action, introduced what he called the practical syllogism to show how actions result from reasoning. A practical syllogism consists of a major premiss, which is a general principle about what it would be good to have, a minor premiss, which is a judgment of how one can realize that good in the circumstances one faces, and a conclusion, which is an action. Thus, one might affirm that it would be good to add calcium to one's diet, judge that milk was high in calcium, and conclude by pouring oneself a glass of milk. Such deliberation leading to action exemplifies the exercise of practical reason, on Aristotle's account. Hume rejects this model. What yields this action, on his view, is not reasoning from such premisses as (1) it would be good to have more calcium in one's diet and (2) drinking milk will provide more calcium. What yields the action is the desire for more calcium in one's diet and ultimately the desire to live longer or the fear of developing osteoporosis in old age. The transition from this desire or fear to action is not, on Hume's view, a transition of reason. It is not an inference. To deny the possibility of practical reason is to deny the possibility of such transitions of reason.

8. Hume's meta-ethics

What meta-ethical views follow from Hume's skepticism about practical reason? To answer, let us replace, as the conclusion of the practical syllogism we just considered, the action of pouring a glass of milk with the directive "I should have a glass of milk" and then ask whether Hume's skepticism applies to the reasoning this new syllogism represents. Plainly, the answer depends on how one understands the nature of this directive. On the one hand, if one takes it as an expression of an idea that could be true in some circumstances, then it could be the conclusion of the reasoning the new syllogism represents. In that case, the reasoning would be no different from the deductive reasoning represented in an ordinary syllogism such as:

(3) New York is east of Philadelphia.
(4) I live in New York.
Hence, I live east of Philadelphia.

It would not, that is, be reasoning that issued in action. On the other hand, if one holds that the directive necessarily guides action in the sense that if one clearly comprehended and sincerely accepted it, one would necessarily be moved to act accordingly, then one cannot by sound reasoning infer it from (1) and (2). This is because the directive, on this second way of understanding its nature, expresses a motivational state of mind, and given skepticism about practical reason, the transition from the ideas expressed by the premises to such a state cannot be one of reason. In short, one must have settled on one or the other understanding of the nature of directives before any definitive meta-ethical view follows from Hume's skepticism.

Neither alternative, however, is wholly satisfactory. To conceive of directives as expressing ideas that could be true in some circumstances is to conceive of them as comparable to factual statements. Yet as Hume himself noted, nothing about factual statements as such moves a person to act. Someone who was totally indifferent to the stated fact would be unmoved by such a statement though he fully agreed with it. Only if the fact pleases or displeases him, only, that is, if it raises his hopes or increases his fears, will his apprehending it dispose him toward one or another course of action. Directives, however, affect those who agree with them. They guide their actions. Hence, a conception of them as comparable to factual statements misrepresents their character.

Consider, then, the alternative way of understanding their nature, the conception of them as necessarily action guiding. To conceive of them in this way is to conceive of them as expressing motivational states. These are states of appetite and passion, desire and emotion, and such states, no less than actions, invite causal explanations according to which they are brought about by antecedent events and conditions. Yet it would be odd, at best, to explain a person's coming to accept or reject a directive by citing prior events and causes. Rather one often accepts or rejects directives in view of considerations that argue for or against them. Someone concerned about the brittleness of her bones, for instance, may be persuaded to drink milk on learning that it supplies calcium that will strengthen her bones. This shows that reasoning from premises about matters that interest or concern one can yield directives as conclusions. A conception of directives as expressing motivational states therefore fails to capture how they can be supported by reason and argument.

Hume himself opted for this second alternative. Because ethics is a practical discipline, he argued, its teachings are meant to influence the behavior of those who receive and accept them. Accordingly, he wrote, "Morality … is more properly felt than judg'd of."[13] A directive to help one's neighbor or keep one's promises expresses a sentiment of approval toward that action; a directive not to lie or take more than one's fair share expresses a sentiment of disapproval. Arguments in support of such directives, Hume held, were arguments to establish facts whose apprehension caused the sentiments of approval or disapproval the directives expressed. That is, he held that men and women were so constituted that upon apprehending facts that pleased them, they felt approval toward actions that brought about such facts and similarly for facts that displeased them. He thus accounted for the place of reason and argument in ethical discourse. Or so he thought.

The problem with his account, however, is, as we just noted, its reliance on cause and effect to explain how we come to see certain facts as arguing for or against directives. For the relation of cause to effect does not explain the connection that holds between a fact and a directive when the former argues for the latter. To see a fact as arguing for a directive means that you cannot consistently affirm this fact and reject the directive unless you see other facts that argue against the directive. If you know that milk strengthens your bones, for instance, and take this fact as arguing for the directive "I should drink a glass of milk", then it would be inconsistent for you to reject this directive unless you saw other facts, such as your being allergic to dairy products, as arguing against it. The reason why you would be inconsistent in rejecting the directive lies in the basis on which you judge that the fact about milk's strengthening your bones argues for it. Recall that on Hume's view a fact can argue for or against a directive only if one is not indifferent to it. In this case, the fact argues for the directive because you are not indifferent to having stronger bones. To the contrary, you want to strengthen your bones. Consequently, you cannot consistently desire to have stronger bones and reject directives to take means to strengthening them unless there are facts that argue against your taking those means. And in general, one would be inconsistent in desiring x and seeing that to have x requires doing y but rejecting the directive to do y, unless one saw facts that argued

---

[13] Ibid., bk. III, pt. 1, sec. ii.

against one's doing *y*. By contrast, if your sentiment of approval toward drinking a glass of milk is merely the effect of your apprehending with pleasure the fact that drinking milk will strengthen your bones, then there would be no inconsistency in your feeling disapproval toward drinking a glass of milk upon apprehending with pleasure that it would strengthen your bones. It would be no more inconsistent than your falling asleep upon drinking several cups of very strong coffee. Such an event would be contrary to what drinking strong coffee causes, but there would be no inconsistency in its occurring after you drank several cups of coffee. By the same token, there would be no inconsistency in your rejecting the directive to drink a glass of milk upon apprehending with pleasure the fact that drinking milk will strengthen your bones. It is evident, then, that Hume's account of the place of reason and argument in ethical discourse fails.

9. Practical reason in modern philosophy

What does the failure of Hume's account show about his skepticism concerning practical reason? One obvious lesson is that Hume goes too far when he denies that actions can be the conclusions of reason. One may, of course, define reason, as Hume and Hobbes did, so as to exclude from its operations any process of thought that issues in action. One may, that is, restrict its processes to those of deductive and inductive reasoning or to the "adding and subtracting" of words. But such restrictions are essentially decisions to define 'reason' narrowly. If one thinks, as Hobbes and Hume apparently did, that reason is best conceived of as that power of the understanding whose workings are the subject of logic and mathematics, then one will so restrict one's use of the term. But if one thinks logic and mathematics reflect only one side of reason, one will then define the term more broadly. Accordingly one may, in light of considerations like those that showed Hume's account to be inadequate, decide to include within the term's scope deliberation issuing in action. Those considerations showed the possibility of inconsistency between one's aims and one's actions and therefore, if one thinks reason is best conceived of as including the cognitive power by which one discerns and corrects inconsistency in one's thought and action, one will extend the scope of the term 'reason' to include both spheres. One will, in other words, add practical reason to the powers that fall under the general concept of reason.

Consequently, to defend Hume's skepticism concerning practical reason one must moderate its categorical denial of the existence of inferences of reason whose conclusions are actions. If one wishes, that is, to continue to deny the existence of such inferences, one must then acknowledge the narrow sense in which one is using the term 'reason' and, hence, the possibility of a broader sense of the term that includes practical reason within its scope. At the same time, one's acknowledgement of a broader sense does not mean that one is abandoning Hume's skepticism in its entirety. For although Hume's argument against the possibility of there being inferences of reason whose conclusions are actions fails to establish this view categorically, there is implicit in the argument a skeptical argument against a different thesis about practical reason, and this implicit, skeptical argument has proven hard to answer.

The thesis it opposes takes us back to the dispute between rationalists and naturalists that we considered in chapter 3. Recall that the question that divides these two schools is whether reason alone can initiate action. Rationalists believe that it can, and accordingly attribute to reason the power to produce motives that conflict with the motives arising from animal appetite and passion. Naturalists hold, to the contrary, that all motives arise from animal appetite and passion and therefore reason's role in action is limited to informing its possessor about the consequences of the actions he is moved to do so that he acts on enlightened motives. Hume in arguing against the possibility of practical reason makes a strong case against the rationalists' hallmark thesis that reason alone can initiate action and for the naturalists' contrary view. This case, Hume's anti-rationalism, is what remains of his skepticism about practical reason once, having allowed for a broad sense of 'reason,' one accepts that actions can be the conclusions of inferences of reason in this sense. Let us call this the modified Humean view.

Hume's case consists in his observing that none of the different operations of reason generates motives of action. Hume, as we noted, divides the operations of reason into those of demonstrative and probabilistic reasoning. With respect to the former, he observes that because it concerns abstract relations of ideas, it never goes further in its conclusions than ideas. When we reason deductively, we begin with premises and pass by inferences to a conclusion either by virtue of the necessary connection between propositions that have the form the premises have and a proposition that has the form the conclusion has, or by virtue of the necessary connection between concepts contained in the premisses and concepts contained in the conclusion. In either case the reasoning as such stays within our understanding or system of beliefs. With respect to the latter, Hume concedes that because it may concern relations of cause and effect, if we have in mind the prospect of something pleasurable or painful, our thoughts will pass, guided by reasoning from effect to cause, to events of a type that would cause it, and we may then be moved by desire to bring about such events or by aversion to avert them. But, Hume then argues, in this case the motive of desire or aversion is due to the pleasure or pain in prospect and not the reasoning that leads us to think of its cause. Indeed, if we neither took pleasure in the prospect of gaining this object nor found it painful, we would not be moved either by desire or aversion in contemplating its cause. "Where the objects themselves," Hume writes, "do not affect us their connexion can never give them any influence; and 'tis plain that as reason is nothing but the discovery of this connexion, it cannot be by its means that the objects are able to affect us."[14]

Suppose, then, we add practical reason to Hume's list of the operations of reason. Clearly, this addition will not affect Hume's anti-rationalism if we conceive of practical reason as the power to discern and resolve inconsistencies between one's aims and one's tendencies to act contrary to those aims. It should be clear, that is, that Hume could say the very same thing about practical reason, conceived of in this way, as he does about demonstrative and probabilistic reason. For the power to discern and resolve inconsistencies between one's aims and one's tendencies to act contrary to those aims operates on already existing motives, and there is no need to suppose that it generates any new motives to understand its operations. You may be inclined, for instance, to take the scenic route on a trip to visit your parents, but if you intend to arrive at your parents' home in time for dinner and you realize that taking the scenic route requires more time than you have, then your interest in having dinner with your parents will prevail. No additional motive is necessary to resolve the conflict. Or you may be planning a vacation and deciding between the Canadian Rockies, where you could ski, and Baja California, where you could surf. You can't do both and therefore you must choose according to which fits best with your larger aim

---

[14] Ibid., bk. II, pt. 3, sec. iii.

of having a pleasurable vacation. Again, no additional motive among the desires to ski, surf, and have a pleasurable vacation is necessary to resolve the conflict.

The modified Humean view, while weaker than Hume's full-blown skepticism about practical reason, is nonetheless sufficient to enable him to maintain the meta-ethical view about the roots of morality that we touched on in the previous section, the view that morality is at bottom a matter of feeling and not reason. His anti-rationalism is one of two propositions on which he bases this view. The other is that ethics is an essentially practical discipline. Its teachings are no mere statements of fact but are rather guides to conduct that should move all who understand and accept them to follow them. Ethics is the study of directives, and directives guide action. Since reason is inert, as Hume liked to say in expressing his anti-rationalism, the teachings of ethics must speak to our desires and emotions if they are to move us. Hence, it follows, on Hume's view, that there is no directive, specifically no moral precept or dictate about what a person ought to do, the rejection of which is necessarily contrary to reason. Whether rejection of a moral precept goes against reason depends on the interests, desires, cares, fears, and the like of the person who rejects the precept, for only if the rejection is inconsistent with the pursuit of some end he is disposed to pursue will it be contrary to reason. Hume's meta-ethical views therefore allow dissent from moral dictates about right and wrong or what ought or ought not to be done that one cannot criticize for being irrational or even untrue. On this point, Hume's views are compatible with those of the defenders of existentialist ethics and opposed to those of Aristotelians.

The opposition between the Aristotelian view and the modified Humean view on the question of the truth of moral precepts and dictates nicely brings out the difference in conceptions of practical reason. To illustrate, consider a simple directive like "You ought to drive more slowly." On the Aristotelian view of practical reason, this directive, like the very action of driving more slowly, follows from your affirming that safety from auto accidents is a good and seeing that slowing the speed of your car will make you safer in the current conditions of the road on which you are driving. Safety from auto accidents is plainly a good in almost any circumstance of driving you can imagine, and hence the directive is true if driving more slowly will make you safer. Of course, if driving more slowly would be hazardous because, for instance, you are driving in heavy, fast-moving traffic and already driving slower than the other cars around you, then the directive is false. By contrast, on the modified Humean view, the truth of the directive depends, not on there being a good that one could realize by driving slowly, but rather on one's having an end – that is, the object of some desire or interest – that one would realize by so driving. For the directive would not guide one's actions unless following it advanced some end one has. A driver who loves to speed and cares nothing for his own safety or that of other drivers would reject this directive (provided of course he had no other end that driving more slowly would help him realize), and in doing so he would not be displaying any defect of reason or ignorance of ethical truth. On the Aristotelian view, ethics is an objective study, and its practical truths are determined through investigation of the human good. On the modified Humean view, by contrast, ethics is a practical study whose results are not certain to be universal truths but rather precepts and dictates whose truth is relative to the particular desires, emotions, and sentiments of each individual.

On the modified Humean view, there are universal ethical truths only if all men and women have in common certain desires whose objects compliance with moral precepts and dictates would further. Needless to say, this condition is not likely to obtain, for there are almost certainly a few adult human beings whose personalities are sufficiently anti-social to make them immune to the guiding force of these precepts and dictates. Nonetheless, human beings may generally share a social nature relative to which moral precepts and dictates are true, and it is upon the supposition of shared human sociability that Hume makes out his argument for morality's being rooted in social feelings rather than reason. The precepts and dictates of morality, on this view, are not universal truths. But they are generally true. That is, for human beings generally they guide their actions.

10. Kant's notion of practical reason

Kant's practical philosophy stands in direct opposition to Hume's on the question of the roots of morality. Kant believes morality has its roots in reason. His account of the Categorical Imperative as the supreme principle of morality is testament to this belief. At the same time, like Hume, Kant holds that moral precepts guide action in the sense that a person who understands and accepts them is moved to act accordingly. Hence, Kant takes reason as having the power to initiate action as well as to inform its possessor about how to achieve his or her ends. Kant thus affirms the hallmark thesis of rationalist ethics and, indeed, he advances his account of the Categorical Imperative as the supreme principle of morality to vindicate it. Just as Hume is the foremost defender of anti-rationalism in ethics among modern philosophers, Kant is the foremost defender of rationalism in ethics.

Kant clearly sees that to vindicate the rationalist thesis requires an expansion of our understanding of practical reason. If the operations of practical reason are limited to our discerning and resolving inconsistencies between our aims and our tendencies to act contrary to those aims, then its role in the production of action will be that of an arbiter among conflicting nonrational motives. In that case, morality would have no more claim to our allegiance than any other object of interest and desire. Consequently, the very operations of reason that validate moral precepts and dictates must also supply the motives to act as they direct. They must supply purely rational motives. This is what Kant calls *pure practical reason*. He did not think, however, that an exposition of morality alone showed that reason was the source of these motives. His exposition consists of an analysis of the idea of acting from duty or respect for moral law that yields the different formulations of the Categorical Imperative as the supreme principle of morality, but the analysis of an idea, as he observed, is not sufficient to establish its realization in human lives or even how it could be so realized. To establish either, one must find in our powers of reason operations sufficient to bring about its realization.

How then can practical reason be reconceived to encompass the operations required for moral motives to be purely rational motives? These must be operations that regulate practical thought just as the operations of theoretical reason regulate speculative thought. Rational action results from practical thinking when it is properly regulated by practical reason. Rational belief results from speculative thinking when it is properly regulated by theoretical reason. This distinction is fundamental to Kant's philosophy. His program of replacing, as the foundations of moral law, substantive standards of right and wrong that we know by an exercise of rational intuition with formal principles of practical reason that regulate the thinking we undertake in determining our actions could not proceed without it. These formal principles must therefore include some – at least one – whose regulation of practical thought yields motives without the help of antecedently existing motives. Kant identifies two mutually exclusive types of formal principle, hypothetical imperatives and categorical imperatives. The former regulate practical thought by transmitting the motive to achieve an end that the agent has resolved to pursue to those acts that the agent sees are the necessary means to achieving it. They cannot, therefore, be the source of purely rational motives. The latter regulate practical thought by testing plans of action, what Kant calls maxims, against criteria of lawfulness and suppressing the inclination to act on those maxims that fail the test. Such regulation may yield purely rational motives provided the testing does not proceed under the influence of antecedently existing motives.

Kant maintains that it does not. When you test a maxim of action against the criteria of lawfulness contained in the Categorical Imperative and determine that the maxim fails, you are moved to suppress whatever inclination to act on that maxim you have. Your motive to suppress the inclination is what Kant calls the motive of duty or respect for moral law. While this motive opposes your inclination to act on the maxim, the conflict between the two is not like the conflict in our earlier example between your desire to take the scenic route to your parents' home and your desire to arrive at their home in time for dinner. In this earlier example, the two conflicting desires are on a par in the sense that you can resolve the conflict by finding some common measure by which to decide between them. Kant thought the common measure in all cases of such conflict was the contribution to your happiness that satisfaction of the desire would make. That is, on Kant's view, you decide between them by determining which desire is such that its satisfaction would give you the most pleasure. But you needn't follow Kant on this point. You might use instead, as the common measure, the importance you place on the desire's being satisfied. Accordingly, you would decide between them by determining which desire is such that its satisfaction matters more to you. Be this as it may, Kant's main point is that the conflict in motives that occurs when one is moved by the motive of duty to suppress an inclination to act unlawfully is different. One cannot resolve it by finding a common measure by which to decide between them. To the contrary, Kant holds, there is no common measure.[15] The motive of duty,

---

[15] Immanuel Kant, *Critique of Practical Reason*, L. W. Beck, trans. (Indianapolis, Ind.: Bobbs-Merrill, 1956), pp. 29–30. Reference is to page numbers in the Preussische Akademie edition.

being a motive to suppress an inclination to act, is of a higher order than that inclination. Indeed, because it inheres in the judgment that interdicts that inclination, the judgment that the maxim on which one is inclined to act fails the tests of lawfulness contained in the Categorical Imperative, its superiority to that inclination is manifest. Its manifest superiority, Kant argues, reflects its origins in the operations of reason.

The argument is succinct. The suppression of inclination that results from one's recognizing that to act on the maxim to which the inclination gives rise would be unlawful exemplifies a person's capacity to step back from the natural desires and emotions that move him and to assess their influence. When the assessment moves one to suppress the inclination, its motive force cannot originate in a natural desire or emotion. Rather it must come from the exercise of reason in which the assessment consists. It cannot originate in a natural desire or emotion because, if it did, one could use some common measure to resolve the conflict. But the manifest superiority of the motive of duty shows that there is no such measure. The motive must therefore originate in reason. Kant thus locates the source of purely rational motives in our capacity for reflective assessment of our natural desires and emotions, when that assessment is not undertaken in the service of some natural desire or emotion. This capacity is exemplified, in Kant's ethics, by the use of the Categorical Imperative to test the maxims of one's actions, but his argument for its being the site of pure practical reason does not depend on the protocols of the test. What is crucial in the argument is that people are capable of reflectively assessing the natural desires and emotions on which they act and of being moved by those assessments.

Of course, even on the modified Humean view, people can assess from an unbiased standpoint the natural desires and emotions on which they act. Indeed, Hume makes such assessments central to his account of virtue and vice, for his account proceeds from the idea that motives are the proper objects of the sentiments of moral approbation and moral disapprobation. Furthermore, one experiences these sentiments from a general or disinterested view of the world, a viewpoint everyone or most everyone is capable of taking. They therefore have the character of reflective assessment. Yet the assessment in each case consists solely in one's being pleased or displeased upon one's discerning or thinking about the inner spring of a person's actions. As such it carries no distinctive authority relative to other natural

desires and emotions. These assessments are states of approval and disapproval, to be sure, but for Hume 'approbation' and 'disapprobation' are
merely names for certain pleasant feelings and certain unpleasant ones.
Consequently, when there is a conflict between the sentiment of disapprobation, say, and the inner spring that is its object, the conflict is similar to
other conflicts between natural desires. One can resolve it by applying a
common measure and deciding between them. It raises no question about
the superiority of disapprobation to the inner spring. Unlike Kant's account,
there is therefore no reason to suppose that the assessments that the sentiments of approbation and disapprobation imply are products of reason.
What secures the rationalist thesis, then, on Kant's account, is not merely
one's capacity to assess reflectively from a disinterested standpoint one's
motives, but moreover the nature of the standpoint from which one makes
these assessments. It must be one of disengagement from one's natural
desires and emotions.

11. Freedom and reason

Kant identifies this disengaged standpoint with human freedom. Were we
unable to assess our natural desires and emotions from such a standpoint
and check those we found unacceptable, we would be at their mercy, so to
speak – and the mercy of the forces of nature generally – in all that we did.
That is, if our natural desires and emotions were the ultimate springs of all
human action, then every human action would be the result of those events
and conditions that produced the motive, and those events and conditions
would in turn be the product of prior events and conditions, and so on.
Human freedom, in Kant's view, requires that men and women be capable
of acting on their own volition, and their power to determine their will
must be independent of the forces of nature. That power, Kant holds, is
found in pure practical reason. It is the power to conform one's actions to
standards by which one's natural desires and emotions, through assessment
of the maxims of action to which they give rise, are themselves assessed and
which issue from reason. These standards, then, are moral precepts whose
authority is universal and whose truth is absolute.

The modified Humean view, by contrast, does not attribute such freedom to
human beings. Naturalism, which this view represents, holds that human
actions are events of nature and as such are explainable by the forces and

conditions studied in the natural sciences and that explain other events in nature. To the naturalist, the idea of a standpoint from which a person can disengage from his or her natural desires and emotions is anathema. It is the idea of a place, free from the forces of nature, to which men and women can remove themselves, and there is no such place. The freedom it promises is incoherent if human beings wholly belong to the natural world. Human freedom is, according to naturalism, the freedom people enjoy when they do what they desire to do, provided that the desires they act on are desires by which they are pleased to be moved. Freedom, on this view, is something to be achieved in life, for it not only requires an external environment conducive to one's being able to do what one wants to do but also requires freeing oneself of internal conflicts that create ambivalence and uncertainty about how to conduct one's life. And internal conflicts are often the most disabling factors in one's life as well as the hardest to overcome. While achieving internal coherence requires practical reason to see the inconsistencies, their resolution does not always come about solely through rational judgment about one's ends and goals. On this view, whether there are any directives that count as universal practical truths depends on whether there is any end or goal that every human being has, and whether there is such an end or goal cannot be determined a priori. In any case, all practical truths are relative to people's ends. There are no directives (and so no moral precepts) whose truth is absolute.

Existentialists, too, deny that any universal moral precepts are absolutely true. The doctrine of radical choice entails as much. Consequently, contrary to Kant, they treat human freedom as incompatible with there being universal moral directives that are absolutely true. At the same time, they agree with Kant in seeing the capacity for freedom as essential to our humanity. Freedom is not a condition human beings achieve. It is rather something inherent in our power of choice. But in opposition to Kant they do not identify that power with practical reason. It is a power one may exercise in reflecting on desires and emotions that are the motives of one's actions, but one exercises it in endorsing or rejecting those motives according to one's decision as to what sort of person to be and what kind of life to live and not in assessing them against standards issued by reason. Human freedom, on the existentialist view, is not coincident with reason. When one exercises it in making the most fundamental choices as to how one should live, one cannot rely on reason to determine for oneself what choices are correct. Even the manifest superiority of the motive of duty to which Kant appeals is open to question, on the existentialist view. Deferring to it as showing the authoritative nature of moral standards for assessing one's natural desires and emotions would be abandoning one's freedom, for the existentialist view is that the ultimate authority in matters of how one ought to live and thus what desires and emotions to act on is the agent's own lucid and sincere decisions. Thus, while the motive of duty may appear superior to every natural desire or emotion with which it conflicts, it is still subordinate to one's decision about how one ought to live. And while the followers of Kant may then object that to go against the motive of duty is to go against reason, the existentialists can respond that ignoring duty is still a coherent, albeit radical choice, even if contrary to reason on Kant's strengthened conception of reason. It is therefore an intelligible exercise of personal autonomy. To think that you may not ignore duty when doing so would be coherent is, on the existentialists' view, to abandon your freedom.

Our study of practical reason in modern philosophy may appear, then, to leave it to us to decide among these three opposing positions. And if so, it may then seem as though we would have to favor existentialism by default, for deciding among these positions appears to require a choice for which there is no standard of correctness. It appears, that is, to require a radical choice. How, after all, can one decide which of the three conceptions of freedom that correspond to these three positions correctly applies to humankind? Such a decision appears nothing short of deciding how to understand one's own humanity and the humanity of others, and what could be a more fundamental and yet indeterminate decision than that? Surely a study that ends by leaving things open to such a decision implies the primacy of existentialism.

Yet such a conclusion would be too hasty. We must not mistake a seemingly indeterminate philosophical question for a first-order question of ethics, and the questions giving rise to radical choice are of the latter kind. What our study discloses, rather, is that the question of the nature of human freedom is itself a second-order question, a question about whether we can find answers based in reason to first-order questions of ethics and what sort of answers they are if we can. It is a question of meta-ethics. To be sure, it may be one for which we will never have enough knowledge about and understanding of our humanity to arrive at a determinate answer. But that possibility should not foreclose our continuing to debate it. Like other major problems in philosophy, only further reflection and argument will tell whether there is a bottom to its depths.

Appendix: Diagram of different teleological theories

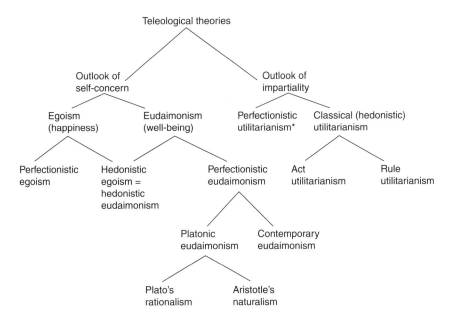

Teleological theories

Outlook of self-concern

Outlook of impartiality

Egoism (happiness)

Eudaimonism (well-being)

Perfectionistic utilitarianism*

Classical (hedonistic) utilitarianism

Perfectionistic egoism

Hedonistic egoism = hedonistic eudaimonism

Perfectionistic eudaimonism

Act utilitarianism

Rule utilitarianism

Platonic eudaimonism

Contemporary eudaimonism

Plato's rationalism

Aristotle's naturalism

*Perfectionistic utilitarianism, like classical utilitarianism, admits of act and rule versions.

Works cited

Aquinas, Thomas. *Summa Theologica*.

Aristotle. *Nicomachean Ethics*.

Bentham, Jeremy. *An Introduction to the Principles of Morals and Legislation*.

Butler, Joseph. *Fifteen Sermons Preached at the Rolls Chapel*.

Camus, Albert. *The Myth of Sisyphus and Other Essays*, J. O'Brien, trans. (New York: Vintage Books, 1955).

Carroll, Lewis. *Through the Looking Glass (and What Alice Saw There)*.

Dostoyevsky, Fyodor. *Notes from Underground/The Double*, J. Coulson, trans. (Harmondsworth, England: Penguin Books, 1972).

Epicurus. "Principle Doctrines."

Forster, E. M. *Two Cheers for Democracy* (New York: Harcourt Brace, 1951).

Grotius, Hugo. *On the Law of War and Peace*, F. W. Kelsey, trans. (Oxford: Oxford University Press, 1925).

Hobbes, Thomas. *Leviathan*.

Hume, David. *A Treatise of Human Nature*.

James, William. *The Principles of Psychology*, 2 vols. (1890; reprinted New York: Dover Publications, 1950).

Kant, Immanuel. *Critique of Practical Reason*, L. W. Beck, trans. (Indianapolis, Ind.: Bobbs-Merrill, 1956).

 Groundwork of the Metaphysics of Morals, H. J. Paton, trans. (New York: Harper & Row, 1964).

Mill, John Stuart. *Utilitarianism*.

Moore, G. E. *Principia Ethica* (Cambridge: Cambridge University Press, 1903).

Plato. *Republic*.

Prichard, H. A. "Does Moral Philosophy Rest on a Mistake?" *Mind* 21 (1912): 21–37.

Sartre, Jean-Paul. "L'existentialisme est un humanisme"; reprinted as "Existentialism Is a Humanism," Philip Mairet, trans., in *Existentialism from Dostoevsky to Sartre*, Walter Kaufmann, ed. (Cleveland: The World Publishing Co., 1956).

Sheinwold, Alfred. *5 Weeks to Winning Bridge*, rev. edn. (New York: Pocket Books, 1964).

Sidgwick, Henry. *The Methods of Ethics*, 7th edn. (London: Macmillan and Co., 1907).

Twain, Mark. *The Adventures of Huckleberry Finn*.

Suggested further readings

Chapter 1

Bennett, Jonathan. "The Conscience of Huckleberry Finn," *Philosophy* 49 (1974): 123–34.

Darwall, Stephen. *The Second Person Standpoint* (Cambridge, Mass.: Harvard University Press, 2006).

Ross, W. D. *The Right and the Good* (Oxford: Clarendon Press, 1930).

Strawson, P. F. "Social Morality and Individual Ideal," *Philosophy* 36 (1961): 1–17.

Chapter 2

Broad, C. D. "Egoism as a Theory of Human Motives," *Hibbert Journal* 68 (1950): 105–14; reprinted in Broad's *Critical Essays in Moral Philosophy*, David Cheney, ed. (London: George Allen & Unwin Ltd, 1971), pp. 247–61.

Gauther, David. "Assure and Threaten," *Ethics* 104 (1994): 690–721.

Kavka, Gregory. *Hobbesian Moral and Political Theory* (Princeton, N.J.: Princeton University Press, 1986).

Sidgwick, Henry. "Egoism," in *The Methods of Ethics*, 7th edn. (London: Macmillan & Co., 1907), bk. II, pp. 119–95.

"Pleasure and Desire," in *The Methods of Ethics*, bk. I, ch. 4, pp. 39–56.

Chapter 3

Annas, Julia. *Introduction to Plato's Republic* (Oxford: Clarendon Press, 1981).

Griffin, James. *Well-Being: Its Meaning, Measurement and Moral Importance* (Oxford: Clarendon Press, 1986).

Kraut, Richard. *Aristotle on the Human Good* (Princeton, N.J.: Princeton University Press, 1989).

Plato. *Gorgias*.

Sachs, David. "A Fallacy in Plato's *Republic*," *Philosophical Review* 72 (1963): 141–58.

Chapter 4

Kagan, Shelly. *The Limits of Morality* (Oxford: Clarendon Press, 1989).

Lyons, David. *Forms and Limits of Utilitarianism* (Oxford: Clarendon Press, 1965).

Parfit, Derek. *Reasons and Persons* (Oxford: Clarendon Press, 1984).

Railton, Peter. "Alienation, Consequentialism, and the Demands of Morality," *Philosophy & Public Affairs* 13 (1984): 134–71.

Rawls, John. "Two Concepts of Rules," *Philosophical Review* 64 (1955): 3–32.

Urmson, J. O. "The Interpretation of the Moral Philosophy of J. S. Mill," *Philosophical Quarterly* 3 (1953): 33–39.

Chapter 5

Adams, Robert M. "A Modified Divine Command Theory of Ethical Wrongness," in *Religion and Morality: A Collection of Essays*, Gene Outka and John P. Reeder, Jr., eds. (Garden City, N.J.: Anchor Press, 1973), pp. 318–47.

Herman, Barbara. "Mutual Aid and Respect for Persons," *Ethics* 94 (1984): 577–602.

O'Neil, Onora. *Acting on Principle: An Essay on Kantian Ethics* (New York: Columbia University Press, 1975).

Ross, W. D. *The Right and the Good* (Oxford: Clarendon Press, 1930).

Schneewind, J. B. *The Invention of Autonomy* (Cambridge: Cambridge University Press, 1998).

Strawson, P. F. "Ethical Intuitionism," *Philosophy* 24 (1949): 23–33.

Chapter 6

Camus, Albert. *The Stranger*, Stuart Gilbert, trans. (New York: Alfred Knopf, 1946).

Hill, Thomas E., Jr. *Dignity and Practical Reason* in Kant's Moral Theory (Ithaca, N.Y.: Cornell University Press, 1992).

Korsgaard, Christine. "The Right to Lie: Kant on Dealing with Evil," *Philosophy & Public Affairs* 15 (1986): 325–49.

Nagel, Thomas. "The Absurd," *Journal of Philosophy* 68 (1971): 716–27.

Sartre, Jean-Paul. *Being and Nothingness*, Hazel Barnes, trans. (New York: Washington Square Press, 1956).

Wood, Allen. *Kant's Ethical Thought* (Cambridge: Cambridge University Press, 1999).

Chapter 7

Anscombe, G. E. M. *Intention*, 2nd edn. (Ithaca, N.Y.: Cornell University Press, 1963).

Árdal, Páll S. *Passion and Value* in Hume's Treatise, 2nd edn. (Edinburgh: Edinburgh University Press, 1989).

Davidson, Donald. "Action, Reasons, and Causes," *Journal of Philosophy* 60 (1963): 685–700.

Frankfurt, Harry. "Free Will and the Concept of a Person," *Journal of Philosophy* 68 (1971): 5–20.

Korsgaard, Christine. "Skepticism about Practical Reason," *Journal of Philosophy* 83 (1986): 5–25.

Nussbaum, Martha. *The Fragility of Goodness: Luck and Ethics in Greek Tragedy and Philosophy* (Cambridge: Cambridge University Press, 1986), ch. 9.

Stocker, Michael. "Desiring the Bad," *Journal of Philosophy* 76 (1979): 738–53.

Velleman, J. David. "The Guise of the Good," *Nous* 26 (1992): 3–26.

Wiggins, David. "Truth, Invention, and the Meaning of Life," *Proceedings of the British Academy* 62 (1976): 331–78.

Williams, Bernard. "Internal and External Reasons," in *Rational Action*, Ross Harrison, ed. (Cambridge: Cambridge University Press, 1980), pp. 17–28; reprinted in B. Williams, *Moral Luck* (Cambridge: Cambridge University Press, 1981), pp. 101–13.

Index